The Fat Man on
GAME AUDIO:
Tasty Morsels of Sonic Goodness

The Fat Man
George Alistair Sanger

New
Riders

201 West 103rd Street, Indianapolis, Indiana 46290
An Imprint of Pearson Education
Boston · Indianapolis · London · Munich · New York · San Francisco

The Fat Man on Game Audio:
Tasty Morsels of Sonic Goodness

International Standard Book Number: 1-5927-3009-4

Library of Congress Catalog Card Number: 2001097872

Printed in the United States of America

First printing: July 2003

07 06 05 04 03   7 6 5 4 3 2 1

Interpretation of the printing code: The rightmost double-digit number is the year of the book's printing; the rightmost single-digit number is the number of the book's printing. For example, the printing code 03-1 shows that the first printing of the book occurred in 2003.

Trademarks

Warning and Disclaimer

Publisher
Stephanie Wall

Production Manager
Gina Kanouse

Development Editor
Chris Zahn

Project Editor
Jake McFarland

Copy Editor
Linda Laflamme

Indexer
Lisa Stumpf

Proofreader
Linda Seifert

Composition
Wil Cruz

Manufacturing Coordinator
Dan Uhrig

Interior Designer
Alan Clements

Cover Designer
Aren Howell

Marketing
Scott Cowlin
Tammy Detrich
Hannah Latham

Publicity
Susan Nixon

Table of Contents

This book is for anyone who realizes that the world is absolutely perfect, and then, somehow because of that perfection, knowingly dedicates everything he or she has toward the absurd goal of improving it.

About the Technical Reviewer

This reviewer contributed his considerable hands-on expertise to the entire development process for *The Fat Man on Game Audio: Tasty Morsels of Sonic Goodness*. As the book was being written, this dedicated professional reviewed all the material for technical content, organization, and flow. His feedback was critical to ensuring that *The Fat Man on Game Audio* fits our reader's need for the highest-quality technical information.

Alexander Brandon has been writing music and creating sound effects for games since 1995, having worked on over a dozen high-profile titles with such companies as Epic Games, Legend Entertainment, and Ion Storm. He is currently the audio director of *Deus Ex 2* at Ion Storm. He is also the membership director for the Game Audio Network Guild and is on the DirectX Audio Advisory Board. He has written articles for *Gamasutra* and *Game Developer Magazine*, as well as starting "The Interactive Audio Journal" found at the Interactive Audio Special Interest Group's website, www.iasig.org.

Acknowledgments

Please forgive me all of you good, good friends whom I've missed here. Your help and your good vibes and your well-wishing have made all the difference to me.

I hereby acknowledge:

Family

Linda, who has consistently been the secret to happiness and success in 100% of my careers in game audio and other livelihoods.

Glen and Sandy, my children, who each gave as much to this book as I did; and they know it, too.

My parents, who raised me with so much love that I was blessed with the full and unshakable confidence that I could do anything at all, which in a way is kind of terrible if you think about it. And then if you think about it, it's the best possible thing.

My sister Wendy, and brothers Rick and Dave, whose laughter, love, companionship, and competition must have been what inspired me to always need to be in a band.

Bands

The CHS Marching Band

Etcetera Rock Revival Band: Ron Mikalson, Paul Ephron, Dave Sanger

Mantis: Keith Coble, Jon Hogen, Dave Sanger

The Phlaix: Pete Marston, Dave Sanger

The Mar-Mars

The Onlys

The Tuesday Night Gods of Music, Los Angeles Branch

The Tuesday Night Gods of Music, Austin Branch

The Adlib Soundblasters

The BBQ Brothers

And Team Fat, the most durable band of all, which isn't even a band: Dave Govett, Joe McDermott, Kevin Phelan, "Spanki" Avallone, and Linda Law

Teachers

MJ Wetherhead, Massage Therapist

Sharon Atherton-Johnson, Yoga Instructor

Mentors

Bob Demmon, high school band director, guitar teacher, and leader of surf band The Astronauts: "When you make a mistake on the trumpet, make it a big one."

Van Webster, recording mentor, Project BBQ facilitator, and co-founder of the Tuesday Night Gods of Music: "Remember—the button says 'Play.'"

Steve Goodheart, fishing buddy: "Sometimes it's not so important what you do, as what you don't do."

Woody, hair stylist across the walkway from Abbey Trails Studio: "Y'all can go to Hell. Ah'm goin' fishin'."

Masters

I've been fortunate to have conversed with a lot of Masters, from many walks of life.

These are the Masters from the game business who have had the greatest influence on me. I'm sure there are some I've forgotten and many more I don't know. But it doesn't matter. If they're truly Masters, they're all tuned in to the same radio station, and they're playing the same incredibly great hit songs over and over and over....

Sid Meier
Chris Crawford
Nolan Bushnell
Danielle Barry
Bobby Prince
"Professor" Brian Moriarty
Richard "Lord British" Garriott
Rob Landeros
Graeme Devine
Dr. Cat
Shigeru Miyamoto
Hal Barwood
Ron Gilbert

The LucasArts Audio Stooges:
  Michael Land,
  Clint Bajakian,
  Pete McConnel
Ernest Adams
Dave Warhol
Tommy Tallarico
Spencer Critchley
Thomas Dolby
Rhonda Conley
Jeff and Stephanie Johannigman
Ellen and Steve Beeman
Steve Jackson

Tell Us What You Think

As the reader of this book, you are the most important critic and commentator. We value your opinion and want to know what we're doing right, what we could do better, what areas you'd like to see us publish in, and any other words of wisdom you're willing to pass our way.

As the Publisher for New Riders Publishing, I welcome your comments. You can fax, email, or write me directly to let me know what you did or didn't like about this book—as well as what we can do to make our books stronger. When you write, please be sure to include this book's title, ISBN, and author, as well as your name and phone or fax number. I will carefully review your comments and share them with the author and editors who worked on the book.

Please note that I cannot help you with technical problems related to the topic of this book, and that due to the high volume of email I receive, I might not be able to reply to every message.

Fax: 317-581-4663

Email: stephanie.wall@newriders.com

Mail: Stephanie Wall
       Publisher
       New Riders Publishing
       201 West 103rd Street
       Indianapolis, IN 46290 USA

Introduction

Read This First:
A Guide to the Book

Here are some things that could help you with this book and give you a better sense of what you will and won't find herein.

This book has the power to change your life.

The book you are holding in your hand might just tell you who you are and where you need to go in your life based on the questions you ask. It could possibly help you to remember that everybody feels that same emptiness that you are feeling right now—that hole that we feel in *here*. It will allude to the fact that most of us try to fill that hole with something—with work or music or answers to questions. But if we are skillful, we might be able to envision that hole as a window, through which the inner light of Holiness might shine out to the world.

This kind of information can be a real drag if you are just trying to get a question answered. Therefore...

You should probably also read a good "normal book...."

I recommend *The Complete Guide to Game Audio: For Composers, Musicians, Sound Designers, and Game Developers* by Aaron Marks from CMP Books.

Aaron's book *will* answer your questions directly.

Almost everything in this book is absolutely true, except the jokes.

Sometimes there's the right thing to do, and then there's the funny thing to do.

I like to tell the truth. It's very important to me.

On the other hand, if a good joke comes up, it's fun to lie. And bragging—that very special kind of lying—is such a Texas Thing that it's even required by state law.

Now here's the rub: Such amazing things have happened to me that people often don't know when I'm telling the truth and when I'm lying. I mean, I'll go on and on about Golden Tickets, Rolls-Royces, famous musicians, and game designers—don't even get me *started* about the talking dog—how are people to know it's all true? Now, I'd much rather people listening to me be enlightened than entertained, so in person, I'll often tell people to *ask* me if something is really true or not, and I will *always* tell them.[1]

---

[1] For those who know me, I am obliged to acknowledge here that, yes, there are two topics which remain exceptions to the "The Truth Shall Set You Free" rule. These are the detailed stories of the alleged zeppelin "Perseverance," and details of the lives of the members of European Sex Machine, which, for good reasons, are to remain cloaked in mystery. The Truth might set you free, but it might put somebody else in jail; know what I'm sayin'?

Since y'all reading this book can't ask that question, we'll need some ground rules. How about this: I'll try to stick to the truth for the most part. If something's funny, though, you might be well-advised to consider not taking it literally. Conversely, if something in the book merely seems like a bold-faced lie, you should consider that it might have been a joke that maybe you didn't get the first time.

Bragging, for instance, is *not* required by Texas state law.

Some of the sentences in this book will end in prepositions.

It's another Texas Thing. Ask your Dad to tell you the one about the Texan at Harvard who asks where the library's at.

It's not about equipment, it's about symbolism.

You can get advice about musical equipment and tips on how to use it from any number of books, magazines, friends, and McDonald's employees. I am not saying that these skills are beneath us; they're essential. But this book is by The Mighty Fat Man Himself (see list of credits), and my Mighty Mind dwells on other things.

Everybody has equipment, Jack, and a good, oh, quarter of them can use it well. Think about how many people get the *Musician's Friend* catalog. (Calling a musical equipment catalog "Musician's Friend" is like calling heroin "Taxi Driver's Friend," isn't it?) What's needed to get straight A's in this business is not equipment—it's something else. Call it Artistry, Common Sense, Symbolic Thinking, Mythology, Experience, Mastery.

Yes, you'll have to master your equipment and your recording skills.

However, your edge won't come from those things, but more likely from a good backlog of experience and stories, and a mind that's willing to apply symbolically the lessons from those stories to every situation that this business throws at you. So don't you be bringin' that *Musician's Friend* receipt over here for *my* stamp of approval before you show Mom.

But if you got something cool, I'd like to see it!

It's not about getting a gig, it's about understanding the supply and demand of the industry.

I'm not going to give any practical advice about how to get a job in game audio. There are just too many variables to be able to build a reliable equation. What I hope to do instead is to arm you with knowledge about what kind of business this is. You'll learn what kind of people you're trying to get work with—how they act and what they need, what's in short supply and what they have just too darn much of.

They say that if you give a man a fish, you've fed him for a day, but if you teach a man to fish, you've fed him forever. I add that if you're going to use that saying, you're actually teaching men to teach men to fish. Set a good example for them by asking first: "Do you like fish?"

If I gave you a job, you'd have a fish for a day. If I taught you how to get a job, you'd be floundering out there with seventy-five thousand other fishermen on a crowded lake, in a boat designed by me, a guy who only built one boat before in his life. If we sat around and fished together and talked about the Way Things Are, you'd understand that there are only three fish in that lake, and you'd figure out how to farm.

It's *not* all about me, it just seems that way.

A great many people have given a great deal to this industry. They've done brilliant things that go far beyond my ability to imagine them.

On the other hand, when The Fat Man does the stuff that he does, I'm standing right there to see it. Fat Man stories are the ones that I'm qualified to tell, and they're the stories that, for some *terribly compelling* reason, beg to be told.

I am honestly sad to say that this book is not going to tell the stories of a lot of very deserving people. Sometimes, out of ignorance, or lack of attention to detail, or infatuation with the story, I may accidentally take credit for somebody else's achievement. For that I am deeply sorry, and I hope I will be forgiven.

My recording mentor, Van Webster, once advised me not to be both Homer *and* Odysseus—at least not at the same time. For those of you who were born after the death of education (probably around 1850), this is the equivalent of his advising me not to be both Dr. Seuss and a Sneetch. Sadly, I was unable to follow this advice, and my favorite stories continue to be the ones in which I say something clever to some famous person, followed closely by the stories in which I turn out to be the hero. A story that has both features gets a bonus multiplier.

I beg you to bear this in mind: There are two kinds of hubris: real hubris and fake hubris. (Again, for you post-1850-ers and fellow Texans, hubris is the kind of pride that, in ancient Greek plays, would cause the Gods to strike down the hero. You know, like what happened to The Artist Formerly Known as Prince, and to God Games.) Real hubris is dangerous. Fake hubris is damned funny, and I heartily recommend it. I'll even try to explain to you how to do fake hubris in the chapter subtitled "The Culture of Game Audio." Hell, it's one of the secrets to our business. It's one of the most prominent things shared by The Legendary Me and The Very Successful Tommy T.

So, be like me, or laugh with me, or laugh at me; it's all good. The Fat Man has the microphone, and the big rhinestone-studded steamroller of his ego is driving right down the signal path into the RAM of your Professional Mythology.

What I mean is this:

Why do I like to brag, brag, brag?

I do not know. Go ask your Dad.

The Strange World

Hearken ye to my song,

Of a Strange World that moves so
  fast along,

A World in which a man can rise from
  nothing,

To become King,

Only to fall from fashion and be forgotten.

After an eternity, found and dusted off,
  gazed upon as a curious relic is he,

And reborn as a Legend after another
  eternity,

And yet, all this can happen so quickly that
  the man is still young,

And nobody in the Strange World

Has ever died.

—*from "Song of the Game World"*

Relics of a strange world.
Clockwise from upper left: Original Ringo button from a gumball machine,
lost on the way to school in first grade, found again in sixth.
Foil wrapper from sandwich bought by Peter Gabriel for Fat Man—
Fat Man later gave Mr. Gabriel his Maurice Gibb Bee-Gees lunch box.
Shell casing from afternoon of shooting with LucasArts music team.
Rubber ear from China shows acupuncture points.
Shrapnel from sister Wendy's army training.
Business card soaked in sweat and rubber from having been tucked in the
belt of Mark Mothersbaugh's rubber suit while The Fat Man was hanging him
upside down for the filming of Devo's video for "Dr. Detroit."
Guitar picks.

About the Author

The Fat Man
wasn't always a
Long, Tall Texan.

George Sanger, nicknamed by his family "The Patron Saint of the Nerds," was born in Maine and raised in the beach town of Coronado, California. Both parents were doctors.

His brother Rick won his school science fair, then won the city science fair, so he was sent to the state competition, which he also won. Then they sent him to Washington D.C. for the nationals, and he won, so they sent him to Japan for the World Science Fair, and he came in first.

Sanger's sister, who is at the time of this writing a colonel in the Army and in command of a 600+ man battalion, taught him to play guitar.

He learned music and confident cowboy-style showmanship from his charismatic band instructor, Bob Demmon, leader of the great, ironically Colorado-based, surf group The Astronauts. The center of his high school life was his '50s band Etcetera, featuring his 11-year-old brother Dave on drums. With the other two band members, Sanger made a deep study of pinball arcades and the Beatles.

The band was a natural outgrowth of his philosophy. Like the Nerd God, Captain James T. Kirk, Sanger had, and still has, a Prime Directive. In his college days, that directive was to work out what it was that made the Beatles so much better than almost anything else in his world, and *do* that beautiful thing, be that cool. To spread the love. To make the world better.

Sanger left the nest to go change the world starting at Occidental College, a small liberal arts school in LA, in the late '70s. He enrolled as a physics/engineering student.

He formed another band, again with his brother Dave on drums, and again set forth to accomplish the Prime Directive. Going to college in the Disco Era, though, he did notice that it might be hard to be a real trailblazer like the Beatles were. All the trees in the forest of Rock seemed to have already been cut down....

Unfortunately for the world of science, George was distracted from his physics/engineering studies by two things. First, his idealistic dedication to the band's success meant that he would have to change his major to music. That was a momentous decision—the music department at Oxy is a tough one and strictly classical.

It is likely that he would have solved many of the world's major problems if he had continued with his science studies, but music alone can't be blamed for the shift. The second distraction had already caused a slipping of his physics studies: It was the beginning of the Golden Age of Electronic Games. *Asteroids. Missile Command.* Sanger was an addict.

They seem amazing to him. Like rock 'n' roll used to be. Parents didn't understand them. Kids had an inexplicable attraction to them. He could think of very few pastimes more satisfying. Would these games be a part of his path?

Well, you and I know the answer, but Sanger didn't at the time.

(*Sheesh.* It doesn't seem right that we should lose the sense of suspense like this. It's just that this writing style sounds so much like a normal foreword, it doesn't work as *a story*. Oh, wait, I know how to solve the problem. I'll switch to present tense, speed it up, and slop up the truth a little bit.)

THE PHLAIX

So, college ends, one more band is formed, again with brother Dave. The band is a hit in the early '80s LA club scene and plays five-encore standing-room-only shows at clubs like The Troubadour and The Starwood. But the unthinkable happens:

The band
breaks up.

George finds himself without a plan for his life. No science degree, no music career. He turns to other things: film school, cartooning, audio engineering. He falls so very, very low, he even tries phone sales.

[handwritten: 59 calls] *[signature: George Sanger]*

BE ENTHUSIASTIC!!!   ENTHUSIASM SELLS!!!   BE ENTHUSIASTIC!!!   ENTHUSIASM SELLS!!!

***SPEAK TO THE OWNER ONLY!!!!!!   *[handwritten: of Las Vegas]*

HI.. THIS IS (YOUR NAME) WITH QUALITY DISTRIBUTORS!! WHO AM I TALKING WITH? GOOD..(THEIR NAME)

MAYBE YOU CAN HELP ME... IT'S BEEN SO LONG SINCE I CALLED THAT I FORGOT... WHO'S THE OWNER THERE?

IS THAT YOU? (GET OWNER'S NAME) THANKS! ... PLEASE PUT ME THROUGH. (OWNERS FIRST NAME) THIS IS

_____WITH QUALITY DISTRIBUTORS! I'M GLAD I GOT YOU.. (SHORT WARM-UP) WELL, LET ME TELL YOU WHAT

I'M CALLING ABOUT. YOU DID A LITTLE BUSINESS WITH US IN THE PAST, AND THIS IS THE TIME OF YEAR

WHEN WE SAY THANKS AND SHOW OUR APPRECIATION TO YOU. CAN YOU STAND SOME GOOD NEWS (FIRST NAME)?

WE WOULD LIKE TO INVITE YOU AND YOUR GUEST TO COME OUT SOME TIME WITHIN THE NEXT YEAR TO LAS VEGAS!

WHAT HAPPENED WAS, WE HAD A MAJOR SUPPLIER HERE IN THE PLANT LAST *[handwritten: night]* WEEK AND HE GAVE US 35 OF THESE

ALL EXPENSE PAID V.I.P. VACATION PACKAGES FOR TWO PEOPLE TO COME OUT TO LAS VEGAS! (PAUSE AND GET

RESPONSE) HE GAVE THEM TO US TO GIVE AWAY TO A CUSTOMER *[handwritten: and]* IT GOES WITH A SMALL BOX OF EITHER HIS

IMPRINTED BALLPOINT PENS OR GLOW IN THE DARK KEYTAGS.

(FIRST QUALIFICATION)

DO YOU EVER GET OUT TO LAS VEGAS? (GET RESPONSE, THEN TALK ABOUT AND EXCITE THE CUSTOMER ABOUT

LAS VEGAS...BE CREATIVE!!!) THEN ASK: WELL, WE COULD TALK ABOUT LAS VEGAS ALL DAY, HOW WOULD YOU

LIKE TO COME OUT HERE IN THE NEXT YEAR? (CONTINUE ONLY IF RESPONSE IS POSITIVE)

[handwritten: Stardust, Landmark - Vegas world] (SECOND QUALIFICATION) *[handwritten: Disneyworld, A Fun ... Ticket]*

GREAT , BECAUSE THIS IS A FANTASTIC OPPORTUNITY TO COME OUT TO LAS VEGAS...THIS IS FOR 3 DAYS AND

2 NIGHTS FOR 2 PEOPLE AND IT'S WORTH OVER $1,000!! SO, LET ME ASK YOU IF WE WERE TO SEND YOU THIS

ALL EXPENSE PAID VACATION PACKAGE, WOULD YOU LIKE TO TAKE ADVANTAGE OF IT SOMETIME WITHIN THE NEXT

YEAR? (GET POSITIVE RESPONSE BEFORE CONTINUING)

(THIRD QUALIFICATION)

YOU DON'T HAVE TO DECIDE WHEN YOU WOULD LIKE TO COME OUT RIGHT NOW. YOU CAN COME HERE ANYTIME

WITHIN THE NEXT YEAR. SO IF WE SENT YOU THIS VACATION PACKAGE WORTH OVER $1,000 WOULD YOU LIKE

TO USE IT...YES OR NO? (CONTINUE ONLY IF YES) FIRST, LET ME TELL YOU A LITTLE BIT ABOUT THE

VACATION. IT'S FOR 3 DAYS AND 2 NIGHTS FOR 2 PEOPLE. NOW, YOU HAVE TO GET THERE ON YOUR OWN,

IN OTHER WORDS, YOU PAY YOUR OWN TRANSPORTATION, BUT ONCE YOU GET THERE, YOU GET DELUXE ROOM

ACCOMODATIONS IN A MAJOR HOTEL...AND THAT'S FREE!!! THE PACKAGE ALSO INCLUDES FREE MEALS, FREE

DRINKS, YOU GET TICKETS TO SEE TWO FLOOR SHOWS COMPLIMENTARY, PLUS YOU GET A GAMBLING PACKAGE

THAT HAS CASH IN NICKELS, FREE PLAYS IN BLACKJACK AND CRAPS, FREE SLOT TOKENS, KENO TICKETS AND

BINGO GAMES. IT'S VALID FOR ONE YEAR AND IT's ALSO TRANSFERRABLE. THE ONLY STIPULATION ON THE

By a miracle, his brother Rick's roommate, Dave Warhol, is working as a producer for Mattel Electronics Intellivision, and Sanger volunteers to empty trash cans for free just

to be involved in the gaming world. His life is redeemed from the slump when he gets one, then many jobs making music for games. Using his scientific background and his love of music and games, he works so hard to avoid another low time that the quality of his musical output goes through the roof. Aided by the fact that so few people are doing what he does, let alone with such earnest effort, he rises to be the Undisputed King of Sound for Games. He may not be feeding the masses, but he gets a remarkable taste of success as the Number One Guy.

Now he is truly among the great Nerds. The old game designers seem to him to be so wonderful—idealistic, philosophical, brilliant. Where they are a little naive in the ways of traditional business, they make up for it by constantly making up new rules and new methods. They even dress like knights and kings on a crusade. It's a golden age, and if anybody can help transform the world into a better place, it's these people. And they'll do it quickly, too. In no time they'll make this game business into a legitimate enterprise, one that will bring to these outcasts of society their longed-for respect and power.

But *because* things move so quickly, Sanger fears that maybe this streak of good fortune won't last. How to avoid falling into another slump? It occurs to George that radio, TV, and film were all star-driven industries, and games have no stars other than characters like Mario and Sonic... yet. He knows that this young field will become crowded, and to avoid falling on hard times again he must use this moment to somehow distinguish himself, somehow secure his value to the business. He concludes that his best bet is to groom himself to be the first *human* star of the games industry. Surely the people for whom he works so hard will value his contributions and proudly promote his name. Surely the players will associate his name with the most entertaining games. Surely when the big budgets come, he'll get to make soundtrack CDs and record high-dollar orchestral scores.

Photo by Teresa "Spanki" Avallone

He names himself The Fat Man, takes to wearing cowboy clothes, and moves to Texas to form Team Fat, a group of friends whose composing skills tower over anything else being done for games. Team Fat lives by an idealistic creed they call "The Manifatso," in which they promise to help the new media always be a safe place for freedom of expression. When they work together, the music is more powerful than anything that any one of them has done alone. Sanger begins to think of Team Fat as the Beatles of games.

A lot of the work Team Fat does inspires and enables other people to get into game audio. Notable among those who enter this world is young Tommy T. He wears sunglasses, and he talks business constantly on the phone. When The Fat Man gets a Rolls-Royce, Tommy T. gets a Lamborghini. When The Fat Man prints coloring books, Tommy T. hands out crayons. When The Fat Man brings Team Fat as an entourage, Tommy T. brings strippers and midgets. Tommy appears to be friendly, and he and The Fat Man share business tips. But there are whispers that Tommy T. is not to be trusted. There's also a Hollywood music agent, Bob, who uses The Fat Man's name to open doors, but never seems to bring in any jobs.

Now comes the terrible twist— a wish comes true. The game industry does mature and become legitimate. Venture capital gives it a huge boost, but the *Dungeons & Dragons* types who so looked forward to this day and worked so hard to bring it are gradually disappearing. They are being displaced by a new breed. Hipper, sharper, business-wise people with real budgets. And for some reason, demand for The Fat Man falls off. His name no longer appears on the boxes. Companies seem either to be ignoring audio, or

Bob the Agent.

hiring in-house composers to work in a cubicle for a pittance, or hiring Hollywood composers and popular bands, and putting them up on that pedestal that seemed to have been built by and meant for The Fat Man. A number of these composers are clients of Bob the Agent.

The Fat Empire crumbles. Real or not, he imagines that the game world has turned its back on him and the others who founded the industry. He finds he can no longer pay Team Fat. They offer to work for free, but he can't accept that, and they move on to their own adventures. One night, he is reading email after email of students and film and television composers asking him how they can do work for games. He has to take a break. He sees an article about Tommy T.'s booming business. The article is in... *Rolling Stone*!!! Something in him snaps.

Years pass, and nothing is heard from The Fat Man.

Then one day, at the old Fat Ranch, an odd, seemingly ragged figure emerges from a dusty, rusted Rolls-Royce. Why, it's him! But he seems strangely transformed. There's some exaggeration to his wild hair, the

cowboy suits are weird colors and bedecked with gaudy symbols; stars and snakes. He's called a meeting of Team Fat. They are there, huddled in the fog, and they're curious to hear where he's been, and what has brought him back.

He's been in isolation, on great adventures and in dangerous places. He's studied with Masters—scientists, musicians, spiritual guides—and learned to conquer his fears. Once, he even had a plan in place to take over every cent of business from Tommy T. and to raid Agent Bob's list of clients, but after a long internal struggle came to the only decision that the Patron Saint of the Nerds could: He put pictures of Tommy and Bob on his shrine and studied them and worked on himself until he could love and trust these two like friends. They became his friends. His fear of them vanished. Eventually, even the fear of having no business at all disappeared completely.

With the distraction of fear gone, he was able to concentrate his powers on a project even bigger than any before. Closely guarding a manuscript, about which he speaks little, The Fat Man makes a revelation to Team Fat: He has built them a command station and studio aboard the *Perseverance*, a huge, if quaint, radar-cloaked zeppelin of his own design.

Now there's a new mission for Team Fat, if they will accept it. They must return the Game World to its original course.

The first step that is asked of Team Fat is that they combine their musical talents to tell their story of what has happened to games. Then, aboard the *Perseverance*, they are to monitor the Game World, and help it. The Fat Man realizes that one person cannot tell this story alone. Together, Team Fat must bring the ancient wisdom of the original Game Designers back, and for the sake of the players, teach these old lessons to the new breed. The majority of his work while in isolation was to compile this wisdom into the manuscript he carries, entitled *Tasty Morsels of Sonic Goodness*. It begins with "The Manifatso."

Perspectives

How to Think

The Manifatso

Multimedia is a frontier for music. Along with the Internet, multimedia will become important in a way that is historically significant, for both tremendous numbers of opportunities for and different and new ways of listening to, creating, and interacting with music.

As the settlers come to this frontier, it is incumbent upon us pioneers to make sure that this becomes a place that is free and open for musical expression. It is Team Fat's intention that the music in this place be expressive, touching, and made for the sake of the human spirit, not repetitive, imitative, mechanical by convenience, nor needlessly enslaved by styles imposed by fashion or limited machinery.

The musical precedents we set, the tools we use and help create, the clothes we wear, the cars we drive, and the things we say should all promote this vision.

—Signed by Team Fat, 8/20/95

Lines and Mirages:

Mistaken Assumptions Commonly Found at the Beginning, Middle, and End ...er...I mean, the Advanced Level of Game Audio Careers

You didn't ask me to write this book, the publishers did. Sadly, you must now read it. I weep for you. And I hope, dear Reader, you will weep for me as well, as I have to write for those who might not want to read my advice. Ah, me. And I, *I,* who was once the Greatest of Them All. You know, audio is always the lowest priority for game developers. Always has been. Probably always will be. It's all too tragic to think about. Poor you. Poor me. How very, very sad. I must remember this tragedy forever.

Or should I just get over it?

I think that as a developer, content provider, or even player, you'll find that finding success in audio for games is largely a matter of getting over things.

I like that.

Begin chapter.

A lot of "expert" authors, such as myself, might get up on a soap box. They might draw a line in the sand and challenge the reader to cross it. Come out fighting. It's a Jungle Out There. I, on the other hand, think it might be more helpful to think of it as a desert... full of mirages and the like. As we travel through this desert, we might see what appear to be lines. And the challenge I'd offer you when you see one is this: "Let's erase that line in the sand, then see if we can get over it."

Let's look at a sampling of the kind of mirages I'm talking about. Here are some mistakes that you might find yourself making at the various levels of your career. Some we'll cover in more detail later in the book, others you only need to hear once to be healed. I would advise, requested or not, that before you even think about moving deeper into game audio, you spend some time learning to recognize, and then eventually enjoy, the *absurdity* of the sentiments represented by the phrases that follow.

Now, I certainly have to admit that one or even all of the purported falsehoods that follow might at some times be quite true. True Falsehoods. *Truehoods*, I guess you'd call them. But, *assuming* that any one or more of them is true before having been proven so can only bring misery to you and me, *ass*. I *think* that's the expression.

Project BBQ T-Shirt.

First time in the studio.

Mistaken Assumptions from the Beginning Level of Your Game Audio Career

- A game needs sound that sounds like "game sound."

- Music should stay in the background and support the game.

- Oh, boy, I'll sure make lots more money in game audio than I would in, say, engineering or pizza delivery.

- The music I like *rocks*. The music that I don't like *sucks*.

- I know what rocks and what sucks—that will ensure my success in the creation of games.

- I deserve my job more than That Other Guy.

- Before I start making sounds, I'm going to need the right equipment.

- We musicians can't let people walk all over us.

- This career will be a perfect stepping stone to the film and TV audio business.

Mistaken Assumptions from the Intermediate Level of Your Game Audio Career

- I have to create game sounds that sound like "movie sounds."

- Let's see, my boss asked for a sound for each action. That means one sound for each. One footstep, one "ouch" sound.... That'll sound *real* good after 40 hours of playing.

- And 40 minutes of music will be just fine for those 40 hours of gameplay, too.

- The company will *never* find anybody else to write this style of music the way I do.

- And certainly nobody with that kind of talent would do the *other* stuff I do.

- And even if he did, he'd never be willing to put up with the crap that I put up with.

- And there's *no way* he'd do it for this little money.

- Before I start making sounds, I'm going to need the right equipment and some decent patch and sound effects libraries.

- Upgrading my motherboard will solve my problems.

- I should repeat my musical themes in order to emphasize them, just as I learned in composition class.

- This is just like the film and TV audio business.

Recording engineer.

Mistaken Assumptions from the Advanced Level of Your Game Audio Career

- I have to write game music that sounds like the radio or those guys on MTV. Better yet, I have to license those songs.

- Music should stay in the foreground of the game so that people will be swept away by the amazing stuff I'm doing.

- They just don't respect us audio guys.

- Something besides repetition is the thing that's making my game sound bad.

- Do you realize how *rich* these people are getting off me?

- Before I start making sounds, I'm going to need the right equipment— more patch and sound effects libraries, a state-of-the-art studio with nice acoustic wood paneling, and the topless intern who comes through occasionally with sandwiches with the crust removed.

- This will save my floundering film and TV audio business.

And the Dreaded:

- Boy, The Fat Man sure knows a lot about game audio! I bet his advice can help me!!!

Getting Over It

Were you already making some of these assumptions? Well, you're not alone, by any means. Is it hard to let go of the assumptions and still feel good about life? Yes, it is. And that's really a good thing. Let it go. Get over it. You'll hear that kind of letting go referred to by Masters as such various things as, "Living at the Edge of the Unknown," "Being in the Moment," and "Knowing Where the Downbeat Is Pretty Well for a White Guy."

We just explored the fact that many of your positive ideas about your situation in the game business are nothing but harmful illusion. The flip side is that your negative ideas are just as illusory.

I'd like to illustrate this with examples from game audio, but there really isn't enough history behind it. Instead, to illustrate more clearly from a richer source, let's borrow from the fact that we're covering music, too, in this book. Let's look at your career as a rock 'n' roller.

Guitar pose.

Your life in the music business can be viewed as a long series of rejections. The rejections come one after the other with no respite in between. Often the only sense of growth in your career will appear to be in the seeming importance of the party doing the rejecting. Here is an opportunity to observe a practical application of The Fat Man's patented Power of Negative Thinking philosophy. Let's break down the various levels of rejection you will suffer in your career, and see how, through acceptance of the inevitable horror that is success, if you hang in there, you will be rejected clear into the Rock & Roll Hall of Fame:

1. The salesman in the guitar shop won't let you touch the instruments.

2. Your mom won't buy you an instrument.

3. Nobody will play with you.

4. Your parents hate your band.

5. Your band can't get a job.

6. *Everybody* hates your band.

7. The only people who go to your shows are from your class in school.

8. Your band breaks up. Your second band breaks up. Your third band breaks up. You go solo.

9. Your demo doesn't sound as good as your live shows.

10. Record companies send you form letters; "We are not accepting unsolicited tapes at this time."

11. Your personal friend at the record company gives you a cleverly veiled rejection; "You have just got to play this for some buddies of mine at Arista and RCA. Tell them I sent you."

12. The record company won't let you play on your own album.

13. Your album doesn't sound as good as your demo.

14. The record company won't let you write your own songs on your second album.

15. Your second album doesn't live up to the expectations set up by the first.

16. The record company won't let you produce your third album.

17. You don't win the Grammy.

18. Nobody can stand you since you "went commercial on them."

19. You come off badly on *The Late Show*.

20. The record company won't let you pose nude.

21. The press thinks you haven't changed with the times. Your comeback album reeks of nostalgia.

22. Your fans think you've somehow, well, changed. Your second comeback album reeks of selling out.

23. You look like a sorry circus freak, still rocking pitifully away at age 80, or you die tragically, a victim of your own fame and insecurity.

24. Of the thousand people who visited your grave this week, only four hundred noticed that your middle name was misspelled.

Now, there's a line to get over.

Death

and

Death

Game

Audio

Let's put things in perspective.

This book is being written in a precious moment in history. The fragile ship of game audio is sailing proudly between a pair of towering twin rocks against which it might scrape uncomfortably at any given moment. I expect this book is also being *read* in a time that can be described similarly. I'll tell you about the rocks of my time now, and when you write your book, you can tell me about yours.

First Rock

On one hand, game audio has been around for a while, and that's starting to have manifestations in our attitude and in our work. As they say in all the news stories, "We've come a long way from the boops and beeps of yesteryear."

True, when we started out we only had those famous "boops and beeps," and got little attention from the rest of the gaming world, let alone that other world, you know the bigger one. What's that one called? Oh, yeah... the "real" world. But things are quite hopeful now. We like to compare ourselves to those who do sound design for movies, and we plan on getting the same kind of budgets and respect that they get. With hope in our hearts, we lay plans to see some of the benefits seen by pop stars and other legitimate music makers. Practitioners of our craft used to encounter surprise and amazement that anybody actually had the *job* of writing audio for games. That's generally become replaced by scads of assumptions on the part of developers and players alike about what a game should and should not sound like. We've been around long enough that some people have made fortunes from game audio. Some have lost fortunes. We have a Guild now, and we have a few beloved veterans who are accomplished, grizzled, and beaten enough to be called Masters. (The Guild currently has two Platinum Members, myself and X-Box's Brian Schmidt.) We even think highly enough of game audio that we think a book needs to be written about it. And we *love* to tell people how far we've come. *Love* it. Like a little kid telling total strangers that he's five now. "*No more beeps and boops! **No more beeps and boops!!!**"

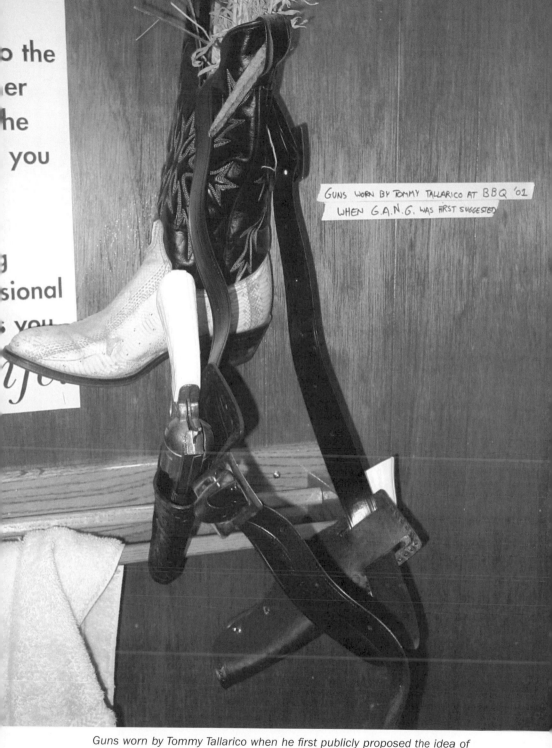

GUNS WORN BY TOMMY TALLARICO AT BBQ '01
WHEN G.A.N.G. WAS FIRST SUGGESTED

*Guns worn by Tommy Tallarico when he first publicly proposed the idea of
GANG, the Game Audio Network Guild, at Project BBQ, 2001.*

Second Rock

At the time of this writing, no notable figure in the business of audio for games has ever died. Not *one*.

Now what kind of nonsense is *that?*

The fact is, yes, we are more mature than we used to be. But who isn't?

I think that in our case the "You've come a long way, Baby," bit is far outweighed by the "But you've still got a long way to go," and this perspective could be used to great benefit. Compared to almost any other human endeavor, game audio has *no* history.

The next time you hear a comparison of games to the movie business, think about the price that's been paid to the movies in human lives. Just the annual "These are the people who died *this year*" video at the Academy Awards show is enough to make you weep, and it's been going on for a long time. Not to mention the fact that these people really, really touched some hearts.

If you're ready for some *powerful* perspective, compare game audio to another profession besides audio for cinema and rock stardom—try something that's been going on for thousands and thousands of years, or at least *more* than a single century.

How about soldiering?

Sanger's sister, LTC Wendy McGuire,
takes command of her battalion while parents look on.

Here are some things you might consider saying the next time you meet a war veteran or a high-ranking military officer:

- Boy, they expect me to work hard.

- I've done some awesome stuff!

- I'm in a noble profession that's finally getting the respect it deserves.

- I'm working on this game that's gonna be, like, the Ultimate. The Game to End All Games.

- I wonder when I'm going to get *my* Ferrari.

- It takes a lot of equipment to do what I do.

- You'd think that, with all this equipment, after a while all the technical problems would just go away and my job would be easy.

- I'm totally dedicated to my job.

- Boy, there's sure a lot riding on audio for games.

So there are your two rocks. On the left is the rock called "People need to pay more attention to our venerable history and give us the respect we deserve." On the right is the rock called "We haven't exactly sacrificed a generation of our sons to this business." Makes me wonder where our ship will end up if she makes it through that gap.

Oh, and back to the fact that nobody from our profession has died at the time of starting this book... the same might even be true at the time that I finish the book. For a few years, it could remain true.

But if this book has a normal shelf life, it's very likely that some readers, hopefully *most readers*, will scan the previous paragraph and say, "Hey, Dude. That's dated. Bunches of these guys have croaked." And the more the better, from my point of view, because if people are still reading this book that far into the future, it means that they're applying the lessons of the next chapter.

Shrine Number One at Abbey Trails Studio.
Every studio needs a shrine and a cat. Other equipment is optional.

How to Understand Everything

Why would you want to read this book if it's dated? Or if it's not even about a field that you're in?

Well, maybe you'd want to do it for some of the same reasons that make you want to focus your entire attention on a movie or play a game that deals with detective work, or a fantasy world, or a war in which you'll never actually take part. It's good for your brain, it's good for your heart, and if you're blessed with a lot of common sense (or can nurture the little bit that you have), these things can expand your ability to understand everything.

They say that if you understand any one thing thoroughly, you understand everything. I read this saying, or something like it, in one of those little impulse-item, cube-shaped, popular-Zen-made-easy-for-everybody books, so in that sense at least it's related to Zen philosophy. I also heard it attributed to the Dalai Lama, and I think he's a Tantric Buddhist, so you see, understanding the first sentence of this paragraph helps you understand both Zen and Tantric Buddhism. This is an auspicious sign. Let's assume during this chapter that the saying is true, and then we can see if it does us any harm.

I know that the Dalai Lama has said many times that his religion is kindness. His Holiness is as sharp a shooter as they get, philosophy-wise. I would sure be gratified if a reader came away from this book thinking that the secret of a good career in audio for games, too, is kindness.

Now I ain't no Dalai Lama, but under close inspection, I think all businesses, all human endeavors are, at their heart, identical, the way all *Quake* MODs are identical. When you play a MOD, you're really playing the same game as the original, but the characters and objects are merely dressed in different skins. Once you've learned to play one version of *Quake* really well, you can play all the MODs. Similarly, understanding the core of all endeavors might be facilitated by a nice focused study of one field.

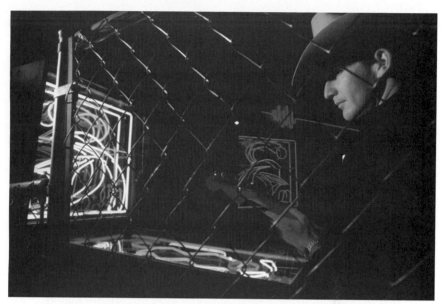

First photo of The Fat Man in his cowboy hat,
by Jack Gescheidt, 1989, at Einstein's Pinball Arcade in Austin, TX.

This was the thought that went through my head in my early days of playing pinball and video games. "If I get really good at this one thing, I'll develop some skills to help me be a more capable person." At that time, I was thinking I'd get dexterity, speed, an ability to focus, that kind of thing. I wasn't quite right, though. I was missing a layer of abstraction. In the end, I am left with the impression that the value of spending all that time playing those games was not in the skills I learned. Most of those were only moderately transferable to other areas. The value for me was this: The process of gaming imprinted certain patterns into my brain that I would see everywhere, in all things, for the rest of my life.

Here's an example of one kind of pattern that happens a lot when a person gets immersed in anything. In this case, a person gains a new perspective on life by playing an arcade game:

"Man, I'd live in this arcade if I could. If only I had more quarters."

"That guy's been playing all day on one quarter—What a winner!!! If I master this game, I could be a winner, too."

"What is it about this game? The more I play, the more I *want* to play. And look, now that I've shown them the game, all my friends want to play, too."

"I'm getting to be kind of a hot shot.... People sure like it when I help them play the game."

"Man, it would be pretty cool to be the kind of person who could *make* a game like that! Wouldn't *that* make people happy?"

"Hey, you know what? Girls don't like boys who spend all day in the arcade. And that guy's been playing all day on one quarter. What a loser!!!"

"Have you **ever** noticed *that when you finally decide that you* **don't** *want to* **play** *a game any more,* you get a bunch of replays?"

It's a known fact that people who become more deeply involved in a field will feel the need over time to alter the way in which they participate in order to maintain interest and a sense of fun. My parents were doctors, and I remember hearing a hint of their pursuit of interest and a sense of fun when they would recite an old slogan that had gone around in medical circles regarding operations: "See one, do one, teach one."

Will Wright, creator of *The Sims*, has a remarkable way of tracking the depth to which his players change their play as they become immersed in *The Sims* games, and he takes full advantage of the knowledge it brings him. He has graphs to show how some percentage of players get very involved in building elaborate structures and playing deeply into the game. Some percentage of those deep players will hit *The Sims* website and download some goody or other for their game. Some percentage of those players who download will get into using special tools that are available from the web community, and will start making their own goodies. Some percentage of those will begin uploading goodies to the web. Eventually, some of them become involved in making their own custom tools, and the elite few of those who go farther—the Masters—become leaders of the web community.

To gain insight into this idea, I'd recommend that you find any middle-aged man and observe him at his hobby. It matters little what the hobby is. Take a hot rodder. Except for the actual apparatus and skills particular to his hobby, he is in innumerable ways identical to the radio-controlled airplane guy, the darts player, the boater, the fisherman, the celebrity stalker, and the electronic game enthusiast.

At entry level, all these hobbyists are mainly interested in the *specifics* of the hobby—to a fault. Each will invest, beyond any reasonable sense of proportion, time, money, and especially attention on these minutiae. What kind of oil do I use in my shocks? What motor proves fastest at high altitudes? What's the best lure with which to snare the elusive Striped-Butt Bass in January? Who was the greatest tenor player, other than 'Trane? How would a fella go about connecting a drive shaft to a sprocket?

Man Facts

Team Fat has identified a cultural phenomenon we like to call the "Man Fact." It first came up when, at a truck stop, Team Fat's Joe suggested that the aerodynamic effect of the spoilers and such on Indy cars allows them to hug the road so well that they could drive on the ceiling if there were a way to get them up there going that fast. In discussing how we would build an appropriate ramp to test this, the question came up: How fast do Indy cars go, anyway?

"Geez, I don't know.
Three hundred?
Five hundred?"

"Gotta be more than a hundred, easy.
Regular cars go a hundred.
But two hundred?"

"Probably two hundred.
Or three."

"Yeah, two hundred fifty, thereabouts."

"Yep."

Now I was mostly just a listener in this conversation, the way I like to tell it, and as I listened my face got redder and redder. In the end, I couldn't help but yell at the team that four guys with no idea at all of the truth had just collectively pulled a number out of the stinkier end of thin air, and then convinced themselves that it was absolutely true. All this was done using no knowledge, no science, and no logic, just strategic use of the word "probably."

Observations since then have shown that almost any time a group of men get together, discuss a macho topic, and lack a fact, they will create a Man Fact to fill in the gap. Monitor your conversations for the word "probably," and you'll see what I mean.

"What was the last year they made good Mustangs?"

"Oh, probably '68."

The best I heard came from my father-in-law. He and his old business partner were visiting my house, and we three had entered the garage to take a break from kids and women, so that Denny and Bill could check out the Rolls, and so that the latter could sneak in a smoke. Eventually, the conversation led to Hemingway's death.

"And that's a hell of a way to go.
You can't miss with that."

"What'd he use? A thirty-aught-six?"

"Probably a 12-gauge."

To rise to the next level, aspirants in any of these activities often "buy their cool." It's as though they are trying to fill a hole in themselves with these things, and that hole is so abominable that they will even make stuff up to fill it. So, when the Man Fact bait is thrown, these practitioners are the ones who answer with Man Facts.

"How **would** one go about attaching a drive shaft to a *sprocket***?**

Hmmm.

Well, **probably** you'd want to use epoxy putty or some kind of welding rig."

Many of us stay at this stage for a long time. Ask a young engineer a question. He *has* to answer. It's like that joke about the guillotine into which I will not go here. (Grammatical error intended.)

It is my observation that most men who transcend this level can be identified by the fact that they have an incredibly earthy nickname, such as "Rusty" or "Red." If their last name is Anderson or McDonald, they'll be assigned monikers like Andy or Mac. (I just met a "Corky" who's been running his jazz band for 15 years. I've never heard them, but based on the name alone, I'd be willing to bet these cats *never* need a second take.) The remarkable thing about the Masters who have made it to Nickname Status is that their wisdom entirely transcends Man Facts. I think they might even transcend facts themselves. Like, if you were to ask one of these plaid-shirt gray-hairs "How would you join a drive shaft to a sprocket?" he might well throw the question back at you: "Well, depends what you're tryin' to do."

I wonder if there is an emoticon for spitting tobacco?

:-9'

There are many compelling reasons for you to seek out these people. First of all, these are the guys who know all the good jokes. Second of all, they will be great mentors. And third, pertaining to the point of this chapter, it will be like getting a peek at the answers in the back of the book. You'll be able to see where the hobby path or career path in which you've taken an interest will eventually lead. And you'll get to see that these people almost without exception have an approach to life and its problems that would make them a great person to have with you when you're shipwrecked, on a cattle drive, alive after the apocalypse, on *Junkyard Wars*, or all of the above.

I challenge you to find an occupation that has *not* got this kind of strata and masters of this kind, men and women alike. Yes, of course women can be and are Masters. I only used men as my example because I wanted to paint a cartoon-like picture in your mind.

Now, I'm not saying that knowing about people makes you know everything. I'm saying that meta-observation of this kind happens in all fields, which means that no matter what field you're in, these things are available to you and will help you in any other field. And studying with a Master, no matter his area, will always help you.

Now since you're reading this book, we might assume that you've chosen a field to study already: game audio. It's a young area, so it could be hard, but with some luck, you'll be able to find a Master in the area, and maybe eventually become one.

I once heard Marvin Minsky, the Great Professor from MIT, the Father of Artificial Intelligence, speak at the Computer Game Developers' Conference. He began by quoting Steve Woodcock, who was one of the Golden Ticket winners (see the chapter "How to Get Work"), which I only bring up here in order to make myself appear to be even more of a vital part of the progress of science.

The VD (venerable doctor) was an amazing thinker. I might be wrong, but he struck me as the kind of older man who's seen some success in contributing toward solving some engineering or national or even global problems, but now feels responsible for every major problem in the entire world. Which is a nice attitude for Zen monks and the like, but it's often not done with suitable grace. The kind of man I'm talking about spends a good part of his life yelling at CNN. ("I *told* them that all they had to do was put a tax on gas, and if they'd have listened, all this trouble in the Middle East never would have happened. Damn it!")

But I don't really know Minsky. It did appear that he was somewhat disgruntled at the lack of progress in AI over the past decade or so. He felt that the problem hadn't been clearly defined, and by God, he was ready to step in and define the thing. He felt that the bottleneck in progress was that computers didn't have common sense and that was a very difficult thing to give to a computer. And, of course, somewhat difficult to give to some humans. Ha. Ha. MIT joke. Okay then, what is this critical element called "common sense?" Now Minsky had cornered himself into having to define it.

Undaunted, of course, he went on to define common sense as the ability to think analogously. To take lessons learned in one situation and bring them to another situation. The computer rarely says, "Aha! This problem can be solved the way I solved that *last* problem!" And doing so would be common sense. In other words, "if you understand one thing thoroughly, you understand everything." And there it is, reflected in the shining radiance of science as one of the cornerstones of human under-standing. Well, machine intelligence, anyway, and now I'm really earning my writers' paycheck because I've made my point in two different and interesting ways.

The punch line to the Minsky story is this: While he was taking his bow just at the end of this wonderful talk, he knocked over his bottle of drink-ing water so that its contents spilled all over his laptop computer. The audience took little note, but as they filed out of the arena, there was Marvin Minsky, Great Professor from MIT, the Father of Artificial Intelligence, cussing under his breath and holding his computer high in the air, water literally pouring out from between the keys. It would have been funny, I think, if he had thought to burst into tears and shouted out to his little computer:

"Ellen, my *Love!* You were so *close* to *completion*, and alas, now *all* is *lost!!!"*

Opposites,' or 'For Every Philosophy,

There Is an Equal and Opposite Philosophy (or Rule of Thumb Wrestling

The George Sanger logo on this tape reel was drawn for me by innovative game designer, graphic artist, philosopher, macro-observer, and inspirational author Scott Kim. He did it kind of on a dare, in ink, during a lunch break at the Game Developers Conference. Hold it upside-down, it says, "He's the fat man." I still used reel-to-reel tape at the time, so it was fun to watch it turn over and over.

I don't trust any philosophy that isn't traveling with its equal opposite. I've heard it said that there's only one thing that's simple—I guess you'd call it God or Love or what-not[1]—and everything else is complicated. Here are some single-pole philosophies that characterize the kind of ready-made phrases that ignore this principle, and, therefore, I tend not to trust:

- Government is bad.

- If a monk swears never to touch a woman, then helps a woman by carrying her across a river, he is going to Hell, and good riddance, monkey-boy.

- There is only one kind of music that will be right for this game.

You can picture, I hope, the kind of person who would whip out one of these single-pointed rules-of-thumb. He would be a focused person. A strong person who knows his mind. A dedicated person. A scary person. In *Man and Superman,* George Bernard Shaw warns the reader never to trust anybody who is dedicated to a purpose. The reason given is that the person would sacrifice himself to that cause... and therefore would certainly not hesitate to sacrifice *you.*

[1] For one of his early birthdays, Team Fat's Dave Govett got a very special gift. His wonderful mom Leta was raising Dave alone, and she couldn't afford anything expensive right then. Instead, she got him a library card. She took him down to the library, and said to little Dave, "all this is yours." Dave took her up on that, and now is as deep a philosopher as they come... but he sure doesn't sound like one. He talks like a Texan, and he's quite likely to say "and what-not" after any sentence. This applies equally well to sentences about UFOs, movies, eastern philosophy, Tarot, computers, music, relationships, what the cat just did, and the kindest words of love. I've found it such a charming habit I've tried to adopt it myself. I suppose it's a sort of tribute to Dave and his mom, and what-not.

By themselves, these one-liners can set in motion the wheels of progress in the game business. They can inspire teams to great levels of achievement. But when the wheels are set thus in pairs facing each other, they better show their illusory nature, dispelling the myth that there exist any formulae for great game design, great game audio, fame and/or fortune. I like these opposed pairs, and the only time I allow myself to think that I'm getting a useful view of a situation is when I understand the qualities of each side.

For example:

"A stitch in time saves nine."

can be countered with

"Haste makes waste."

Both slogans have merit.

Anything Timothy Leary says can be handsomely argued against by G. Gordon Liddy, and anything Gordon says can be as elegantly put down by Tim.

The great *"All we are is dust in the wind"* can be refuted

with the **equally** potent

"You are everything and **everything** is you."

It goes on and on, continuing into the world of games and audio, creating dichotomies that can wreck any and every rule of thumb ever tossed off by a producer trying to rationalize his Super Mario Kart–like graphics and his Daikatana-like schedule.

I suppose that some people sporting one-sided philosophies do have some clarity in their view of the issue. When the Dalai Lama says fighting is bad, he backs it up with profoundly well-thought-out decisions, actions, a book or two and... hey, come to think of it, I don't even think he *says* fighting is bad. I think he just prefers not to do it. Whereas

if, say, an elementary school kid or a 19-year-old game designer says fighting is bad,

I might tend to think that he hasn't thought the whole issue through.

When he was about six, my son asked me, "Daddy, are guns good or are they bad?"

"Uh, well, Son, guns *are* the thing that killed Bambi's mother. On the other hand, if that guy Hitler's troops came to your elementary school, a gun might be just the thing needed to save your family."

"Oh, I see, Daddy. Then they're a little bit good and a little bit bad."

"I think so."

"They're GOOD-BAD!!!"

And he made this sign with his hands:

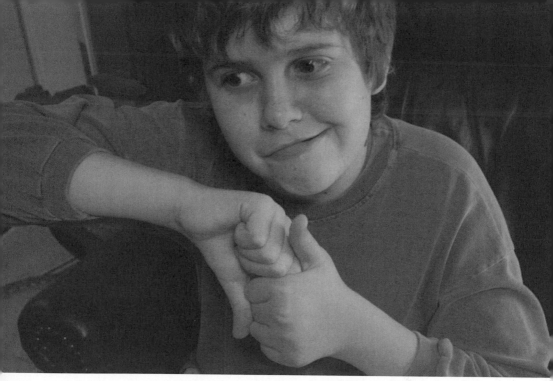

He was half this age at the time of the story.

That conversation, and the fact that it came so naturally to such an uneducated mind, had a profound effect on me. I continue to see in those words the power to lend great clarity to many of Life's situations.

Therefore, it is my sincere hope that you will think on this chapter during your career, during your creative moments, during the critical decision-making moments of your life. And it is my hope, especially, that when you note that several of the chapters and the concepts in this book fall into contradictory pairs, you will think on this chapter and consider that, maybe, I did it on purpose.

Sideways Smiley Face.

Insurmountabl

Problems

and how to

deal with

Them

I broach this topic for the most practical of reasons: In order to conquer audio for games, you are going to have to face certain problems that appear fairly insurmountable. And, whereas every occupation has such issues, the very freshness of game audio as an occupation, the inherent nature of audio as an art, and certain special qualities of the gaming industry (described in the next chapter) add up to a very impressive list of problems. At some point or another, they will seem insurmountable. At some point or another, some problem, probably one of these, will actually *be* insurmountable. You will have to deal with that.

Right now, I'd like you to do a little mental exercise with me. Take a moment, if you will, to think of yourself as a mountain climber, and I'm going to join you in an attempt to scale Everest. I am pointing at the mountain that we are about to scale and proudly noting its height.

As we approach this game audio metaphor-thing together, we mustn't be misled by the jumble of distractions and illusions scattered at its foothills.

See over there to the left of the path: It's Tommy Tallarico and The Fat Man having a race in their fancy cars! And over there is Trent Reznor in his expensive studio, casually speculating in front of a camera crew on how technology and artistry can deeply affect the player of *Doom III* in a unique and wonderful way. There are the young people reading Aaron Marks' book, *The Complete Guide to Game Audio*, and planning their glorious assault on the Peak.

But look! Over to the right of the path is quite a different scene: It's Bobby Prince, the kindly southern gray-haired public defendant who did the music for the original *Doom* that was loved so well—and today I don't think he's happy about Trent's theories. There are the members of the Video Game Musician's list server, and it seems that at least in today's thread not one of them, *not one*, is getting the respect or compensation he deserves. I especially don't think they're happy about Tommy T. and The Fat Man's cars. And they are flanked by the scores of older composers

What if I see a Mountain Lion?

What if I get lost?

Rick Sanger is a ranger in the backcountry of Kings Canyon National Park.

Jeffrey didn't know what to expect when his family took their first trip to the mountains. He'd certainly never dreamed of anything as exciting as their ride on the Palm Springs Aerial Tram. Come along! Float up past huge granite cliffs and into the heart of the Mt. San Jacinto State Wilderness. Discover a place that offers joy, wonder, beauty... and unexpected adventure! Join Jeffrey as he learns a few wilderness basics, and asks the question that fascinates both children and adults alike: *Are There BEARS Here?*

ISBN 0-9653149-0-1

For curious adventurers of any age!

Meditating on the mountain metaphor, literally and literarily, Sanger's brother Rick figured out that writing childrens' books pays slightly better than climbing mountains.

who succeeded, did great things, and left their mark on the business, and who still couldn't make it work out and had to move on to other things. Including Team Fat!!! How will *they* feed their families when the young readers of Aaron's book get their dream jobs? How will they feel about you, sitting there reading your little book by their former Fat Team Mate, planning to ascend the hill that they once took by storm?

Well, my friend, reader, and fellow mountaineer, there is something to this configuration of paths that is not unfamiliar. According to Joseph Campbell—a man so smart that he could have been a game audio guy—

every very holy place, every Great Temple in every religion, is guarded by two angels, and these angels represent Fear and Desire. You've got to get past them if you want to make it to the Cream-Filled Center of Mount Mixedmetaphor.

So, we look past Desire—the dreams of cash, glory, groupies, fancy clothes, and an easy life. And we look past Fear—the fear of a difficult and a wasted life. And this being done, we're ready to look at the mountain and get up it.

So here's the mountain: a list of our own Insurmountable Problems, some of which have been solved by others, but they can't share the solution; some of which will be solved by you and others quickly and easily, but not by me; and some of which will Eat Everybody's Lunch.

Bobby Prince, composer for Doom, agreed to help the Project BBQ staff solicit sponsorships to help musicians attend the conference.

Game composer and minister Chance Thomas of HUGEsound.

The Great List of Insurmountable Problems Begins Here

There Is No Tool for Doing What We Do

Are you ready for this one? Believe it or not, folks, almost every person making audio for games today is like a blacksmith in the days before the invention—or at least the availability—of the anvil.

A few castles (companies) have their anvils. Some are big, some are little, some work well, and some don't. But as of this writing, the independent game audio guys, and most in-house artists as well, have access to *no* tools to allow them to create audio for interactive situations.

An independent sound designer can create linear audio (the kind you'd hear on a CD, on TV, or in a film) to his heart's content, and the tools for helping him to do that are downright glorious. Listen to the music on the demo CD from one of the many composers attempting to make the move from being a film composer to being a game composer. Fantastic! The thing that is missing is the ability to map those linear pieces into an interactive context. When a piece of music has to change in midstream based on what a gamer does, or when a stream of sound effects has to play in rapid succession, or when the volume has to dip down while an announcer describes a play that just happened, there's nothing[1] that allows him to compose for those situations, edit his ideas, or listen to them, or even pass his ideas on to the programmer who will implement them. Tools (if he's lucky) and even methods of communication, all have to be somehow cobbled together from scratch for each project.

This is not unlike requiring that a classical composer describe his piece to the orchestra via email, rather than using musical notation, and in a different language for each orchestra with which he works. The results can be every bit as pleasant.

---

[1] See the chapter "Integration for Beginners," for a disclaimer about Microsoft Direct Music Composer.

The Fat Man

From: The Fat Man
Sent: Tuesday, March 18, 2003 11:51 AM
To: Programmers
Subject: Insurmountable problems

Dear Programmers,

I KNOW that you guys respect me, and I am constantly gladdened by the fact that you are willing to sacrifice the integrity of the product we ship, just so that I can have one or two more amazing and unbelievable anecdotes for my upcoming book, "Tasty Morsels of Sonic Goodness."

For those of you who weren't in on the joke, try this:

on [certain games, names omitted]

Make sure your GameSettings.ini is not read-only.

Set MasterVolume = any number other than 100.

Run the game.

Quit the game.

Read your new volume setting. It's ONE LESS!!!

You guys are such the Jokesters!!!

;)))

Love,

FAT

Game Audio Is Not on the Creative Radar

This is an actual email from The Fat Man to his favorite game programming team, who had created a hitherto unnoticed routine that would automatically and very slowly turn the volume *completely down* on all their products.

A game developer is a very busy person.

Like a movie producer, he has to consider all of the normal "making a film" things: visuals, music, story, budget, that stuff. Audio is a small but significant slice of that pie.

Nobody *doubts* the significance of audio,

nor its ability to create immersion in an alternate universe. We've all seen somebody on the phone *trying* to drive a car.

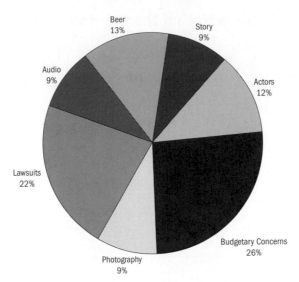

Making a normal movie.

But consider now that the game developer *also* has to keep in mind gameplay, interactive arts that have never been explored, and about five cutting-edge areas of computer science. If you've ever tried it, I'm sure you'll agree; it's hard to keep up on even *one* cutting edge. Add to this that he has probably got less pay than the movie producer and more kids wanting his job.

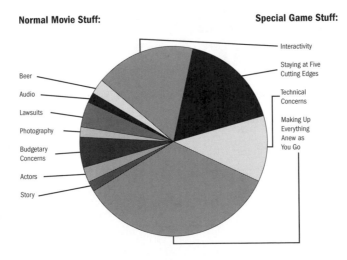

This second chart was drawn to represent the mental bandwidth of the game designer, but it also reflects audio's tiny share of other resources such as disk space, processor cycles, budget, space on the credits, and order in line for pie at the company picnic, creating a beautiful symmetry to the otherwise prosaic "pie chart" analogy.

Picture a rocket being prepared for an impending launch date. The eyes of the nation will be on this rocket very soon, and it is imperative to the nation's administration that this launch be remembered forever. High up the gantry, there's a trap door open on the side of the rocket, and a scientist is leaning into it up to his waist, muttering things about capacitors, liquid oxygen, relativity, and rubber seals. Unbelievable pressure plagues his every move. This is the game developer.

Far below, there is a younger guy jumping up and down, yelling "Paint it PINK! Paint it PINK! It should look like a slice of WATERMELON!!! Nobody will ever forget THAT!!!" This is the audio guy.

The audio guy, of course, is dead right. But the developer can hardly be blamed for yelling, "Get that nut off of my launch pad... *NOW!!!*"

Producers Are Often Unfamiliar with the Vocabulary and Subtle Skills Necessary to Coax a Good Performance from a Composer

And they shalt ask for the music to be a little more green. And it shalt ever be thus.

Game Producers Have Come to Think in Terms of a Very Few Styles of Music

As I have stated, we are a Simple People, and that simplicity can lead to frustration for the musician who wishes to compose his own style when the game developers have been thinking in terms of "Great Game Music."

At the time of writing, the following six styles comprise the Golden Six, the six styles considered to be "Great Game Music" by most (precisely 74.32%, in fact) game developers:

1. Orchestral imitations of John Williams' or Danny Elfman's film scores.[2]
2. Techno/repetitive beat dance music.
3. Atmospheric Beatless Music. That's Beatles with an extra "s."
4. Whatever was currently on the radio, but not composed by a game musician. Rather, this music is to be licensed from big artists for a small amount of money or licensed from small artists for nothing.
5. Music made by a friend of theirs.

And I'm *sure* there was a sixth.

Repetition

Game audio repeats. This problem has caused literally millions of people to hate game audio, and even games themselves.

The most important root of the problem is that there is simply no way a game developer can afford to pay for enough audio to adequately entertain a person for 40 hours of gameplay.

Even with the most brilliant adaptive scores, tunes that change over time, and well-thought-out licensing schemes, we find that after ten hours of listening to any game, the people in the next room (read "Mom") are ready to sign into law any bill prohibiting the sale and distribution of game audio.

Far More Audio Gets Created for Games Than Is Ever Heard

Although perhaps 100 games containing 100 hours of music are created per year, no more than three of those games, therefore three hours of music, get played; over and over and over....

---

2 Historical note: For a short while, after *Wing Commander* and *Ultima Underworld*, there was another style on the list: FM Imitations of Team Fat's FM imitations of John Williams' film scores.

A shocking thought, isn't it? Bad for composers, worse for players.

And it's made worse by the fact that I entirely made up the statistics, grossly underestimating them—100 games my foot. How many games do *you* think had an hour of music composed and then either rotted on the shelf or never even made it there? Makes it tough to be a composer, since most of your music—and your credits—will be unknown to the public.

And as I said, it's worse for the players. For them, it matters not what games aren't getting played a lot by the public, it only matters how many aren't getting played by an individual. Let's put it this way: How many games that were ever made have *you* not played? That's the music you aren't getting to hear, all the time you are having your nose rubbed into a 30-second loop of "High Tension Battle.WAV."

There Is No Business Model for Game Audio

Nobody in the world, even the most successful people in our business, has a sense of how much money a person should get for audio, nor do they know where that money is to come from or how they are to ensure that they can get some of it. In this sense, the business of game audio is starkly unlike the risky but relatively established businesses of TV audio and film audio. In those businesses, there are time-honored laws, rules, and conventions, and when somebody does the work but doesn't get paid (which happens, I understand, a terrible lot), it is generally agreed that that person was screwed. We haven't come that far. We don't have the laws, rules, and conventions, and therefore when *we* don't get paid for the work, there is no general sense of our actual "screwedness"—no general agreement that any wrong has been done. Of course, the bright side of this is that we have far, far fewer horror tales involving lawyers and long, twisted legal battles.

So, I would say that in the sense of its sophistication, history, frequency of legal battles, the guidance and protection available to businessmen, all that kind of thing:

I think the
business
of Game
Audio
can most
accurately be

compared to the
business of, say,
mime.[3]

[3] Now that I think of it, mime and game audio are also roughly matched in terms of supply-and-demand (although mime has a certain edge insofar as mimes in search of work are certainly more rare than musicians in search of work). And, in most test-beds and many gaming situations, the two are quite equal in terms of volume level.

There Is No Standard Creative Chain of Command for Game Audio

Who is the guy whose job it is to determine what kind of audio goes in the game? Whose responsibility is that in the end? Who answers to whom? What are good procedures for making sure that it happens? What does one do when the whole project goes all "yard sale" on you?

Well, a lot of guys will tell you the answer to these questions. But are they right? NO. Ask 15 guys, and you'll get 15 answers. Your Fat Friend in the Funny Suit has worked on 200 games, and he's got *lots* of answers, by crackey.

I've seen publishers force development teams to use person X to make the music or sound effects, swearing all the time it was "standard procedure." I've seen developers risk their chance to release a game with the publisher by ignoring such requests, claiming that such procedure was unheard of, unfair, and ridiculous. I've seen final audio decisions rest on everyone from the development team's boss to the lead designer, the manager, the programmer, the lead audio guy, the project's audio guy, corporate, the investor (!!!), the test-bed, the dreaded "Everybody" (as in "let's see what Everybody thinks"), the even more dreaded Focus Group, and occasionally the musician, which means that the final decision probably lands on his girlfriend, because she's smart enough to hold down a normal job, which has to be the case, because he's the musician.

The spontaneous nature of this part of production can be seen by the enlightened mind as a refreshing break from the more rigidly structured aspects of Life in the Business World. But it can be a problem if you're trying to, oh, say, make audio for a game.

Come to think of it, the **enlightened** *mind is kind of ill-suited* **to making audio for games.**

It's amusing to remember that when I first started doing this, the musician was almost always the game's programmer/designer himself, and he usually lived in his mom's garage. That's our roots, our DNA.

The tangled branches of this tree grew,
literally,

from a single nut.

The
Secret Elixir

It's good, hard work. Without it, this business will eat you alive. With it, you can elevate your mind to not even *see* the GLIP (see previous chapter) as problems.

Have you heard the old business adage, "Fast, Cheap, Good: Pick Two?" I've never heard anyone refute the wisdom of that saying, but then, I don't remember having discussed it with other successful game musicians.

Last month, I experienced a convergence of so many of the issues that are listed on the GLIP, all in a single job bid, that I found myself writing this to the client:

> "Fast, Cheap, Good, Technically-so-difficult-it's-not-likely-to-work-the-first-few-iterations, Unnecessary-because-the-programmer-has-special-tools-that-I-can't-have-and-considers-himself-an-audio-guy-so-he-has-already-done-a-version: Pick Four."

The facts that the end result was going to play back on a one-inch speaker using tones I'd never heard before and that I was limited to under a second for each composition were not even counted on the "pick four" list—I actually *love* those challenges.

That describes the fundamental character of the business of audio for games. They say you have to draw the line somewhere, and I'm proud to tell you what it took to finally get me to draw one after 20 years of saying "You bet!" There is a great feeling of pride in being able to participate in a business that allows this kind of story to be told without exaggeration. Maybe that's why I tell the stories with so much relish. Maybe that's where the Texas bragging comes from. Maybe that's why it's cool to climb the Big Mountains.

Working hard is cool. There's only one thing we're entitled to in this world, and that's doing our work with love. I like to do big jobs. I like small ones, too. It's Good-Bad.

I think that *is* success, and **everything** else is like the icing on the...
well, on the

rotten fish.

No matter how gifted and dedicated and such we are, we're not entitled to money and fame and a Ferrari. Sometimes we get those things and sometimes we don't. Whatever money and other gain that we get will be compensated by an exactly equal and opposite burden that goes with all stuff like that. Whatever pain we have from being fearful isn't something we're entitled to or deserve. It either comes or doesn't, and if it does come, it will be compensated by the strength of character, the bragging rights, the earthy cool that gets built by that kind suffering.

So, in review: There's Camp Fear on one side of our trail and Camp Desire on the other. You can go camping there or not. But the mountain is always there for you. If your mind is on the mountain, and you do your work and *love* it—experience it with unconditional acceptance—you will not only be certain to scale the mountain, but you'll find yourself instantly transported to its peak. Access to that peak is always available to you. Always unblocked. Nobody controls it but you.

I was very happy with my work one day, and Brian Moriarty, then in the deepest part of what he calls his "Obnoxious Zen Phase," said something very true. He simply said of my happiness, "It can always be like this."

This authentic piece of the South Pole was cut from the bottom of the actual pole and sent to me on my birthday by Brother Rick. Rick's goal was to go to the South Pole, and he heard they needed a cook. With great audacity, he signed on as a cook, then proceeded to teach himself cooking, all to freeze his butt off in the snow. Truly, he passed between fear and desire, did the work, and got the prize. My birthday, he realized later, is the anniversary of the exact day Man first set foot on the pole.

What to Expect from an Industry Based on Games

Things Happen Fast

If any one thing sets the game industry apart from others, it is the speed at which things happen.

Things happen quickly in the world of computers. Things happen quickly in the world of entertainment. Things happen quickly in games. Put it all together, it's kibbles-through-a-kitten fast.

This situation was most eloquently described by cyberpunk pioneer and author Bruce Sterling in his keynote speech for the GDC conference of 1991.[1]

Sterling said, "My art, science fiction writing, is pretty new as literary arts go, but it labors under the curse of three thousand years of literacy. In some weird sense, I'm in direct competition with Homer and Euripides. I mean, these guys aren't in the SFWA, but their product is still taking up valuable rack-space. You guys, on the other hand, get to reinvent everything every time a new platform takes over the field. This is your advantage and your glory. This is also your curse. It's a terrible kind of curse really."

In other words, a writer will often convince himself that his work might possibly be read and loved five hundred years from now. Maybe thousands of years from now. Like cave paintings. In most cases, of course, this is purely a delusion. It's a common one, and it's a beautiful and useful one. An author with the madness of self-importance will approach his art as though it were important. He'll use care, sensibility, and responsibility toward the future, as though he were writing his book to be read by millions and millions of thirsty eyes. I'm convinced that the early game developers approached their art with that kind of tenderness. I did. My friends did. Many of my friends still do.

[1] The full text of this speech is thoughtfully included in the appendix, "Bruce Sterling's Famous GDC Speech."

But now, 20 years later, something special has become dreadfully clear to us: We are not making cave paintings, we are building sand castles. The authors are too, but, for better or worse, they don't have their noses rubbed in that fact over and over the way we do. Every three to five years, in fact, the greatest games don't just fall out of fashion as a book might. They become unplayable. In the case of console games, there is some mercy. A player might find an old working Intellivision and one or two of the classic games at a garage sale and, without too much fussing, get a wonderful gaming treat. But computer games are a bust. My first days of glory were captured in *Wing Commander* and *The 7ᵗʰ Guest*. Now, I can't play either of those games, not even the later Windows versions, on any computer that I own. Since the days he was in diapers, my son hasn't played or heard anybody play those games of which I'm so proud. My daughter has never heard them played. She might not ever.

I'm just the sound guy.... Think of the situation facing the greatest of the game designers. The best gaming experiences I've had in the past months were two rounds of the multiplayer game *M.U.L.E.*, played against old-school producer Jeff Johannigman and his sons and mine. It's a good game. Four people in the same room, laughing out loud, "accidentally" bumping each other's controllers (per the instruction manual), my son driving down the price of food, causing a hilarious and unexpected dip in commodity values, joyously wandering the planet's surface in random circular movements, using the hitherto untried "headless chicken" strategy. I have two copies of *M.U.L.E.*, given to me by its creator Danielle Berry. One disk has become demagnetized, and there is no way to fix it. One still works, but my Atari 810 disk drive is broken. Jeff has two drives, but one is broken. I'm trying to parts-swap between the two broken drives to create a new one. I would try to make a copy, but I'm not hopeful. Jeff thinks it's too hard to do, and I think I would be wise to listen to him. He was in charge of copy protection at EA when *M.U.L.E.* was produced.

So you can see why I might just think twice before I wholeheartedly recommend that the reader or his friends delve into gaming as an occupation. It comes with a bonus that not everybody can accept gracefully. When you join the world of gaming, you sign up to get more than free games and a chance to drink Jolt Cola for a living. You tell the Universe that you are ready to learn the biggest and scariest lesson of all: perspective.

Mark Miller, the night he received the first ever Lifetime Achievement Award from GANG. I think he looks pretty good for a Lifetime Achievement Award recipient. Where's the wheelchair and oxygen tank?

A true game player knows that his world is temporary, his character is an illusion, and if it's a good game and he gives it his all, he and his foes will all be able to laugh about it when the game is over. But it's only fun if, at the time of the game, it's all as real as real can be, so he gives himself a kind of temporary amnesia, turning over every fiber of his being to the illusion that he is actually in the game.

Game designer Ernest Adams addresses other high-level game developers on the topic of immersion:

"These discussions... have taught me something about myself, and that is that the game's fantasy world is more important to me than to just about anybody else I know. That's why I'm repulsed by the brutality of *Grand Theft Auto III*, et al: I don't consider it just a little Monopoly-set car moving around a Monopoly-set world, a purely iconic abstraction with no emotional significance to me or cultural relevance to the real world. Computer games aren't 'games' to me in the board-game sense; they're more like movies—still fictitious, but a world that I enter into personally, and the more so since they're interactive. When I'm playing a game like that, the car is real, the victims are real, the avatar is me, and I take its moral challenges very seriously. I immerse myself as totally as I can. And that's where, I realize, I part company from a great many other players. To you, Scott, changes to the theme don't constitute game-play innovation; to me, the theme is an essential part of the gameplay, the part that enables me to be *in* the world rather than just a guy in a room staring at a screen and twiddling some buttons.

"Or, to sum it up in one sentence: To me, every alien in *Space Invaders* was an individual with a home and family somewhere, and I regretted the necessity of killing them. :)"

—Ernest W. Adams
Designer for *3DO Madden* and *Dungeon Keeper 3*,
in an email to game designers

A true game developer learns that his career can be such a game. He is faced over and over with the truth of the fact that nothing he does in this world will last. He has eaten the fruit of the tree of knowledge and cast himself out of Eden.

And yet, the poison tree gives its own antidote. For how could he have gone into games without knowing that to be totally immersed, to care about people, to live every moment as though it were the only thing that mattered, is a way of glowing, of loving, and of praying. To live like that, with full knowledge of the rules of the game, allows a person to give off the kind of colors that can heal the planet.

That is the gift that we game developers bring to the world. It's not that complicated. To bring our gift, we limit our perspective.

Simply put, we like to design and play our own games.

We choose what's important, we pick our rules, and then for much of our lives we deliberately set aside the rest—the irrelevant things, the things that detract from our immersion in the Big Game. Women. Social skills. Subtleties of art. Exercise. And especially The Past... the painful, painful past. Then we share the purity of this vision with everybody else who loves games.

We are a Simple People.

We move toward the future and burn our bridges to the past.

We chase bad guys, or **we** pretend we're bad guys.

We like a palette with millions of colors, but given the choice, **we** always pick black. **We** like guns and breasts, and in most cases **we** are quite certain that **bigger** is better.

Sidebar: Barefoot and in the kitchen with DragonLord

DragonLord, also known as John Myers, exemplifies the very powerful and unique life-as-a-game attitude of the archetypal game developer. In an effort to find distribution for his creation, Bite Me™, he wore a hat shaped like a giant shark head to GDC. Is DragonLord in it for the money? You decide. I have known him long enough to believe that he did not run out and buy the props in the photo below. He does survive on tuna. Those are real bills. Likewise, he did not borrow the Corvette in the photo at the end of the chapter "Venture Capital: Angel or Devil," nor is he lying about his income.

He sends me presents on my birthday. He has familiarity with Asian cultures and languages. He hired my friend Adam Holzman, who used to play keyboards with Miles Davis, to transcribe pop songs into one-beep-at-a-time ring tones for telephones. He takes sitar lessons from Hiro-sensei, an Osakan Master who studied under Ravi Shankar. It's my great honor to be the friend of somebody who paints in broad strokes.

But hark... we hear the DragonLord about to release some wisdom unto the world, and his voice is saying this:

Life is an Adventure.

Remember this always.

Life is a grand game of *Dungeons & Dragons*, in which YOU are both the GM and the main player.

It's your responsibility to design a good module for yourself.

When you don't, you have only yourself to blame.

You can make it funny, or you can make it exciting; you can make it romantic, or adventuresome, or educational, or evil, or holy. You can make the story come out however you want. YOU get to decide what the adventure will be like. It is completely up to you.

Again, life is like a parade. Many people spend their life as couch potatoes, watching the parade of their own lives on TV. Never bothering even to change the channel if it gets boring or if a horror show is on by mistake. Some people take the trouble to get out of the house and show up. Watch the parade outside. Chat with their neighbors and watch the real people marching by in front of them. However, a few people choose to march in the parade—they get to dress up and be glorious, do something that *matters* to themselves. Wave at the people watching by the side of the street or watching on TV. Run their own lives and MAKE it a parade. Make it glorious!

Me, I'm marching right up there in the front, with my leather superhero cape, my wizard boots, and my dragon on my shoulder. Casting spells left and right. Creating joy and humor and fun and adventure for humanity. Because that's what it's all about.

I believe everyone should be the leader of his or her own parade.

There are many other things that a young game designer must know.

Creating art, creating value in the universe, is much more important than eating or sleeping or earning money. You must understand your priorities and then follow through. However, if you neither eat nor sleep nor make any money, then you cannot make any games, and you will be unable to accomplish your mission. This is a paradox, but it is true.

Therefore, you must take care of yourself first and keep yourself strong, in order that you may take care of others.

Here Mr. Bite Me Shark, you must eat protein to keep your strength up.

Eating a tuna sandwich every day keeps you feeling happy. One of the cheapest sources of protein is those large cans of salmon for $0.75 each; you can live for close to a week off of one of those if you push it. Potatoes also offer a wonderfully cheap source of energy. Instant Ramen noodles also give an extremely cheap meal (eat with a lettuce leaf and a single slice of lunchmeat ham immersed for that Japanese flavor), and chopsticks are a lot faster to clean than a fork.

Canada Dry ginger ale provides a soft drink without all that nasty caffeine.

It's important to develop a ritual to tell your brain when it's time to work; mine involves opening a can of soda. My religious beliefs make it a sin to throw aluminum away without recycling it; unfortunately, there is no recycling bin at the apartment complex where I live, so a special trip has to be organized out to the recycling center in my spare time. Haha. Hahahaha. This illustrates in a graphic manner the inventory storage problems factories encounter when their processing flows are not balanced properly.

The shirt says "CGDC '96." Wearing the competition's T-shirts keeps you inspired, saves money on unnecessary things like clothes in favor of necessary things like food and rent, and allows you to go for another day (or two!) without wasting time on something unproductive like washing clothes. If you visit enough booths at the conference, you can acquire a whole month's worth of T-shirts. It's okay, because a decade later you will be wasting thousands of dollars giving your own T-shirt out for other starving developers to wear in the privacy of their own kitchens. And you should only give T-shirts out if you can afford to. This is thus a metaphor for charity in life. Think upon this every time you put on a T-shirt, and grow wise.

Above my head are lots of bottles of juice for the Y2K bug. Everyone knows that on January 1, 2000, all of the planes are suddenly going to fall out of the sky, traffic lights will fail and cause massive collisions, and banks will forget everything that you own or owe. Thus it is a good time to be net negative. Fortunately, I owe somewhere around $50,000 to $100,000 total to various credit card agencies, so I'm going to be just fine. Kids: Don't Try This At Home. The one lesson I learned in business school is DON'T RUN OUT OF CASH. I have six months left before I run out of credit completely, hit The Wall, and have to punch the ejection button. Fortunately, I pull down an easy $140,000[1] a year consulting for dot-com companies, when I have to work for someone else and don't run my own company; I've never had to look for a job longer than two or three weeks in my life; and the economy looks absolutely wonderful for the next five or ten years.[2] So even if I were to max out, it is inconceivable that I could spend six or eight months searching nationwide for any kind of consulting job over $100K. I know how much credit I have and how much my food/rent burn rate is, so I'll just have to punch out a month or two before I deplete everything completely, and it will work out.[3] Besides, I'm just about to get a check for a million or two from a Japanese publisher, just as soon as I get an edutainment company to pick up my game. Japan is the world's number two economy, and I'm sure it must be full of edutainment game publishers.[4] At least I assume so.[5]

The CDs and the videotapes are to keep your spirits up on the Death March.

Depression can kill you. *Urusei Yatsura* (*Lum*), written by genius lady Rumiko Takahashi (who also did *Ranma 1/2*), has always been one of my favorites.

I use Manowar music to work by; it is laden with the skull-crunching, testosterone-driven, We-Will-Prevail-No-Matter-What attitude that you need to keep you working late nights past 3:00 a.m. It lets you deal with The Fear.

The Fear is what Evel Knievel felt when he was driving his motorcycle up to the ramp to jump the Grand Canyon, he looked down at the gas gauge, and he realized that he'd forgotten to refill his tank and there might not be enough gas for him to make it across to the other side. He realized that either he was going to jump the Grand Canyon and make it across, or he was going to fall to his death screaming horribly with the end within sight. Except Evel Knievel only felt The Fear for five minutes, whereas game developers learn to live with The Fear for months on end. It is a direct consequence of taking financial responsibility for your company, especially when you don't know what you're doing and have never formally studied risk management.

Moms: Don't let your kids grow up to be untrained, self-funded entrepreneurs. Only let them be entrepreneurs if it's in their blood; there are easier ways to make a living. Always insist that they go the first four rounds using OPM (Other Peoples' Money). And make sure that they get the training that they need to be able to survive on their own. And remember, always:

DON'T RUN OUT OF
CASH!!!!!!!!!! "

---

[1] This was in 1999, when we still had dot-com companies.

[2] This was before the bubble burst and top computer programmers became virtually unemployable. Haaa ha ha ha ha ha.

[3] "Famous Last Words."

[4] Inconceivably, the world's second largest economy was full of entertainment software companies and education software companies, but in 1999 there were no edutainment companies. The concept was foreign and was summarily rejected by the host body. Extensive market research failed to take into account the most important customers of them all: the publishing executives.

[5] Bad assumptions can get you killed faster than just about anything else except running out of cash. However, it is impossible to operate without making some assumptions. Try to keep them to a minimum as much as possible, though, and always double-check and triple-check when it's really important. Never assume when it's possible to avoid doing so. Remember: "Anything that *can* go wrong, *will* go wrong" [Murphy's Law].

A

Simple

People

SPOKESMAN OF THE NERDS:

I appear before you, oh mighty Oracle, to beg for guidance for my people. My people are the Nerds, the Gamers, oh Oracle—and we are lost.

We are a simple people. Our clothing needs are simple: anything black. Our nutritional needs are simple: caffeine, salt, fat, and sugar in any combination will do nicely. But nothing about us is nearly so simple as our aesthetics.

It has to do with our roots. We are not like the Television People. They came from the Radio Men, who came from the Book People, who called Shakespeare their father. Shakespeare is complicated, and he does "to be or not to be," which makes us think about decisions. He is not the guy for us. Nor are we like unto the Big Screeners, whose ancestors were the Photo Makers, who came from the Painters, whose way was watched over by the Van Goghs and the Warhols and the guys who draws *Doonesburys*. We despise the Big Screeners and Television People and their soft jobs, in which they can just point a camera at something and it shows up on a screen and people laugh and cry and pay money.

Many years ago, in the Before Time, our ancestors, the Life Givers, created the first games, and our people were born and we thrived. The first games were good and, being a simple people with little tiny computers, we were happy to have what we had.

What we had was white text against a black background, describing a few rooms in a dungeon. In these dungeons, we could find and pick up swords and things and kill dragons and things, and the more things we picked up, the more powerful we became. We liked becoming powerful, because it enabled us to kill dragons.

Then the computers got a little bigger, and a game that described more rooms and had more things for us to pick up, like shields and potions and stuff, made us more powerful, and therefore it was a better game.

Then a game came out that had two rectangles and a flying square, and that was even better. Then there were little eight-pixel-high blocky guys who looked like they were running, and those games were better still. The bigger and faster the little blocky guys got, the better we liked the games.

And so the little men got bigger, and they ran faster through bigger dungeons, picking up more and more kinds of stuff, and the dragons they fought had pixels and pixels and more pixels.

And as the games got better, the people who made the better games made more money than the people who made worse games. Soon, they even made more money than artists, than photographers—more than pretty much anybody in their high school classes. That was good.

Then they made more money than their teachers. That was even better.

Then they made more money than the Television People and the Big Screeners, because they made the best games. And by then they—and in fact all of the Simple People—all knew exactly, precisely, without a doubt what a good game was. We still do.

A good game is a fast game. A good game is a game with lots of rooms in its dungeon. A good game is a game in which the little guy and the dragon have countless pixels. And if you can pick up lots of things, countless things, innumerable things—even the flies and the silverware—then that is the best game of all.

Faster is better. Bigger is better. More is better. More realism and better physics is better. That is our wisdom to this day.

But, oy, Oracle, have we got troubles now.

Because now our computers are big. Really, really big. And we can make things really, really, *really* big, fast, and plentiful.

And there was this one guy last year, Prometheus, who decided that he would make the best game of all. He started to make a game that had all the rooms in the world in it and all the guys in the world in it, and that would run as fast as the world runs. And do you know what he discovered, Oracle?

There are a *lot* of *things* in the world.

I mean, Prometheus, he didn't make more money than other game makers. Even after he had built a machine that could simply point at something and bring it into the game, he still *spent* money on modeling all those rooms and guys and flies and footprints and *all that silverware*!!!

And the game wasn't very fun. The flies were bothersome, and nobody knew what to do with all that silverware.[1]

So my people, the Nerds, the Simple People, had a meeting of the Elders, and at that meeting, this problem was discussed for a long time. And it was concluded, painfully, that perhaps more, faster, and bigger are *not*, after all, better. Because you can't make everything, and if you do, it's not fun or profitable. And the Elders realized that they would have to decide *which* things to make, *how fast* to make those things, and *how big*.

Oh Oracle, that brings me to why I have come here. I represent a people who are humbled. A people who thought they knew the answers, and who found out that they were wrong.

The guys making smaller, less, and slower games sometimes make better games, and it confuses the heck out of us.

We are a people who need to learn something. We need to learn that, if big, more, and fast aren't best, what *is*?

[1] Long after the death of Prometheus, the question of what to do with all that silverware was discussed amongst the intelligent and bored members of lower society. It was eventually correctly hypothesized by members of a secret society, PSI (Persistent Silverware Inc.), that the only way to defeat the gigantic dragon in the final level of the game was to use all the knives, spoons, and forks to build an intricate exoskeleton with which your hero could become as powerful as Sigourney Weaver in the final battle scene of *Aliens*.

The game was revised and shipped in this form, hailed as gaming's greatest achievement, but still nobody liked it—except one player, an eight-year-old beta tester named Jimmy, who could not be convinced to leave the computer. Researchers discovered finally that little Jimmy had found among the myriad of virtual objects in the game a perfectly accurate working model of a first-generation Gameboy handheld, and he had been spending his hours battling virtual Charizard against virtual Pikachu.

Go figure.

We need to learn *what* to point our camera at to make people laugh and cry. We need to learn *how* to make people think about decisions. We need to be, or not to be. We need to learn to *decide*.

How do we *do* it, oh Oracle? We beseech thee.

ORACLE:

William Shatner is not in the office right ***now***.

Please leave a **brief** message at the **sound** of the

communicator beep.

beep

What Gamers Do

In February of 1997, a match was held between two players, and many felt that it determined who was the best Quake player in the world.

To everybody's surprise, the winner turned out to be a charming young lady. Her name was Stevie Case, but online she was known as Killcreek. She came to Texas from Kansas to challenge John Romero, founder of Ion Storm and the closest thing the game world has to a celebrity. They played, and he lost.

Killcreek worked on a Quake Mission Pack at her own company, Primitive Earthling Games. By the time she applied for a job in QA at Ion Storm, her gaming prowess was known to the company. She got the job in QA, then moved up to other levels. She dated John.

She made great money at Ion Storm. She bought herself some new boobs. She did a center spread in *Playboy*.

When the game *Age of Mythology* was released to manufacturers, Ensemble Studios threw a very nice party in Dallas, Texas. There was a mechanical bull. The Fat Man was there to participate in a celebrity tournament of the game. He and his friend Jamal arrived early and played two rounds of the game, getting instruction from a quiet, excellent gamer named Blue. Jamal did have the pleasure of using the Curse power to turn The Fat Man's most promising invading army into pigs. Then he fed them to his villagers, which was a classy move. However, by the end of both games The Fat Man had beaten Jamal quite soundly. He made a promise to himself to rub this fact in by writing about it someday in a book, because that's the kind of thing Real Gamers do when they win.

Later at the party, The Fat Man was surprised to find out that the only other celebrity in the tournament was to be the famous John Romero. When Romero showed up, he asked The Fat Man if he was ready to be crushed. He introduced his partner, whose name was not entirely unlike "Evil Death To Your Mother From Hell." Fat asked if John played the game much, and John responded by saying that he and Evil Death played it all the time and were quite good.

Mr. Romero wanted to know who The Fat Man's partner was to be. The Fat Man had never played with a partner. The Fat Man, trying not to shake, let his eye wander past Jamal and then land upon the other person he happened to be hanging around with, Blue. "I believe this is my partner. Is that okay with you, Blue?"

It was a good game. The Fat Man created an invading fleet, landed it on the other island, and when his army refused to attack, the entire room burst into laughter. He had accidentally invaded Blue's island.

In the end, Fat and Blue crushed their enemies. Fat liked the part where Blue leaned over to him and whispered, "I think we can relax. All I have to do now is make it look good." He also liked the part where he delivered the turn-them-into-pigs curse on John, shouting at the top of his lungs, "SoooooooEEEE!!! Eat Musical Death!!!" He liked planting an earth-quake on John's city. He liked that his individual score was higher than John's or Evil's. He liked that the food was free.

The Fat Man plants the earthquake on Romero's town center.
The Fat Man's score at this point: 6734 to Romero's 2635.

On the other hand, The Fat Man was humbled by the fact that in the rematch, which pitted John, Evil, and him against Blue, Blue trounced them all. But then he went and rode the mechanical bull a couple of times and forgot all about that.

And it is said that by the Grace of Hera, The Fat Man won a beautiful trophy that night, and furthermore, something magical happened. It came to pass that nobody would ever be able to accuse The Fat Man of not being a real gamer. He beat the Great John Romero.

And The Fat Man spoke, saying:

"**Now** my future is clear and my **fate** is sealed.

"I'm going to get some **new boobs**, then do a **spread** in *Playboy*.

"Because that's the kind of thing that **Real Gamers** do when they win."

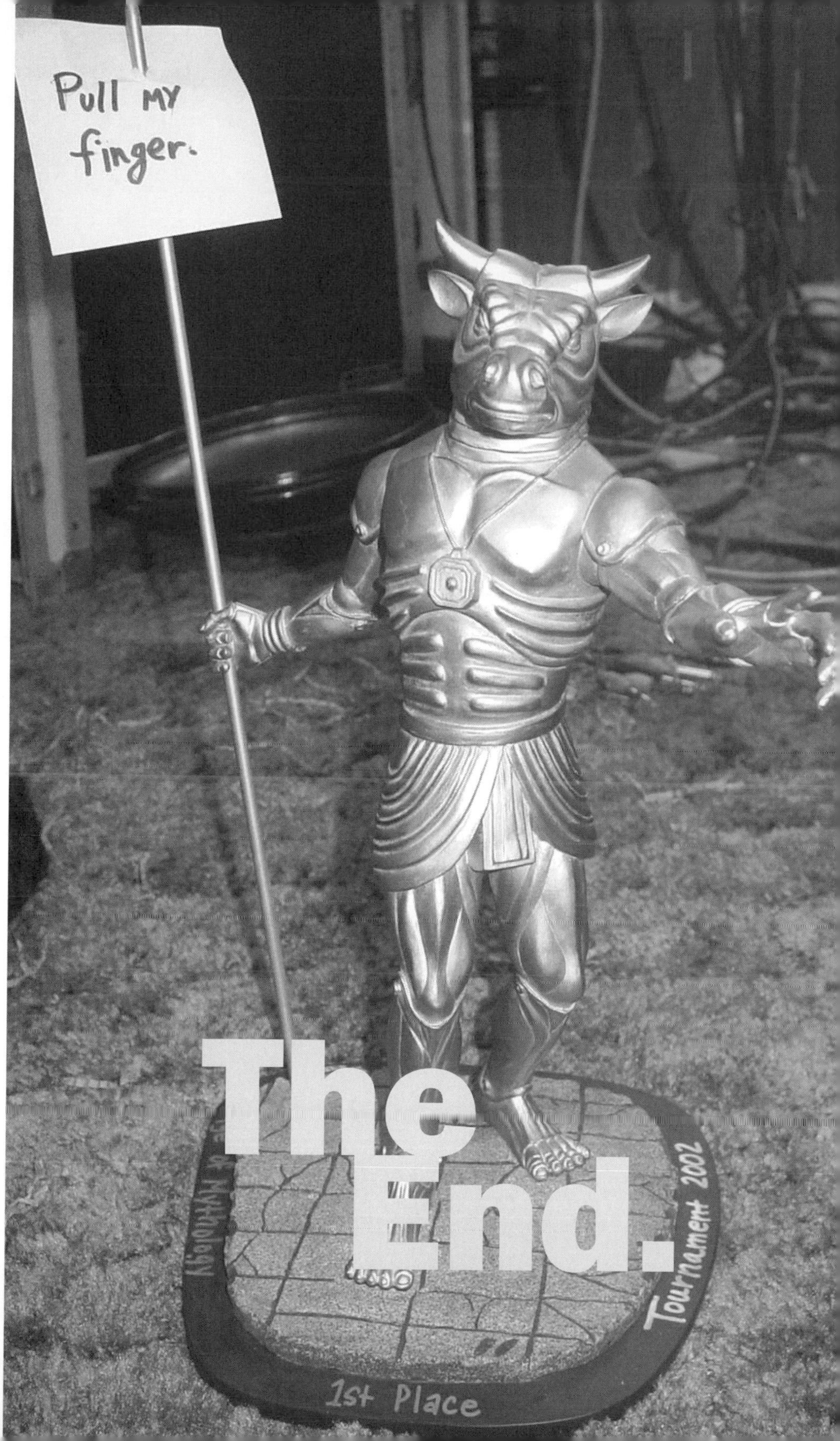
Pull my finger.
The End.
Tournament 2002
1st Place

Q:

Where Do Competitors Come from, Mommy?

For most of them, The Wild Basin Expedition was their first hi-tech job:
The Origin Systems team that created Savage Empire poses in the beautiful
lobby of the old, old, old Origin building, circa 1990. Clockwise from lower left:
Keith Berdak, Jeff Johannigman, Jeff Dee, Marc Schaefgen, Denis Loubet
(rear), Aaron Allston, 'Manda Dee, Phillip Brogden, John Watson, Jason
Templeman (rear), Bob Quinlan, The Fat Man, Glen Johnson, Mike Romero,
Richard Garriott, and Stephen Beeman. Dan Bourbonnais not shown.
Don't even try to find all the companies these guys have been in since.

How did Austin, Texas become such a great place for game companies? Origin Systems. And what did they do? They created a perfect competitor-generating machine. An environment ideally suited to spinning out huge numbers of its own brilliant likenesses.

I don't think you or I could have done a better, more noble thing for the city of Austin if we'd tried.

Let's say that we set out to create an incubator that was especially suited to spinning off as many brilliant competing game companies as possible. How would we start?

Well, let's work backward. Since we eventually want the people to spin off and form their own companies in a massive fit of discontent, they really mustn't be too contented where they are. We'd have to pay them less than they think they're worth.

There are two ways to do that. We could pay them too little, but that's not nice, and it will earn us a bad reputation. We can try it for a little while, which is nice for sowing the seeds of discontent. But our company really won't last that way. Sooner or later, we'll have to start paying people industry standard.

So the only way to pay people less than they think they're worth is to hire people with no idea at all what they are worth. Smart enough to do a great job, but naive enough to think they'll get amazingly rich right away. I think you'd have to hire them straight out of college before they'd ever worked another job in their lives, don't you?

To make sure that they left in a huff, though, you'd have to work the hell out of them. Naturally, you can't *ask* them to overwork themselves. *But,* if the work is inspiring and fun and cutting-edge, they'll set up little cots in their offices, and they'll *never* go home.

That's right. Hire brilliant, egotistical people with no idea of what it is to work for a boss. Hire people to whom every inter-office memo is a Kabala, full of secret meanings and importance for the future. People who *expect* that they are only a month or two away from getting the Ferrari that life owes them. Give them their dream job so that they overwork themselves, fueling the fires that heat the indignation.

And to crown the whole thing off, hire people who are always thinking of ways to better their lot. To whom all the world is a game. Hire gamers.

If these suggestions tempt you to take action, Dear Reader, I must remind you not to bother. This was all done to perfection in the early '90s by Origin Systems. There were years—yes, *years*—in Austin during which you could not allow a group of three or more game professionals to gather lest it turn instantly into an interminable, indignant rant about the atrocities perpetrated upon poor them by the heartless management of this terrible, terrible company. They left in packs and droves, taking their friends with them, starting brilliant little empires and enterprises that would glorify Austin in years to come.

And enough water has passed under the Congress Avenue bridge that today when these same people gather, they no longer speak with unbounded venom, hatred, or remorse. No, generally it's a sense of nostalgia, admiration, and thankfulness that a company was able and willing to take them under its wing, even at a time when they themselves had no stinking idea at all what it was to wake up with the rest of the world and put in a normal hard day's work.

God bless the aptly named Origin Systems. The city of Austin is a testimonial to the remarkable good that can come from a determined policy dedicated to that defiance of reality so characteristic of gamers, a policy so deeply ingrained in this group so certainly destined to spread its seed far and wide, that even the company's mission statement declared it.

"We create worlds."

"Good-bad," The Fat Man's '58 Rolls-Royce Silver Cloud, covered in ashes from the bonfire that burned the six-foot-high stack of design documents for Ultima Online II. The project was cancelled on the day it was finished, and the wild, sad party that was thrown for it on founder Richard Garriott's lakeside property was widely seen as a final passing of the old Origin Systems.

A: Define "Competitor"

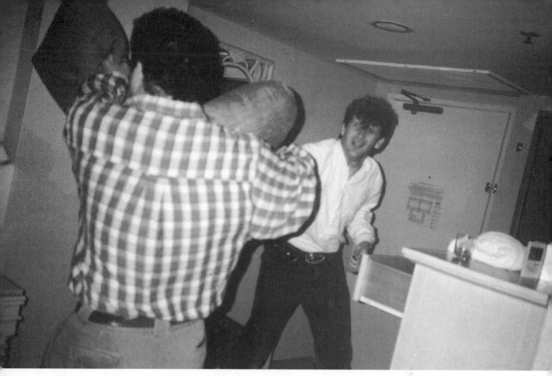

I womp "competitor" Clint Bajakian upside the head with Weapon Three, the Deadly Laser Pillow. Yes, Mom, we broke the lamp. It happened just as you said it would. We fixed it, and for the sake of archaeologists to come, we also sealed a nice cigar inside.

My particular sob story during the aforementioned Era of Austin Griping was that Dave Govett and I had written music for *Wing Commander I*, *Wing Commander II*, and several other games for Origin Systems. While some of Origin's forces, under orders to do so, assured us that we were never to be replaced, other forces installed an in-house music department to replace us.

Surely, if anybody ever in the world would qualify as a competitor to The Fat Man, it would be the evil bastard who got the job of writing music for *Wing Commander III* and up, George Oldziey.

I met Evil George. I met his wife. Our sons became friends in Cub Scouts. I heard about George's remarkable career as a world-class professional trumpet player. I heard about how it was cut short. And when I heard that he had been just about to take a job selling insurance when he heard about the opening at Origin, I was ashamed to think of the harm that would have come if I had successfully landed the *Wing Commander III* gig. The world would have been short one very cool composer.

Fierce competitors of the future: Yu-Gi-Oh club founded by my son Glen, far left, and George Oldziey's son Nick, far right.

This year, my son was hit by a car while he was riding his bike to school. He's okay, don't worry, but we didn't know that at the time. My wife and I drove down to the scene of the accident. There was an ambulance and a fire truck, and everyone was gathered around our Glen, who was lying in the middle of the street. Linda was having a terrible time of it. I couldn't comfort her while I spoke with the paramedics. There was only one person on the scene who was a close enough friend to do that: George Oldziey.

People, unless you want it really badly, there is no such thing as competitors. Get over it.

How can it be called collaborating with the enemy? What enemy?
Me and my "biggest competitor," my rich brother Tommy T.,
getting over it at an all-game-musician jam hosted by the IA-SIG.
Everybody's wearing their new GANG vests.

Venture Capital: Angel or Devil?

Brian Moriarty once took me aside and confided,

Part 1:
the Devil.
"Venture Capital **is**
"

I look at it like this: In the "good old days," people used to call me up and say, "we're going to make a really great game, and we'd like you to help us with the sound." Then, one day, they started saying, "We're going to make a demo that's just going to *blow those investors away,* and we'd like your help." If, indeed, there was a moment at which things changed, *that* was the moment at which things changed. Making great demos requires a completely different process than making great games, but if you have investors, making demos is a process in which you are strongly encouraged to participate. Sometimes, it seems to me, at my most bitter, that every decision I've seen made that was associated with making a great demo might have been set out upon with a good spirit, but eventually eroded into a compromise, a half-measure, squeezed painfully by the developer from his reluctant accomplices by appealing to their greed and fear. Every decision that I associate with making a great game has been one of growth, freedom, exploration, and blossoming forth of creativity.

From time to time, especially during the dot-com boom, I would be called by Venture Capital firms. At first, I didn't fully realize what they were offering. As I looked into it, I found that we would fall into this conversation:

"Hi, George, we heard about your exciting business. We're going to be in town next week, and we wanted to know if you'd be interested in our taking you to dinner and discussing a possible relationship with us."

"So, I'm not too bright at these things, but from what I understand, in exchange for some participation in my long-term profits and some control over my company, you would be willing to give me all the money I've ever dreamed of, right?"

"Yes, George, actually, that's pretty much the size of it."

"Oh, cool, thanks! But I'm sorry, I don't really *want* all the money I ever dreamed of right now. But if you still want to go to dinner, I'd love to talk."

Brian Moriarty also took me aside and confided,

Part 2:
"But if they invite **you** out to dinner, always take them up on it. They buy *great* meals and at the *best* restaurants."

DragonLord Writes

People think that venture capitalists (VCs) are there to bring joy into the world and help a company blossom. It is a common mistake of perception. A VC's job is to make money. A VC is nothing more than an extremely bright investment banker or fund manager. Very rich people have given the VC lots of money, with the expectation that the VC will make even more money for them. The VC has a mandate to do this. By whatever means possible. When you sell "35%" of your company to a VC for a couple of million dollars, that means that the VC owns your company. And that means that the VC can and will replace your butt as president and CEO of the company once it actually grows up and becomes mainstream, or if it starts to implode and needs to change directions. Your only hope for managing your own company is to have it be above mediocre, but not excellent. Anything less or more means you will be replaced. The VC might own only 35% of the company on paper, but he or she will have the final say in actuality. You think of your company as being a unique flower. The VC sees it as wheat: You grow it, you harvest it.

Professional VCs are only interested in companies that are absolutely sure to reach a $100M value. This means roughly $10M in sales per year. There are about 300 to 1,000 startup companies that cross the desk of a typical pro VC every year, but he or she only funds about three a year. All of these look perfect on paper. This means that if your company is less than perfect, it is never going to make the cut. There are 20 more companies better than yours coming in next week.

Unless you can show that you are the next Apple, there is no way that you will ever get funding from a professional VC.

Does this mean you are wasting your time talking to one? No, because it will provide a humbling learning experience as to just how far you have to go before you can be considered "real."

You might get an amateur VC, but you wouldn't want to deal with someone like that.

Game companies have a better chance of being bought by Microsoft or some other huge gaming company that is strategically interested in acquisition than they do in getting funded by a VC.

The alternative to VC or strategic funding is Angel funding. An Angel is a bored rich person who wants more excitement in his or her life. Angels can write six- or seven-figure checks without blinking. Most Angels will want to see a return on their money (rich people generally are not stupid), but some may do it mostly for altruism, speculation, or pride of ownership. Angels can be a lot better than VCs, because they don't have a board of billionaire investors breathing down their neck. On the other hand, Angels can be a lot more unpredictable than VCs.

The Fat Man doesn't know much about *this* kind of Angel, but the other kind seems to respond well, albeit indeed unpredictably, to being recognized and thanked, especially out loud. By way of illustrating the importance of this point to daily life, The Fat Man refers his indulgent readers to the story in the appendix of this book entitled, "The Nudie Suit Story."

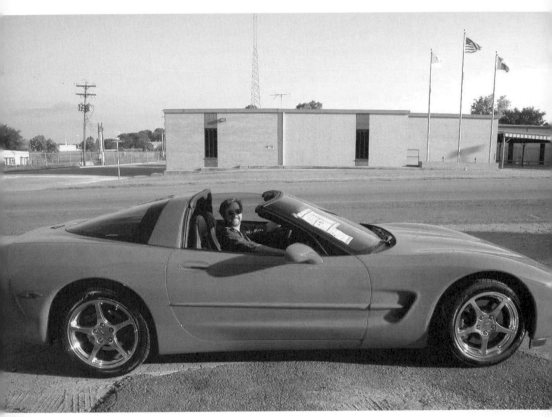

DragonLord, as much at home behind the wheel of his new Corvette as he is behind a checkbook, a computer keyboard, or a fork stuck into a can of tuna.

The Culture
Game
of Audio or
If You're Gonna
Be Portin'
You Gotta Look Like You're Portin'
or,
Better Still, Tell Me
How To
Be Like You
Fat Man!!!
or Lead, Follow,
or
Get Out of
the Way

I like to imagine the early days of surfing, when there were only, like, four guys who surfed. They had to decide what length to wear their shorts. They had to decide if sandals were cool. They had to figure out if short hair was better in the water than long hair. What words would they use? Which one thought of "Gremmie?" Which one coined "Wipe-Out?" Must have been fun. Did they ever think about the future?

"Hey, Dude, ya know what's funny? In, like, the *future*, Dude, maybe everybody's gonna, like, use the words 'like' and 'dude' a whole bunch because of *us*, Dude!"

Thanks to them, we know how to pretend to be surfers. We wear sandals. Long hair is best. Shorts should be baggy. If it weren't for those brave pioneers, people pretending to be surfers would not know how to dress and talk. Think about it. A moment of silence, please.

Team Fat found itself in a similar position in game audio, and we *did* think about the future. You can see this reflected in "The Manitatso." We were making up a profession as we went along, and we couldn't bear the idea that someday an aspirant such as yourself would have to invent his own culture. We were joined by Tommy T. and a few others who had a sense of style, and certain cultural traits took hold.

It has been said by people high up in the conference throwing world that the only subgroup of game developers who has a real community is the audio guys.

If you hope someday to be a game audio guy, or portray one in a television series, or if you merely wish to be able to identify one as he approaches so that you might avoid him, you will certainly need to know about our culture, follow its rules, change its rules, or get a real job.

Tony Goodman gets into The Fat Man's car to pretend he's a cool game audio guy.

Aaron Marks, author of the other book on game audio worth reading, realizes that it's important to look like a good game composer.

Jay Semerad, student and staff member of GANG, walks a mile in my shoes, and I in his. Jay honored me by asking me to decorate his GANG vest. There is a way these things are done.

It was the Science that did that thing to his eyes: Thomas Dolby Robertson tries in vain to match The Fat Man's famous "lights-on-but-nobody's-home" look.

You probably know Thomas from his hit songs, especially "She Blinded Me with Science." He's done a lot of other things, including films and producing other great artists. He created Beatnik, which stands out as one of the best ways to play audio on the web. But most importantly, he attended Project BBQ in 1999.

Story: It had been about five years since he'd played a live show, the one exception being that he had played a few songs for a friend's wedding. At about two in the morning we kicked off a jam with about seven people in the band, and no audience. After a few covers, Thomas pushed a button on his keyboard, and "She Blinded Me with Science" kicked in; he still had it sitting in there from the wedding gig. So we did the tune, and when it was time to yell "Science!!!" he pointed at me. So I got to yell "Science!!!" Pretty cool. When it came up the second time, he gave me the cue again, but I'd already done it once. Game Audio Guys pass the good stuff around.

First
and least
important,

the official blade of the Game Audio Guy is the Gillette Mach III razor. Bobby Prince (*Doom*) turned me and Alex Brandon on to them. He gave me his. Stan Neuvo (Ion Storm, Retro Games) picked it up from me. The Mach III got passed around at the first meeting of the GANG. As Bobby said, "Mah face hasn't been this baby-butt smooth in *years*!"

We dress like early '70s funk bass players.

*The Great '70s Funk Bass Players Mark Miller, Dave Javelosa, Tommy Tallarico,
and Fat, at a jam party in Las Vegas hosted by Sierra Online.*

We drive either cheap-looking piece-of-crap

cars or ...

expensive-looking *piece-of-crap cars.*

The venerable members of the community are, almost to a man, maniacally pro-active, like the members of GANG and the Brothers of BBQ. The newbies act like they are the last surviving original blues musicians. Never has there been a whinier, more downtrodden group than the three-year veterans of sound for games. Luckily, because things move so quickly in this business, they become venerable in their fourth year, and all is changed.

We own melodicas. It started when Michael Land brought one to BBQ for jamming around the campfire. It spread to the rest of the Stooges, then to Tommy, and then me. The best deal I was able to find is the Color Boy Melodihorn pictured in the chapter "Creating Your Signature Sounds." It costs half what the competing brand does, so check it out.

We have our own language. And if we didn't before, we will after this book catches on.

Clint and Tommy duel to the death on melodicas after the first GANG kickoff meeting. Clint says, "Beat this: Beethoven."

The First Ever Glossary of Game Musician Words

Alsihad (*Pronounced Al-see-hod*): means Pro Tools. The term was coined by an old-timer named Fletcher who once described a session in which "alls ah had was Pro Tools." Some newsgroups and listservers feature filters that automatically change the phrase "Pro Tools" to "Alsihad" (http://recpit.prosoundweb.com/viewtopic.php?t=2281).

> **Alsihah:** The one who uses Alsihad.
>
> **007:** The free version of Alsihad.
>
> **MOA:** Short for Mother of Alsihad.
>
> **666s:** MOA's proprietary ADDAs.
>
> **NYPD:** MOA's proprietary digital clock.

BBQ: Project Bar-B-Q, the conference we throw in Boerne every year. See the appendix, "Projects," of this book for a description of BBQ.

Cables: What it always is. See the chapter "Methods (Superstitions) of Efficient Audio Production."

Cinematic: A little noninteractive movie that can be scored as though it were normal video, using no special techniques that are unknown to TV and Movie guys. I worked on three of the early games to make significant progress in establishing the *cinematic*, and it was tough because we had no word for them. I put in a bid to call each one a "finite amount of theatre," or FAT.

Content: Music.

Content Provider: Musician. As in, "Beethoven is my favorite content provider."

Excellent: Good, but either in an evil way, per *The Simpsons*, or bad, as in sarcastically. The idea of starting a union was brought up once many years ago between a bunch of broke musicians. Bobby Prince said, "Excellent strategy. Let's kick 'em while we're down."

Excrement: Really good. Like "bad-ass."

Fucked: Super good, for the reasons listed above.

Fuckcellent: The best of all.

Game Musician: Sounds too much like "gay musician" to say out loud, so we are still looking for something to call ourselves. Speaking of which, how can a magazine call itself "*Game Informer*?" It sounds too close to "Former Gay Men."

GANG: The Game Audio Network Guild. This is a remarkable trade organization that covers audio "content providers" for games. Started by Tommy Tallarico at Project BBQ 2001, the GANG seems so far to be characterized by the broad strokes that we associate with its founder. GANG might save the world, and it might ruin us all. As Alice Cooper says, "You bought a ticket for a roller coaster. It's gonna go up. It's gonna go down." I am Member Number One of GANG. Certainly it makes sense to become knowledgeable about GANG. If you think it's very good, you should join and ride the gravy train. If you think it's very bad, you should join and change it (http://www.audiogang.org).

IA-SIG: The Interactive Audio Special Interest Group of the MIDI Manufacturers' Association (MMA). The IA-SIG is the trade organization that covers hardware and software for game audio. It also stands for "I Actually Started It—George." I heard last week that there will likely be some reorganization happening within these groups, so if you want to be on top of things, you should do a quick web search before throwing around terms like "MMA" and "IA-SIG."

IMUSE: The best integrator (see below) ever built. It was built by the Stooges (see below).

Integrator: A tool for mapping linear audio into an interactive context. You can't get one.

Mission Control: Linda Law of Team Fat.

Miyamoto's Foot: The thing that indicates great success. The Stooges and Dave Sanger went to great lengths to perform the theme from Super Mario Brothers for an awards show, and Clint observed that if Miyamoto-San's foot tapped, it all would have been worth it. To answer your next question, "Yes."

Movie Quality: That which uses an orchestra, even if composed by a three-year-old and recorded by an orchestra of monkeys for a game that it fits like Pink's clothes on Roseanne.

Musiks: An English-as-a-second-language term for more than one music file. "Fat Man, I am loving your musiks so much, it bring me tears of joyce."

Muso: One of the electronics-only, European-school game musicians. I think. How can I love these guys if they won't let me *in*?

My Ferrari: What's coming to me. "Where's *my Ferrari?*" I wrote a song called "Where's My Ferrari?" for a demo disk, and a surprisingly large number of people in the business assumed it had been written about them.

Noise: Sound effect. The client says, "We'll need 500 *noises* for this game."

Project Bar-B-Q: See *BBQ*.

Sharpshooters: I was feeling humble about Team Fat, because of all the great music that the LucasArts team had made. They made me feel better by saying that they always thought of Team Fat as "*emotional sharpshooters.*"

Sleeping with Britney: To *Sleep with Britney* is to record an orchestral score. All your life, you've dreamed of doing it. Now the moment has come, and you finally get your chance. You give your all working up to the moment. Will it actually happen? Will this be your last chance? Will you be good enough? Will you be as good as all the others who have gone before? The *agents*! The *publicity*! The *pressure*! *It kills you.* The schedule is all too short... and then... You're *doing it*! *You're sleeping with Britney!!!* Afterward, you try to figure out how much that cost you, and what exactly you got for your money. But the bottom line is, you did it, and they can never take that away from you.

Somebody Like Jay: Jay Semerad is the King of the Students Who Help Gang. When something needs to be done, President Tommy says, "We'll just get Somebody Like Jay to do it."

Spanki: Teresa Avallone of Team Fat.

Spaunch: The Frisbee Golf term for very bad or drunk.

Spanuch: A misspelling meaning super-duper drunk. Like when you write on a napkin, "I am SO SPANUCH."

The Spiritual Drum: The drum, owned by Somebody Like Jay, that determines a candidate's suitability for membership in GANG. The elders beat the drum, then Clint Bajakian yells, "What makes this you think of?" When the candidate says, "ummmm...," an elder is to say, "You're IN!!!"

Stooges: Michael Land, Clint Bajakian, and Pete McConnell. They were the audio team at LucasArts from 1990 through 2000, joined in the later years by Larry the O. This small team is the only one whose reputation can be compared to that of Team Fat in the PC audio world. No brag, just fact. They didn't do *that* many games, but consider the impact that these soundtracks, all by just three guys, had on the PC world:

- *Monkey Island*
- *The Dig*
- *Grim Fandango*
- *Outlaws*
- *Full Throttle*
- *Indiana Jones and the Fate of Atlantis*
- *Day of the Tentacle*
- *Sam & Max Hit the Road*
- *Force Commander*

Come to think of it, y'all should buy their CD, which celebrates 20 years of LucasArts games by showcasing seven years of the works of these three guys who didn't even work there any more at the time that this CD was released (http://www.lucasarts.com/companystore/misc/cd.htm).

That's how great these guys are. *That's* how much good music means to gaming. *That's* the kind of thing The Fat Man says about you if you buy him a nice meal.

Next week I'll be going to Las Vegas to run the pit band in an awards show. The band, "The Players," will consist of these three guys and my brother Dave and me. We figure that a pit band's job is to react in real time to what other people do and make it sound intentional. It's pretty much like being a Human iMUSE.

The Meal: An annual event at the NAMM (National Association of Music Merchants) show at which the Stooges would celebrate Life, Friendship, and Having a Gig Making Music. The Fat Man and Spanki were invited to join a The Meal, and became a part of the tradition. That gesture was taken as a great honor and cemented the goodwill between Team Fat and the Stooges forever. And the Stooges paid.

The Thing That Made That Noise: A specific home-made lap steel, made from toilet parts and two-by-fours. My brother Dave had heard it on a Joe McDermott children's album. When he saw the real thing, he gave a gasp of recognition, saying, "That must be the thing that made that noise."

The Thing You Need: An RCA-to-1/4-inch phono adapter. You can never have enough of *The Thing You Need.*

To Torque: To turn the bass knob all the way up, turn the treble knob all the way up, and then to think or say, "There, that sounds better."

The Ultimate Music Creation Tool: A paid gig.

Workahol: Coffee.

To Yacht: To take one's sweet time in the studio, making poor decisions for reasons of ignorance, all under the pretense of doing a good job. "Gee, I'm just not sure. Let me hear it both ways one more time." *Yachting* was named for people who think they are getting exercise while out on their yachts.

Yachtsman: One who yachts.[1]

---

[1] The opposite of yachting:

My first job as a second engineer was to place microphones for the great drummer Louis Bellson. The album was for high-note trumpeter Paul Cacia, and the engineer was my mentor Van Webster. Louis' brother Frank set up the drums, I set up the mics with Van's help, and we proceeded laying the tracks to a click. The room was filled with very critical listeners, and I got to witness Van making some amazing punch-ins, sometimes of one or two notes at a time.

We finished cutting the tracks on time, and Louis showed up as scheduled right on the dot, five minutes early. He and Paul talked for a few minutes about where Paul might get a new limo. Louis laid out the eight-page chart on the floor, murmured to himself for a few seconds, and asked if there was anything special he should know. He popped in to the music room, and played the part with tape rolling.

Every jaw in the control room dropped to the floor. He had aced the solo, played the melody on his toms, nuked the groove, talked the talk, and walked the walk. After a moment of silence, Louis said into the mic, "Is there anything you'd like changed for the second take?"

Paul and Van looked at each other. Van pressed the talkback button, and Paul said, "Well, frankly, Louis, I can't imagine how you could possibly do it any better."

Louis replied, "Well, I could play the same thing, but with my clothes off."

The importance of all these identifying characteristics takes a far distant second place to the fact that we jam.

A History Of Game Musician Jams

The first jam at a Game Developers' Conference was around '92, with a bunch of the Top Doggies from Virgin in a hotel room. I remember that "Doc" was there, Graeme Devine, Peter Oliphant, a bunch of other great people. Mostly we sang Beatle songs and got drunk, and somebody wanted to do it again next year. It was a wonderful moment, and I keep meeting people who claim to have been there. It was pretty much me and some other game developers playing guitar and hitting beer bottles with pens. There weren't a lot of musicians in the business.

The next year we had a jam with a similar group of folks, and it's where I first met Michael Land, who sat in on guitar. The thing became a GDC Hotel Tradition. "Is there a jam this year?"

One year, possibly '92 (whatever year *Warcraft* came out), Team Fat flew out and played the GDC's "Big Event," which was a dinner, party, and awards show. We were the pit band for the awards ceremony, and as people came up to accept their awards, we played, in surf style, the theme music from each game that won. I don't think a single person recognized a game theme or realized what we were doing. Team Fat played the "dance" afterward. Not much dancing went on, as the industry only had five women at the time, and two of them used to be men.

The following years, we were asked to play at several of the game conferences, usually in somebody's booth on the show floor. But one magazine that wanted Team Fat to act as a surf band in their booth for the Intermedia Conference couldn't afford to fly us out. That's what led to my calling around to find out if anybody in the industry could actually play instruments and just meet me at the show. That led to the first Multimedia Jam.

This is a picture of the first Multimedia Jam, where most of us met and jammed publicly for the first time: The Intermedia Conference.... I think it was 1993. We played for about five hours with no set list. There *is* video-tape, and it sounded great.

Left to right:

Jim Donofrio. An award-winning independent composer for games. I had met him a few minutes before in the parking lot, and he ran home and got a guitar.

Dave Javelosa. Then head of music for Sega of America. Many other credits. You must know him.

The Fat Man.

Neil Grandstaff. Then head of music for Sierra Online.

Michael Land. Then head of music for LucasArts, creator of iMUSE.

David Albert. Bigtime Producer. Then at Sega.

Don Griffin. Independent game musician. One of the early ones with a lot of credits.

Al Lowe. Creator of *Leisure Suit Larry*. Sierra's first musician.

After the "Multimedia Jam," Dave Albert started making sure that we had amps and PAs for GDC, and we'd regularly set up a big electric jam either in private rooms off to the side or one year at the top of the escalator. Some people who are doing quite well now got into the business simply because we seemed at those jams to be "cool guys," who let the new guys jam with us.

I think it was '97 when we played the Main Event in the Tent, and had about 20 people on stage. It was like riding a whale, but I understand it sounded pretty good from the audience. That was the first time Tommy T. sat in, I think, on "Great Balls of Fire." Even Rob Hubbard did some licks. One of the best performances was in about '99, when we (by now known as the Adlib Soundblasters) found out that the very successful *Leisure Suit Larry* games had been cancelled. Since the creator of that series was our friend and sax player, we gave Larry his "wake" in a ballroom off of the Fairmont Hotel lobby. I think we skipped 2000; some other company hosted a none-too-successful "The GDC Jam," and we had a real nice one in 2001 in a big room with a fairly big crowd, and we even finally got some support from the people who throw the conference.

The cool guys hang out after the Great Dance of Venture Capital, our GDC jam for 2001. It was too late to get a milk shake, so Tony Goodman (between the exit signs) ordered milk and ice cream and made the shakes.

That's all the history I can remember, but we should try to list all the people who have taken part in these things... they're all great, they've contributed a lot to the great spirit in our community, and they've moved a *lot* of amps.

The Adlib Soundblasters "Get Your Heart On" Tour

CGDC 1992: Spontaneous Room Jam, Westin Hotel

CGDC 1993: Less Spontaneous Room Jam, Westin Hotel
InterMedia 1993: THE FIRST PUBLIC GAME MUSICIANS' JAM

CGDC 1994: Guerrilla Jams in Lecture Theater, and Atop the Escalator

CGDC 1995: Official CGDC Lecture Theater Jam and Banquet Room Jam
CES 1995: Sierra Online Game Musicians' Jam, Riviera Ballroom

CGDC 1996: Pass: Team Fat Hogs the Stage as Pit Orchestra for Developers'
Choice Awards

CGDC 1997: The Whale Jam: 21 People On-Stage in a Tent

CGDC 1998: Pass: Nobody knew anybody in Long Beach with amplifiers.

GDC 1999: Leisure Suit Larry's Wake, Fairmont Lobby

GDC 2000: Pass: Tired of hauling amps.

GDC 2001: The Great Dance of Venture Capital, Fairmont Hotel
GDC 2001: Coolernet Suite Jam

GANG Launch 2002: Acoustic Room Jam, Argent Hotel
GDC 2002: You Are Here...Get Your Heart On!

Commemorative T-shirt for the 2002 GDC jam,
dubbed the "Get Your Heart On" Tour.

The Coolernet hotel suite jam.
Left to right: Orpheus Handley, Michael Land, Tommy Tallarico,
The Fat Man, Rod Abernethy of Slackmates, and Peter McConnell.

She Branded Me with Silence

Dolby Labs (not Thomas, the other one) generously sponsored Project BBQ, and generously gave each attendee a fine branding iron. They are, after all, the last word in brand awareness. This taught us another thing about game audio guys.

Game audio

guys cannot be

trusted

with hot branding irons.

The LucasArts backpacker guitar.

A Gallery of Greats

Dave Albert (left) was for a long time a big producer at Sega. A wonderful guitar player, he was heavily involved in the first game musician jams, was even a brainstorming facilitator at Project BBQ. On the right is Dave Warhol, my brother's roommate in college, respon-

sible for getting me my first gig in the business as well as *Wing Commander*. The two Daves worked together for a while at Warhol's company Realtime.

I bet you don't recognize these guys. It's the Blue Man Group, not wearing their blue face paint. I asked them for their permission to play one of their songs. Since there are several "Blue Man Groups" on tour at any one time, I think this was like asking Santa at the mall if it was okay that I shaved the cat. They were very serious, considered my request quite deeply, and nodded their approval, just as any good Santa would have done.

Classic übergeek Ernest "The Guy in the Top Hat" Adams and his patron saint, George "The Guy in the Cowboy Hat" Sanger. Each is wearing neither hat nor blue face paint, yet somehow it makes them no less like the Actual Santa Claus. Ernest resides precisely at the juncture between commercial success and artistic success, between wild individualism and comfortable conformity. Anybody interested in studying the transition between Old School and New School gaming would do well to examine the magnificent paradoxes that surround both of these guys.

Alexander Brandon, composer of music for Unreal, head of audio at Ion Storm, and Technical Editor for this book. Blame him for the mistakes, please.

Brian Moriarty, gaming's greatest sage, and me. I have sworn never to reveal that Brian was also Team Fat's record company, and created the wonderful artwork on our CDs. When his game *Loom* came out in 1989, the ad proclaimed to the world that this game incorporated "art by real artists." And the soundtrack was my careful arrangement of eight movements of *Swan Lake* by Tchaikovsky, so I suppose that would be "music by real musicians," too.

A rare shot of some of the most talented women in Texas music all in one place. They were recording a Dave Sanger-produced project at Abbey Trails studio, under the name "Henhouse." Left to right, Rosie Flores, Cindy Cashdollar, Sarah Brown, Pimp Daddy Fatty, Becky Hobbs, and Lisa Pankratz.

On the left, Interactive Storytelling guru Chris Crawford. He founded the Computer Game Developers Conference—its first meeting was in his living room. On the right, pioneer of synthesized music, Morton Subotnick. This could only happen at BBQ. Between them, playing the part of The Great Gazoo, Dolby's Kristoffer Larsen.

Will Wright invented *The Sims*, and is one of the most conspicuous leaders in the fight to create games that jump off the conveyor belt and make people happy in new ways. He judges the "Stupid Fun" factor of various activities by multiplying the "Stupid" factor by the "Fun" factor.

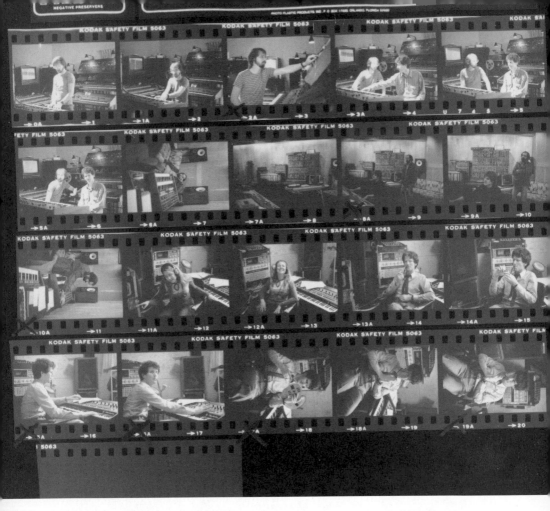

Before I ever wrote music for a game, I interviewed film composers Alan Howarth and Basil Poledouris for an article I wrote for the movie trade, *Millimeter* magazine. The article explained the importance of audio to motion pictures. That's Alan and me in the top row, and Basil in the second row. The young lady is Mission Control.

Years before that, Alan happened to have had the luck to live next door to where my band, The Phlaix, rehearsed in Glendale, CA. This must have poisoned his young mind, for Alan has made a strong commitment to gaming. He now runs the music department at Electronic Arts.

Sid Meier. 'Nuff said.

Christa. A very nice follower of Krishna whom I met at the airport in LA, on my way to the E3 conference. And what Krishna was doing at the airport, I'll never know. I only put her picture here because I suspect her parents are looking for her, and this might help. We went shopping for Rolls-Royces together.

Bruce Shelly, a game designer's game designer. Father of *Age of Empires*. Years ago I talked him into adding handicapping to his games so I could play against my very young son. The handicapping feature finally made it into *Age of Mythology*, but by then Glen was so old I was the one who needed the advantage.

I'm glad I was able to return a favor and introduce Bruce to my brother. Bruce is a big fan of Dave's band Asleep at the Wheel. I think he's happier in this picture.

The Fat Man

From: The Fat Man
Sent: Monday, May 5, 2003 9:51 AM
To: Sheldon
Subject: weddings

Dear Sheldon,

I need to ask your opinion as a professional in the Weddings Industry.

You know how sometimes I try to describe how much I like working for your company, Sedans Inc., driving my Rolls for weddings? Well, you see, what happened is this. I tried to go see a friend's performance on 6th street before my wedding run last week. I got to the club at 9:00, but the show started late, at 9:45, so I had to leave slightly disappointed. As you know, I was to pick up the couple at 10:30 at the Barr Mansion. I don't like to be late for weddings.

I got there in plenty of time, and the couple climbed in. They were wonderful—we became friends instantly. As I've said, I think that the driver at a wedding is in a better position than even the preacher... he is the first person to be alone with the couple when they are married! So I try to respect that moment, and with the magic of the Rolls-Royce and the wedding night, sometimes very cool things happen.

Well, the subject of 6th street came up, and I told the couple about the show I missed in order to pick them up. They knew somebody who knew the performer, too! So, and here's the funny part, rather than go to the Honeymoon Suite and make time, these two decided that it would be even more cool to see if we could drop in on the show instead. The only thing that would have kept them from trying to go would have been an increase in my rate, and I sure as heck wasn't going to do *that*! We got there just as the show was over, the crowd was gone, and the performers were signing autographs for the stragglers.

Fortunately, Margaret Oritz had a camera ready to capture the moment, and we got a second set of wedding photos for the happy couple.

I think it's a pretty nice picture. That's me on the left. The fellow with the kindly smile and the full-body blue puzzle-piece tattoo and horns surgically built into his head is The Enigma, the friend I went to see. The gentleman with the neon piercing through his ears, that's the Neon Cowboy. At his crotch, that big metal phallus with the two doorknobs hanging off the bottom is actually a flamethrower. I was surprised to hear that. Of course, I don't have to tell you that the woman in white with her hand on the flamethrower is the Bride, and behind her in the tux is her proud new husband, who had just suggested to her where to put her hand! Moving to the right, there's another friend, The Enigma's lovely and kind wife, Katzen. You can tell her by the nylon whiskers pierced through her upper lip. She stands out from the crowd as the only woman in the world with a full-body theme tattoo. And that's Muramasa, I guess from my autographed poster, with his hand on Katzen's butt. We didn't get to meet, I'm sorry to say. But that's often the case at weddings, don't you think? The Bearded Lady (far right) was quite charming, if a little shy, and I regret that her lovely dress does not show up well in this photo.

My question is, how would you advise me to crop this photo for best effect?

Ever your friend and servant,

The Fat Man,

George A. Sanger

Jeff Johannigman, star producer of many early Origin titles. At the time, he knew more people in the business than anyone alive, with the possible exception of Ellen Guon.

Watson Wu, game audio musician guy (but he spells it, "Director of InfraStructure Studios [audio production services]").

Tony Goodman, CEO of Ensemble,
the Age of Empires and Age of Mythology guys.

Before Tony was successful, he was a nice guy. Tony and I spent a memorable evening on the rides at Great America talking business. It was all about how he couldn't possibly ever hire me because he's loyal to his friends, and about how I thought he was biting off more than he could chew making a game with too many damn civilizations. Now that he's successful, he's an even nicer guy. I left my golf clubs at his place, which is a blessing for those with whom I like to play golf.

Tom White, MMA president, way back when he was the guy you talked to at Roland if you were a musician and were trying to get answers or free gear.

You can do what you want in the audio world, but if you want to do it right and get the audio manufacturing community to buy into it, you'd better run it past Tom. The day I met him, I was so proud of what *Loom* and *Wing Commander* were doing for the Roland MT-32, I introduced myself as his "new best friend." It's been about 10 years now, and we're just about new best friends. My wife bought Tom a nice cake last night to help him celebrate 20 years of MIDI.

Chuck "Chuckles" Bueche, co-founder of Origin Systems. Now he roams the country in an RV with a satellite dish, doing Gosh-Knows-What, and calling it "consulting." Kids, don't be ashamed of your nickname. It might just work out in the end.

LucasArts audio Stooges Michael Land, Clint Bajakian, and Peter McConnell.

Once when I visited them, they celebrated my visit with an afternoon of shooting guns at the range at which they had recorded the sounds for *Outlaws*, followed by some excellent single-malt whiskey. Shooting *then* drinking? These Californians. I did so well, they put my target on display in the LucasArts commissary. True story: I once killed a fly with a Lugar. And how he got that Lugar, I'll never know. That's twice.

We stopped off at the Alamo after BBQ one year to salute the fallen heroes thereof. Clint is a world-class idealist.

The third Stooge, Clint Bajakian.

He gets sad and **nervous** if conductor Seiji Ozawa gets *sick*.

Infogrames producer and good friend Jennifer McWilliams.

The teeth are authentic. I got them while on an audio consulting gig in Kentucky. I saved the company.

But then it fell apart any-way.

I forgot to wear black. On the right is Tommy Tallarico, on the left is Joey. Joey does a great deal of the composing for Tommy's company, and he's widely respected as a behind-the-scenes treasure. As proof that I could never hire Joey away from him,

Tommy once had Joey show me the Rolex watches that he'd bought for him. I took the story home and then tried to get Team Fat's Joe to show somebody the cheap little watch I'd bought him. Joe said, "I'm not your *God Damned Joey.*" So I'm thinkin', Man, if I could afford better watches, I could get the *good* Joe. Between Joey and me is Peter Alau, who was at that time the person at Sony to whom you talked if you made sounds for the PlayStation. This photo was taken when Peter and I had just finished singing a complete rendition of *Trouble in River City.*

My brother Dave is here shown playing drums more drunk than he ever has been in his life. The band is Asleep at the Wheel, and they are opening for the George Strait country music festival. I am not in this one picture, but the chicken hat makes up for it, don't you think?

The two on the left, Kurt Sehnert and Jason Rubenstien, had been sent by Intel to this conference with one mission: to find and foster applications that would "chew up MIPS." Why doesn't Exxon send people to car shows to encourage gas guzzling? On my right is Mark Miller, who did more for game audio than anybody. He founded the first independent music composing house for games. He created the GEMS music authoring system for Genesis. He established the music track at the GDC. He ran music at Sony. He ran audio at Rocket Science. He helped establish the IA-SIG, and acted as its chair. He got so mad at me for putting down the IA-SIG in an article that it inspired me and Spanki to start BBQ as a way of helping the community. He is a good man. I think he sells real estate now. At his final game industry conference, we took a long walk as friends, and he did me this great and singular honor: He has only smoked one cigar in his life, and it was with me that night.

Bobby Prince once said I was the smartest person he knew, next to Mark Miller. It was meant as no insult, and it was taken as none.

"An industry mainstay, Sandy Petersen is a member of the Gaming Hall of Fame, and he was crucial in the production of such award winning game titles as *Doom, Doom 2, Quake, Command*

HQ, Lightspeed, and *Civilization*. As seems to be the rule with successful computer game designers, Petersen's roots are in the board game industry. His illustrious portfolio includes *Runequest, Call of Cthulhu, Creatures of the Dreamlands*, and *Petersen's Field Guide to Monsters*. As an internationally recognized game designer and writer, Petersen's works have been published worldwide."

I didn't know who he was when this picture was taken. I searched for his name on the web, and found the quote above.

But of course he's a top dog—just look at him. Some people, you can just figure out they're bad-ass from the suspenders and everybody calling 'em by their first name, which sounds like an earthy nickname. See the chapter "How To Understand Everything."

Elen Guon, who knows everybody and everything about games. She's one of the good ones, folks!

The Ladies of Mary-Margaret.com, the greatest agents in gaming. Not counting Melanie. I love these girls. Ah, the stories I could tell.

Melanie, the greatest agent in gaming, not counting the girls of Mary-Margaret.com. Now I think I need a picture of Jill Zinner of Premiere Search, also the greatest, or she's gonna get pissed at me. Jill, where were you when the camera was out?

*Great game designer Noah Falstein writes the wisdom column
"Better by Design" for* Game Developer *magazine.*

If Noah is more comfortable with quotes around the word "wisdom," we can change that in the second printing. Noah and I have been sniffing each other's butts for 20 years and *still* have never worked together. For the first 18 years or so it bothered me, but now that I'm doing okay, it's not a problem for me, and it's bugging the crap out of Noah. I guess I wIn.

Victory dance!

A hell of a good-hearted man, Rex Baca, head of audio for Sony in San Diego, and the woman who has made far more vocal sounds on games than any other woman in the world, Lani Minella of Audiogodz.

Underground comix artist and co-creator of *The 7th Guest* and *The 11th Hour*, Rob Landeros. His website, Skreed.com, is responsible for reviving the music of the European Sex Machine, the artists who performed the theme song for *The 11th Hour*, "Mr. Death."

The closest thing gaming ever got to a celebrity, Ion Storm's John Romero, back when he liked me, before I cracked open a can of musical whoop-ass earthquake death on his village.

The behavior editing software development team for Aibo, the robot pet. Clockwise from the left, my wonderful friend, wrestling fan, and game producer Dana Hanna, programmer John DeCuir, Brett Spivey, The Fat Man, and a prototype Aibo. This picture was taken the day that Aibo was released in the U.S. Just the night before, Jon Stewart had announced on *The Daily Show* that "Aibo" was Japanese for "Metal dog good lick lick friend." I made the sounds for this team's work. If you program an Aibo using the computer-based software, one of the sounds you will hear when you press buttons is me hitting myself really, really hard on the head with my knuckles. Joe took forever to set the levels on that one.

Mike Wilson, founder of God Games, a.k.a., Gathering of Developers.

At the E3 conference one year, a young, underemployed Alexander Brandon was desperately trying to meet important industry connections to get his garage-sized game development team launched. I wasn't having any luck with my career at the time, but I figured I could at least help Alex out, so I took him over to the mighty God Games booth to meet Mike. Mike was surrounded by reporters, so to get his attention, I asked if I could get my picture taken with him. He answered, "only if you give me that shirt." Poor schmuck should have chosen his words more carefully. He had to wear the flames for all his interviews the rest of the day. Of course, I had to endure threats from Aggies fans all day. Mike then founded Substance TV. He denies that the shirt was the inspiration for it, but for a couple of years, that exact red-yellow-black flame pattern was the theme for the Substance TV booth.

Now Young Alexander Brandon is head of audio at Ion Storm, and the technical editor of this book.

Mike unplugged Substance TV last fall, but he writes, "Take 2 called me the following week to lure me back to this whacked industry. I signed a deal in January with 'Gathering of Developers, a Texas Corporation.' Funny world indeed."

*Devo member and cartoon soundtrack king Mark Mothersbaugh
saw the red suit and asked if I had change for a twenty.*

A Fat-Centric History of Game Audio Hardware and Software

The Fall from Paradise

This is a **game audio** story in four parts.

Heaven

Back in the day, compositions for games were compositions.

The first game I did, I submitted the music on manuscript paper, and the programmer put the tune into the game. It was a simple time, and each of us knew his job and how to do it. I got good money for that game—$1,200 for a single ten-second song.

For the second game, I used an Atari Music Composer cartridge, and the game's programmer hacked into the resulting file, found the pitch and duration values, and placed those into the code in his game. I was still very much a composer, but now sitting at a computer keyboard using a commercially available program. I received pretty good money, albeit a third of what I had asked for, and it came after many, many years of pressing from a good friend who was a lawyer.

By the time of my third game project, the downhill slide had begun in earnest. I was given a custom-written composing program written by some smart kids just out of high school. It was command-line-based and all but impossible to use. The project, a demo cart for the Atari 800, did not see the light of day. I was not paid.

When MIDI sequencers became affordable, I had the idea to submit the songs I wrote for games as simply MIDI compositions. People generally did not know what MIDI was, and I was all too happy to explain it to them. There was no General MIDI to assign program changes in the code to specific instruments, so I would compose a MIDI file that would play back well on an MT-32 sound module. I'd label one channel "trumpet," one "bass," and so forth, and Dave Warhol would hack into the MIDI file, find the pitch and duration values, make "trumpet" and "bass" sound algorithms, and place those into the code in his game. Dave was known for his excellent ear for music and sound, and his work was consistently good, even innovative.

The music I wrote for Origin Systems was the same. Good people on staff interpreted the MIDI files I would send, and would carefully and lovingly place each note—by hand—into the code of the game.

I got the illusion that the erosion had ceased, that a composer could use an efficient system to write music for games, charge a reasonable rate, and make a reasonable living. It was not so. I had failed to realize that the erosion was continuing to eat away at the ground beneath me. It was only the talents, the musical awareness, the sincere efforts of Dave Warhol and the audio staff at Origin that had been holding up the thin strip of soil beneath my fancy custom-made-but-for-somebody-else boots.

The first thing I hadn't realized was that I was spoiled. There were not a lot of people creating games who were at the talent level of Warhol and Origin, and I was about to find that out in a big way. The second thing I hadn't realized was that the hardware for game playback was about to change radically, making it impossible to be a mere composer.

The Snake: MIDI Track Zero

It happened one day: A developer chewed me out. He said I didn't have any idea about how to write music for games. He was angry at me because two notes overlapped very slightly, resulting in my having more than one note playing at once on "MIDI track zero."

Oh my **foes** and oh my *friends*, when the Devil counts, he starts at *zero*.

The programmer had built a music driver that would automatically convert my MIDI files to code, thus cutting out the drudgery of converting the notes by hand. Dave W. had built one, too, but his was elegant and musical. This particular misbegotten monster was the programming equivalent of a robot nursemaid that had gone mad with a chainsaw because it had been hastily built by an all-too-busy scientist father. When I finally heard that game, the music that played over the title screen was a horror. Literally, squeaks, squawks, and buzzes. Bass notes I wrote that went lower than the expected range did what any spaceship did in those days: It screen-wrapped and showed up at the top of the range as whistles.

I note with a grimace that this game was the only one ever of the 200 I've contributed to that sported, in the first screen, the words "Music by **The Fat Man**."

The Apple—The PC

Those were days in which you could tell that somebody was using a computer in the next room by the occasional loud swear word, followed by the phrase "I just lost a week's work," and another swear word.

Those were days in which the Apple Macintosh stood out like a special-forces soldier picking up his kid from nursery school. The Mac, very much unlike the PC, worked well and dependably. This was the case because everybody who contributed to its design was required to exactly follow certain rules, which were laid out in a single big fat book called *Inside Macintosh*. Over the years, *Inside Macintosh* grew to be many volumes of big fat books. If a person did not follow the guidelines in those books, Apple would not approve his program, and the program would not be included in the world of Macs, simple as that.

Game developers do not like to follow rules, so nobody made games for the Macintosh. Simple as that.

And that is how the strong, dependable, disciplined, and regimented Mac lost the support of game developers, and working on a game turned to the path marked by the chaos of rampant and unregulated third-party development that led to the eternal bond that exists to this day between swear words and computing.

Sound on the PC was at first made by the internal speaker, which could only beep at a single volume. Yes, musicians were required to support that as an output device.

When this was replaced by an FM synthesis chip made by Yamaha, conditions arose that happen very seldom in the marketing world. Yamaha was capable of charging a premium price for the use of their chip or the license of their technology, and was selling into a market that was growing conspicuously more quickly than any other market ever had. This did not go unnoticed. An executive at Tandy (Radio Shack) described Yamaha's pricing as though he were describing somebody selling a $30 cup of coffee. See, there are *ways* that things are done in the electronics world. You don't charge a premium price because of what the chip can do, you charge *by the "micro acre."* Unless, it seems you're Yamaha. So demand for a product was high, Yamaha was doing something historically significant with the supply, and the industry and the entrepreneurs alike took sudden and intense notice. Like when Clapton and Beck went to see the new kid in town, and it was Hendrix. Whoops. What're we gonna do about *that*?

What followed started us on the gold-rush-lost-in-the-hills-in-hostile-territory adventure that Audio for Games now is. I think every grad student at every business school in the world did his thesis on "potentially profitable underserved markets" and audio for games popped up as the best bet on about half of them, and those kids took their results to various investors.

The investors saw that Yamaha money and tried to get into audio. Sometimes they'd play ball and buy the expensive Yamaha chips, and distinguish their cards from others with exciting new features. Sometimes they tried to compete with Yamaha's FM, but Yamaha's patents were so tight that the new sound cards had to, by law, operate completely differently from Yamaha's design.

The fallout for game audio guys? Pure Hell. A composer who wanted to be at the cutting edge of PC audio would have to create a different file for each piece of music times the number of sound cards supported. Since most people did not know about, much less have, what we now might call ".WAV playback capability," sound effects, too, had to be created multiple ways for the various possible playback devices that might be out there.

05:14   P.7

Table 1

Board	Manufacturer	FM chan	Digitized chan/res	Audio Input	Adlib Comp	MIDI Cap.	Connection	Installed Base	Price
Internal Speaker*	ALL machines		1/6 bit	no	no	no	Internal	All machines	NA
Speech Thing*	Covox	0	1/8 bit	no	no	no	Parallel port	100,000+	$99.95
Voice Master*	Covox	0	1/8 bit/DMA	yes	no	no	PC bus	100,000+	$149.95
Sound Master II*	Covox	11	1/8 bit/DMA	yes	yes	yes	PC bus	10,000+	$229.95
GameBlaster	Creative Labs	12	none	no	no	no	PC bus	NA	$69.95
SoundBlaster*	Creative Labs	12	1/8 bit DMA	yes	yes	yes	PC bus	430,000+	$239.00
SoundBlasterPro	Creative Labs	22	2/16 bit/DMA	yes	yes	yes	AT bus	NA	$299.00
Fantastic Audio	Artisoft	0	CODEC	yes	no	no	AT bus	NA	
Adlib Music Card*	Adlib, Inc	11	1/6 bit	no	no	no	AT bus	200,000+	$119.95
Adlib Gold*	Adlib, Inc	20-st	2/12 bit/DMA/st	yes/st	yes	yes	AT bus	NA	$299.95
Roland MT-32	Roland Corp	32	none	no	no	yes	MIDI interface	NA	$550.00
Echo II*	Street Electron	0	1/8 bit	no	no	no	AT bus	NA	
Sound Source*	Walt Disney	0	1/8 bit	no	no	no	Parallel port	NA	$39.95
Digispeech*	Digispeech	0	1/8 bit	no	no	no	Serial port	NA	$129.95
Tandy EX/TX/IBM PCjr	Tandy/IBM	3	1/4 bit	no	no	no	Internal	NA	NA
Tandy SL/TL*	Tandy Corp	3	1/8 bit DMA	yes	no	no	Internal	NA	NA

'Digitized Sound Support from THE Audio Solution
st - Stereo

Audio Board	Bundled Software
Internal Speaker	BEEP
Speech Thing	Text to speech, demos.
Voice Master	Voice Recognition, Digitized Sound Recording, Playback and Editing Software, developer tools.
Sound Master II	Voice Recognition, PC Lyra Music Program, Record, Playback, special effects, and editing, with libraries
GameBlaster	Intelligent Organ, Silpheed
SoundBlaster	Sound recording and playback, Docter SBAITSO, Talking Parrot, Intelligent Organ
SoundBlasterProc	Mixing Chip, CD ROM Interface, Sound Recording, Playback, & Editing, SBAITSO, Talking Parrots, Organ
Fantastic Audio	
Adlib Personal Music	Jukebox music playback program, developer tools and documentation.
Adlib Gold	Jukebox gold, VoicePad record and playback, Multimedia utilities, developer tools, documentation.
Roland MT-32	EASE music software
Echo II	
Sound Source	None
Digispeech	None
Tandy EX/TX/IBM PCjr	None
Tandy SL/TL	DeskMate, Digitized Sound Recording, Playback, and Editing Software

This list was made by John Ratcliff to alert the development world of the problem, for which he was proposing a solution. The list represents the various platforms that the programmer—and composer—had to keep in mind when supplying music for PC games. This chart was made even before the huge explosion of General MIDI sound cards.

ATTACK SUB FILES

	ADLIB				MT-32				SOUND CANVAS		
FILENAME	.DES	.MID	.XMI	FILENAME	.DES	.MID	.XMI	FILENAME	.DES	.MID	.XMI
AATT1V3	✓	✓	✓	RATT1V1	✓	✓	✓				
AATT2V1	✓	✓	✓	RATT2V1	✓	✓	✓				
AATT3V2	✓	✓	✓	RATT3V1	✓	✓	✓				
AATT4V2	✓	✓	✓	RATT4V1	✓	✓	✓				
AATT5V2	✓	✓	✓	RATT5V1	✓	✓	✓				
AATT6V1	✓	✓	✓	RATT6V2	✓	✓	✓	SATT6V3	✓	✓	✓
AATT7BV1	✓	✓	✓	RATT7BV1	✓	✓	✓	SATT7BV2	✓	✓	✓
AATT8V2	✓	✓	✓	RATT8V1	✓	✓	✓				
AATT9V2	✓	✓	✓	RATT9V1	✓	✓	✓				
AATT10V2	✓	✓	✓	RATT10V1	✓	✓	✓				
AATT11V2	✓	✓	✓	RATT11V1	✓	✓	✓				
AATT12V1	✓	✓	✓	RATT12V2	✓	✓	✓	SATT12V2	✓	✓	✓
AATT13V1	✓	✓	✓	RATT13V1	✓	✓	✓				
AATT14V2	✓	✓	✓	RATT14V1	✓	✓	✓				
AATT15V2	✓	✓	✓	RATT15V1	✓	✓	✓				
AATT16V2	✓	✓	✓	RATT16V1	✓	✓	✓				
AATT17V1	✓	✓	✓	RATT17V1	✓	✓	✓	SATT17V1	✓	✓	✓
AATT18V1	✓	✓	✓	RATT18V1	✓	✓	✓	SATT18V1	✓	✓	✓
AATT19V1	✓	✓	✓	RATT19V1	✓	✓	✓	SATT19V2	✓	✓	✓
AATT20V1	✓	✓	✓	RATT20V1	✓	✓	✓	SATT20V1	✓	✓	✓
AATT21V1	✓	✓	✓	RATT21V1	✓	✓	✓	SATT21V1	✓	✓	✓
AATT22V1	✓	✓	✓	RATT22V1	✓	✓	✓	SATT22V1	✓	✓	✓
AATT23V1	✓	✓	✓	RATT23V1	✓	✓	✓	SATT23V4	✓	✓	✓
AATT24V1	✓	✓	✓	RATT24V1	✓	✓	✓	SATT24V1	✓	✓	✓

This spec represents the music files we were to supply John Ratcliff for a game he was producing. Note that to deliver 24 pieces of music, we had to deliver 216 different files, via mail or phone-to-phone 300-baud modem. Despite our best efforts, I must confess that more energy was expended on organizing and converting files for this game than was spent composing.

"The Fat Man and Team Fat are proud to be associated with this game. John has given us tremendous freedom and encouragement, and displayed and animated our sound with remarkable software. The music is linked not only to what's happening in the game, but to the possibilities of what might happen next, and the memory of what has already been. While you're operating the SONOR, notice how sound is used to create an interactive experience that movies, TV shows, and amusement parks can only dream of achieving. You'll scroll at will through a soundscape of time, space, and emotion. Put on your ear goggles and turn it up… He who listens wins the game."

—FAT

We were happy to endorse the game for its great innovation and care, many aspects of which remain unmatched to this day. Sadly, the end result of those 216 music files was 14 minutes of pretty good music. Despite fantastic implementation in the game, over a 40-hour adventure the player would be subjected to quite a few repetitions of that 14 minutes. Bear in mind, too, that John was far ahead of his peers as far as realizing the problem and implementing generalized solutions. Other developers merely ignored the issue of audio.

A Brave Knight and a General Solution

John Miles created the Miles Sound Drivers, the software layer that nearly every PC-based game uses to drive its sound. The day that Microsoft hired John Miles to help with their audio marked the first day that Microsoft did anything in the world of sound that made the least bit of sense. Of course, such software would have to have been made by a remarkable man. John Miles is such a man.

Okay, story where I turn out to be hero: One day back when he was relatively unknown except for at Origin and in his hometown of Antlers, John Miles asked me out to lunch, and told me he was going to make a set of audio drivers for the PC, and he wanted my advice. Among the things he asked me were, "What does MIDI stand for?" and "Why are there black and white keys on the piano?" *That's* how important *I* am. Also, I'd like to brag here that John kept his BBS server computer set up at my house, because this was before the web. The deal was, I could make my FM General MIDI emulation files available to whomever wanted them without much effort on my part, and John would save the cost of paying for the phone line for his BBS.

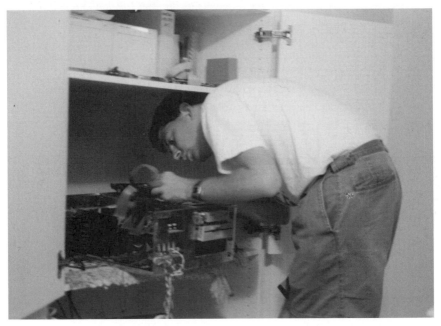

Legendary Audio Programmer John Miles installs his BBS at my house. Note the five-inch floppy drive and lack of a mouse or CD-ROM. The cases above his head are not CD-ROM cases, they are for big floppies that actually flopped in more ways than one. There was a monochrome text-only monitor, and a phone line that would ring every time a developer decided to use the Miles Tools, thus properly supporting audio. Remember, every time you hear the ringing of a bell, it means that somewhere a fairy is getting its wings. The Miles drivers, now distributed by RAD software instead of a 286 on my living room bookshelf, are still generally regarded as the industry's best.

Makes me look great, doesn't it? Where would we all be if it weren't for The Mighty Fat Man?

And so it came to pass that John Miles and I took a fateful drive together, and during the course of that drive, we were musing about what would be needed to solve the problem of having to write so many files for each piece of music and "noise" (see glossary in "The Culture of Game Audio").

Catalyzed by the enlightened discourse with John, I began to realize that all possible ways of making interactive sound on computers shared a few common elements.

If there were a way to use **MIDI** to trigger .WAV files of any length and then store both in a new, **standardized** file format that would also contain the **"rules of interactivity"** for the game, we'd be home free.

We could use one set of tools to create and audition and play back all of our music and sound effects files, regardless of the playback platform. We could turn in one file to the client. It would even guarantee correct playback.

Thus The Fat General Solution was born.

I
Actually
Started
It

—George

Early Delusions of Grandeur. George, Wendy, Dave, Rick.

One of the presidents of the United States, let's say Lincoln, was said to have had a plaque on his desk. It read: "There is no end to what we can achieve when we stop worrying about who gets the credit."

I would like to claim credit for having made that quote.

Still deluded, George prepares for the Senior Prom. That's Big John in the background. Note the height of his head compared to the doorknob. We had two of those. We had two Great Danes, too.

In the year when I took that drive with John Miles, there was no professional organization whatsoever for game audio content providers. Nobody cared about *that*, of course. However, there was also no organization to address the needs of the exploding number of hardware manufacturers, and that meant that money was falling through the cracks.

The closest thing we had to such an organization was an audio "town meeting" organized at the Computer Game Developers' Conference by Tom Rettig.

That year it went smoothly. So smoothly, in fact, that at one point Tom asked if there were any more topics, and the room went silent for a full ten seconds.

I raised my hand. I spoke. As I spoke, I was literally grabbed by a hand on my shoulder, and the owner of the hand whispered loudly to me the whole time, "We have it under control, George. Don't worry. We have it under control."

"I've been thinking about it," I said, "and I think that if there were a way to use MIDI to trigger .WAV files of any length, and then store both in a new, standardized file format that would also contain the 'rules of interactivity' for the game, we'd be able to have one system to author and play back audio for any and all of the crazy ways that people like to make sounds on computers."

Every hardware guy in the place went nuts.

"We're **thinking** about uploadable samples."

"**We're** thinking about uploadable samples, **too!**"

"Yeah! Uploadable samples! What about **them?**"

"Uploadable samples," which were, naturally, later known as "downloadable samples," were a small piece of the Fat General Solution I had just described, but they were the piece everybody in the hardware business was looking for. It seems that RAM had just become a viable thing to add to a sound card, and these companies were looking at this write-able memory as a way to add sounds to the computer's palette—a way to expand beyond the limitations of sound cards that had built-in, immutable General MIDI sounds.

When the meeting finally dwindled to its end, an excited Tom Rettig approached Tom White, the head of the MIDI Manufacturers Association. He expressed that he and some others were so inspired by the flurry of activity that they were considering starting a trade organization: The Association of Interactive Audio and Music Professionals, I think, or AIAMP. I was sitting at the table; I heard it.

The sign.

I went to the first meeting of the AIAMP, and somebody handed me the horribly misspelled sign from the door of our meeting room. "This should be yours," he said.

I can't remember who it was who said it. Anybody want to claim credit?

The AIAMP became the IA-SIG, the Interactive Audio Special Interest Group of the MMA. It's our professional organization to this day.

But the people who were there know that IA-SIG really stands for:

"I actually started it."
—George

General
MIDI
Rides
to
Texas

So, trying to solve the problems associated with having to write all those different files for those different sound cards led me to the idea of a Fat General Solution, a way to author any kind of audio regardless of the demands of the interactive context, and regardless of the hardware that happened to be present. The concept had the interesting side effect of starting the IA-SIG. But what good does that do me as far as having to write all those *files*?

So, I get this call to do a "multimedia" game called *The 7th Guest*. The word "multimedia" is used to distinguish computer programs that use stuff like pictures, sound, and a CD-ROM. At this time, "multimedia" was a joke and referred to as "The Zero-Billion Dollar Business."

Now, even though no CD-ROM based game ever sold more than 20,000 copies, I get a feeling from looking at the demos that this was going to be a major project. So, I calls Tom White, my new-best-friend-to-be at Roland, and I says to him, "Now, Tom," I says, "If I trust programmers to convert my compositions to work on all that hardware out there, some of it is going to sound really awful. But if I do the conversions and testing myself, that's a lot of work, and I won't be able to concentrate on composing, right? So, what do I do to avoid all this *drudgery*?"

And so Tom says to me, he says, "Why not just use this new Roland thing called General MIDI? It's a way to write one MIDI file that can then play back on lots of different sound cards."

So I says to him, "How do I do that?"

And he says, "You just write your music on a Sound Canvas, which is the only General MIDI sound card there is."

So I did, trusting that someday a lot of other sound cards would come out that would play back General MIDI, and all my nice *The 7th Guest* music would sound good on all those future sound cards forever.

And, just in case somebody didn't have a Sound Canvas, I had "Professor" K. Weston Phelan help me make a set of FM tone algorithms that would sound as much as possible like the ones required by the General MIDI (GM) spec. Kevin was the newest member of Team Fat and had demonstrated a great skill at programming synth sounds. John Miles' drivers allowed us to map the right sounds to the GM patch numbers. We then made a similar set of General MIDI-like patches for the MT-32, and an initialization file that would shuffle our GM-like patches to the right slots in the machine, so the right tone would sound when the right program change number was called by the MIDI file. We tested the sound files up and down, and by the time we were done, we could play any of our Sound Canvas files on an MT-32 or an FM card and usually be quite pleased with the results.

For the instruction manual of *The 7th Guest*, I wrote four pages of thanks to the developers for taking a chance on this new thing, General MIDI, which had never been used in a game.

The 7th Guest sells a million and a half copies right out of the chute, and "multimedia" is suddenly a viable business.

The **hottest** thing in business is **computers**; the hottest thing in computers

is **multimedia**;

the hottest thing in multimedia is *The 7th Guest*; and, according to some reviews, the hottest thing in *The 7th Guest* is the **music**.

So I'm the hottest thing in business.

CUE THE WOLVES.

Now I start getting calls from all these hardware companies trying to squeeze out product through the bars of the Yamaha patents, and they all want my endorsement for their General MIDI sound cards, and I start getting excited about the prospect of my picture on the box, and free equipment, and that kind of stuff, until I try one.

Every one of the GM cards I got for the next year was awful. I mean, it sounded good if you wrote music especially for it, but if you played back stuff that was written on a Sound Canvas, it was dreadful.

Entire passages would be lost. Instruments would be an octave off. Some sounds would blare out suddenly at five times the volume of any other instrument playing.

The problem turned out to be that there had been no specification for General MIDI, just a set of suggested guidelines, and these guidelines had no indication of how loud the instruments should be, compared to each other, nor how slow or fast the instrument's attack should be.

For a day or two, I hung my head in the dark thought of not becoming a celebrity endorser and at the even darker thought that I had recommended to 1.5 million players a "standard" that would make my nicely composed music sound bad for them.

Photo by Teresa "Spanki" Avallone

"Professor" K. Weston Phelan operated Fat Labs for many years.

Eventually, the light bulb came on. Team Fat decided to create Fat Labs, an independent testing company that would help give chip manufacturers the assurance that their GM sound hardware would work in a musically responsible way when playing back GM files.

Fat Labs stepped on a lot of toes with its early promotions, brashly announcing that it was "establishing a new standard." I learned quickly that in the hardware world, "establishing a standard" is something best left to trade organizations. The particular trade organization for this kind of thing was the MIDI Manufacturers' Association, headed, in fact, by the selfsame Tom White as above.

Worse, Fat Labs suggested that volumes and attack times for all GM instruments should match those of the Roland Sound Canvas. We didn't suggest imitating the Sound Canvas' tones, or matching the quality, or anything like that. It's just that the fact that Roland was mentioned in the same breath as the word "standard" was received very, very badly by all the MMA member companies who weren't, in fact, Roland. Which happened to be most of them.

It was a very slow process to earn the trust of the manufacturers and the MMA. I joined the association, and with the able assistance of Roland's Mike Kent headed a working group to address the non-generalness of General MIDI. Years later, well after the use of GM had peaked, the president of the IA-SIG of the MMA reluctantly mumbled a verbal announcement that "the Sound Canvas should be the standard."

Fat Labs tested a lot of cards. Kevin worked hard and helped fix some major stupid errors that showed up in each card he tested. He eventually tested enough chips by enough major manufacturers that today, almost any GM sound set you use will create a musical effect that falls within Fat Labs' standards.

The GM-emulating MT-32 and FM tone algorithms found their way into hundreds of games, because we decided to let developers use them in exchange for a dollar and our name in the credits of the game. John Miles packaged the tones with his widely used drivers, and so a huge percentage of GM games were made possible by Kevin's good ear.

To this day, if a person were to play a file made for FM through the drivers that come with Windows, he will hear Kevin's GM tones. How did the Team Fat FM tones get into Windows?

Because Microsoft changed the last paragraph in the last iteration of the last contract I signed with them. It's a long story. Maybe it'll be in the next book.

Fat Labs never made a profit. It performed some good services for the game world, spread our name around very well, and gave Kevin a job for a long time.

My favorite part is this: For a while, no chip manufacturer could sell a General MIDI chip to any sound card manufacturer in Taiwan unless it was approved with the Fat Seal by Fat Labs. We can truthfully claim to have, for a moment, held a billion-dollar industry by the balls.

And we were so cool that we didn't even threaten to squeeze.

80025 75540

Adaptive Audio:
A Report

by Alexander Brandon

Video game music is finally coming into its own and finding its voice. EMI and other major record labels are starting to jockey to place their hot artists into the soundtracks of the best selling titles or use their music in cross promotional deals. The movie composer Harry Gregson Williams scored the recent release *Metal Gear Solid 2: Sons of Liberty*. Some of us may venture the opinion that video game music has finally found its voice, as Journalists are comparing the quality of some of the latest soundtracks to those of movie and TV shows.

From the perspective of the public at large, video game music is certainly no longer necessarily something to listen to only as part of a game but as "good quality," "well done" music unto itself. More and more people who before would scoff at the four-voice (or less) synthesized sound of such games as *Elevator Action*, *Mario Bros.* and the thousands of others that graced the 1980s are now buying game soundtracks by the millions. (The *Final Fantasy* game series by Squaresoft, which now uses a full orchestra, sold over half a million copies of its soundtrack in Japan for its latest installment alone.) They're even reading the new monthly section in *Entertainment Weekly*, "EWInternet," which contains at least 10 pages devoted to video games and, of course, their sound.

Despite this new and growing worldwide popularity for video game music, somewhere in the back of every game composer's mind is a lurking question:

"How can I make my music unique?"

Game music can easily mimic the theater and TV. We all know the green producer who comes to us with the dreaded request "make my game sound like John Williams!" Well, who can blame them? It's a benchmark to shoot for. Those industries have been around for decades, and it isn't as though they'll say "make my 3D immersive game sound like *Pac Man!*"

Nevertheless, where game music truly comes into its own is in its interactivity, and I'm not just talking about whether the music switches depending on the player's situation or not; we all know that old trick by now and we'll discuss it here in a moment. What do we really mean by "interactive music?" I'll not only give some examples, but also nail down some actual definitions. For those out there just entering the industry, for God's sake read this. You can talk to a company and sound like an expert even if you haven't fully immersed yourself in the biz yet. But make sure you're ready before you dive in. This is a pretty hefty read. A lot of pretty cool information, no matter what your level of experience, is coming your way. Grab a cup of coffee or a Jolt and sit back and enjoy the ride....

We're going to begin with a brief history of game audio, citing the most popular soundtracks. Note that my examples are in *no way comprehensive*, and I do hope some in the audience will notify me of other notable examples (What? He didn't include *Crysalis* as the best Nintendo soundtrack of all time? The FOOL!). The game geeks among us who have been with game music since the beginning will probably enjoy this trip down memory lane, but this might also be interesting for someone who wishes to learn "from whence we came."

The history that follows is categorized into generations, but remember, my friends, that these are approximations.[1] Years before Nolan Bushnell (founder of Atari and creator of *Pong*) tinkered in his garage, there may have been someone else on Earth who had already created game audio. I've talked to many a veteran whose favorite phrase is "That? <snort> I did that 10 years ago." Well, it wasn't in a national syndicated press release, so here's your chance to let the world know you really DID do it 10 years before anyone else, buckos. Write me and let me know the truth if its grossly misrepresented here.

---

[1] For an excellent short history of game audio, look at "A Brief Timeline of Video Game Music" by Glenn McDonald at http://gamespot.com/gamespot/features/video/vg_music/index.html. I also based some of the information presented below on my interview with Atari's Brad Fuller in the third IA-SIG newsletter.

Generation One: 1970–1980

From the mid 1970s to 1980 or so, video game music started as the most horrendous, static-filled movie soundtrack might have started in the 1920s. Simple electrical components and transistors were used to create one or two sounds at a time.

To tweak the sound, you had to actually engineer these components by hand. It is uncertain (by me, anyway, don't count me as the expert in this era, I'd hardly been born by 1974) just when the microprocessor chip entered the video game audio arena, but by 1980 it was in fairly widespread use. Most of us shudder at the thought of such primitive days, but it was a tremendously exciting time for the engineers involved.

Console, Arcade, and PC Systems

Before we get too far, I want to make a distinction between *console* systems, *arcade* systems, and (slapping my forehead before I forget) PCs. They are all separate sets of technology unto themselves and should be, in any comprehensive analysis or timeline, considered separately. For the purposes of not boring readers to tears, though, I'm going to lump them together.

Just keep in mind that during the years of video game audio's history, these three markets evolved at different paces. Sometimes arcade audio held a triumphant upper hand over the poor quality of home systems and sickening quality of PCs (such as in the 1980s). At other times, PCs have been able to compete with the best of arcade and console audio—such as now, believe it or not (just something to think about as you read this history).

Example games in this era are *Pong,* of course, and the other earliest arcade games:

- *Gunfight* (Midway, 1975)

- *Amazing Maze* (Midway, 1976)

- *Space Invaders* (Midway/Taito, 1978)

- *Galaxian* (Midway/Namco, 1979)

- *Asteroids* (Atari, 1980)

- *Pac Man* (Midway/Namco, 1980)

Keep in mind that the United States and Japan released blockbuster hits right around the same time period. If you want to play these games, I'd suggest you get MAME (the best arcade emulator available for home computers), but if you don't contact the original game companies and buy the ROM chip of the title you play on MAME, using it is illegal. As an alternative, head to Cedar Point Amusement Park in Ohio; they have one of the largest operating collections of vintage arcade games I've ever seen.

Yes indeed, by this time it's obvious that Midway (who recently released a remake of their classic *Spy Hunter*) and Namco are damned old companies. A round of applause to them and the other dinosaur companies that are still around and still going strong, and a moment of silence for the (as of this writing) recently deceased SNK, whose first title was *Ozma Wars* in 1979. They produced dozens of the best titles, and they'll be sorely missed.

Generation Two: 1980–1990

Video game music grew by leaps and bounds in this period, as did all aspects of game technology. Vector graphics began, using lines to draw objects instead of the blocky pixels; moving cockpits were used in various titles (Sega's *Afterburner II*, for instance); and audio turned into full-fledged chip processing.

Some of the best artwork ever produced digitally was done for games during this period, before 3D rendering began. The home market exploded as well. Not only did Atari flourish and then flounder, but on Christmas of 1986 the Nintendo Entertainment System was released. Thanks to its new technology and outstanding games, it outsold everyone's wildest expectations. Because this is Brad Fuller's domain, check out his description of Atari audio and FM sound in Issue 3 of the IA-SIG newsletter to learn just what horrors the game audio folks had to endure for arcade machines. They still had tremendously catchy pieces for the most part. The best pieces of this age still stack up compositionally to the best popular tunes of the present age. 'Tis sad that they only had the weak voice of FM synthesis to sing with, but look at some of the accomplishments.

This description of interactivity comes directly from an interview with Brian Schmidt, head of the audio department at Microsoft's Xbox division, about his title *Black Knight 2000*:

> "From the time you press Start until the game's over, the beat continues.
>
> "Music always changes at a musical boundary (beat, measure, 1/2 measure, etc.).
>
> "Some sound effects (the pop bumpers on the upper playfield) are timed to 1/16th notes when you lock a ball, the sound is on a beat boundary. Also, the key of the sound effect matches the underlying chord of whatever the background music is playing.... If you have the glass off, try looking the ball when you know the chord's about to change, and you'll hear the sound effect transpose in mid-stream. Graphics (lights, flashes, visual display) are all very, very tightly synchronized with the music.
>
> "A further trick... the vocal singing (the aaahs in particular) ...Memory was *really* tight. The main song is in E minor. I recorded a vocal aaah of an EMin chord. I use that same sample as EMin chord, CMaj 7 Chord and Bsus, so it sounds like there's a lot more singing samples than I actually have.

(Listen to the part in the main music where after the '...beat the Black Knight!' is sung... chords go Em, CMaj7... Bsus... B7... EMin.)

"Each mode has it's own music... main play... one ball left for mball... mball... jackpot... ball in shooter (waiting to plunge)... they are all harmonically related, move from one to the other seamlessly. Also, as the music progresses, if you go to another mode (say a timed mode), when the mode's over, it doesn't always go back to the beginning of the first piece. It might pick up in the middle."

Example Generation Two games include:

- **Wizard of Wor (Midway, 1980):** Notable because it was among the first, like Stern's *Berzerk*, that used voice synthesis to mimic speech. *Vanguard* by SNK did this too, but it wasn't released until 1981.

- **Legend of Kage (Taito, 1984):** Notable because it was among the first video games to use far more accurate synthesis of real instruments, primitively reproduced though they were, in its soundtrack. Give it a listen; its quite impressive for the time.

- **Lifeforce (Konami, 1986):** Not only did this game use samples in its soundtrack, but it also used recordings of voice. *Kid Niki: Radical Ninja* (Irem/Data East), among others, did this as well.

- **Afterburner (Sega, 1987):** Used distorted guitar samples to score a very impressive soundtrack.

- **Skull and Crossbones (Atari, 1989):** According to musicians Brad Fuller and Don Diekneite, "The music becomes more intense when boss guy appears, more triumphant as his health goes down, more dire as your health goes down."

During this time, the Atari 2600 and Colecovision home game systems were sweeping the world. The Colecovision featured a Texas Instruments chip that enabled three tone channels and one noise channel. Although not up to the standards of the coin-operated Gyruss class machines (the coin-ops, as they were known in those days), it preceded by about only two years the next wave of technology, spearheaded at home by the Nintendo Entertainment

System. Released in February 1986 in the U.S., the Nintendo system had a 2A03 integrated processor with two square waves (that's a kind of synthesizer for the boys and girls out there), a triangle wave, a noise, and sample generators, totaling five channels in all. Dozens of excellent soundtracks emerged that were so catchy they have been remixed by full live orchestras, among them the infamous theme to *Super Mario Bros.* by Koji Kondo and *Metroid* by Hirokazu "Hip" Tanaka.

Generation Three: 1990–present

As 1990 came around, several events turned games from a multi-million dollar industry to a multibillion dollar industry in a matter of a few years. This was because of changes in technology, and even more importantly, radical changes in game design itself. The first major coup was the release of *Wolfenstein 3D*, and subsequently *Doom*, by Id Software.

Because the advanced technology gave legendary programmer John Carmack the power to render worlds in three dimensions instead of two, people found themselves losing thousands of jobs due to the addiction formed from this new sense of virtual reality. Many games were doing 3D, but none used bitmaps the way *Wolfenstein 3D* did. Only solid colored polygons were used, and even mediocre realism was difficult to achieve with that limitation.

But game music and sound were making minor leaps of their own. For the first time, at home with the Commodore Amiga PC, in the living room with the Sega Genesis and the Super Nintendo, and in the arcades as well, games could play back prerecorded sound from any source without much hassle. Games certainly had accomplished this before, but in bits and pieces. The four-channel Zorro chipset on the Amiga leapfrogged the first IBM PC based Ad-Lib sound cards (released in 1987). The Ad-Lib sound cards had more channels but only used sub-standard Yamaha OPL chipsets to synthesize sound, whereas Amigas could use PCM-based samples in the newly developed .MOD format to mimic 1980s hits such as *Axel-F* and *Rockit* with frightening precision. With the introduction of Creative Labs's SoundBlaster 2.0, IBM PCs could play digitized sounds as well. Game music, which before had underground and closet fans in the thousands, saw those numbers climb steadily into the hundreds of thousands. The music was growing with the technology and evolving with just as much stride. More from Brad Fuller and Don Diekneite on *Gauntlet: Dark Legacy*:

> "All the music is streamed, but we were able to still make it somewhat interactive.

> "On the Haunted House level, the organ music fades in/out depending on how close you are to the organ. It was written to go with the existing music bed regardless of when in the music you happened to go near the organ.

> "Maze Of Illusion—the music changes when the playfield changes.

> "In the Carnival of the Lost, the music changes as you pass through various sections of the playfield."

Adaptive Audio... What Is It?

Some people call it "Interactive audio," but for the purposes of this chapter, we're talking about a segment of this broad field: audio that isn't just interactive, but adaptive. What's the difference?

Thomas Dolby Robertson, who runs the company Beatnik and who released several pop hits in the 1980s, such as "She Blinded Me With Science,"[2] said it best at an IA-SIG meeting in February 1997:

> "Adaptive audio systems provide a heightened user experience through a dynamic audio soundtrack which adapts to a variety of emotional and dramatic states resulting, perhaps, from choices the user makes."

---

[2] He'll never live that one down, but check out his *Retrospectacle* for other hits and lesser known gems such as *Budapest By Blimp*, for those of us who can tear our eyes away from MTV for more than 10 seconds.

What does this mean to the pro as well as the layman? *Interactive audio* is audio that happens when a user does pretty much anything with any kind of device, whether it be to click a mouse or hit a key. *Adaptive audio* refers to something that happens most often in video games (at times in websites as well) when the user influences the audio, and the audio influences the user.

In the years that have elapsed since Mr. Robertson's speech, adaptive audio in video games has taken some very dramatic steps, as you'll see in the next section.

Early Adaptions

The simplest form of adaptive audio (AA... not to be confused with the group that uses bumper stickers that say "Easy Does It") is found in such titles as the original arcade games. It's an easy concept to get your head around: Music and sound effects would match things players did. Because, for the most part, sound effects are designed to be as closely related to actions as possible to maintain continuity, the adaptive aspect of them is instantly recognizable, but not necessarily a new concept. The explosions of *Asteroids*, the gobbling of *Pac Man*, and the heavy thud as Donkey Kong hits the girders all corresponded best to the actions onscreen using whatever technology was available to reproduce them.

The next step, therefore, in AA was to explore music. Music in its purest form can be incidental or absolute. That is, it is like sound effects in that it corresponds to what is seen (incidental) or exists independently (absolute). The magic of music is that both of these techniques can work in live music just as much as games.

An early example of adaptive incidental music is seen in *Vanguard* (SNK), when the player flies through a fuel depot (a lovely little pixellated flashing tunnel with the word "FUEL" written above), the music changes from the main theme that begins the level (derived from Paramount's *Star Trek: The Motion Picture*, music by Jerry Goldsmith) into a triumphant theme (derived from Thorn/EMI's picture *Flash Gordon*, music by Queen) that lasts for as long as the player is invincible—around 15 seconds, during which the player can fly through anything and destroy it.

Even in *Pac Man*, there is use of a soundtrack that kicks in when a little muncher reaches an energizer and eats it, indicating that it, again, is invincible and can munch anything that stands in its way.

This technique of switching a single background soundtrack was employed by roughly 90% of games that used adaptive audio at all. Because games themselves were in their infancy, no one thought to employ very advanced audio techniques, and no one could with the limited technology available. Concentration was on adding audio, period.

Various games in the 1980s used adaptive audio in increasingly new ways, but on a very small scale. I have heard tales of brilliant interactive concepts in Commodore 64 titles as well as other systems, but few (and so help me if you don't inform ME of them, they'll still remain shrouded in cult fantasy, so write me!). It was not until the early to mid 1990s that AA really started to take root and grow. The switching of a single background soundtrack was all that was used until such games as *Fade to Black* (Delphine Software), *Ultima Underworld* (Origin Systems), and *System Shock* (Looking Glass) actually switched the game's music in response to events using such techniques as fading and mixing.

Now, let's examine a select few games that use AA in some obvious way and try to reason where the value of it lies. For years, audio professionals have tried to academically catalog interactive techniques and lump them into various terminologies. This method is proving ineffective, and I'm only just now realizing why. Although it might be useful in the future to label techniques used for interactivity such as "transition" and "sequence," people who create adaptive scores do so individually to create a unique experience on each new game.

Console Examples: Music Games

For those who haven't played *Parappa the Rapper*, it was, and still is, a groundbreaking title. While other titles may have done the same thing in the past, *Parappa* and its successor, *Um Jammer Lammy*, based the entire design of the game on the musical score. Because of *Parappa the Rapper*, AA took command of design, and so it is at the top of my list for AA achievement. Check out my interview with the game's creator, Masaya Matsuura.

In *Parappa the Rapper,* you listen to music and then tap your PlayStation controller buttons to match the lyrics of a song as it is being played (the button presses scroll across the screen so you have a visual cue). Matching the lyrics makes your character "rap." The goal is to make your character rap as close to the beat as possible. If you do so, you get bonuses and higher points. If you fall behind or miss the beats entirely, you lose points. The soundtrack of this game is interactive in the strictest possible sense: You must pay attention and press buttons in synchronization with the rhythm. If you fail to do so, the soundtrack becomes obviously distorted and more negative. If you follow the rhythm and beats perfectly, the soundtrack gets even more full and satisfying.

This game was hugely popular. While I wasn't able to find sound clips, you can check out the game online (http://www.scea.com/games/categories/stratpuzzle/parappa/index2.html) with some streamed audio. The audio quality isn't great, but at least you can get an idea of the happy-go-lucky goofy soundtrack.

Since *Parappa*, other titles have used this technique too, from *Samba De Amigo* to the latest music-based title, *Frequency*.

Console Examples: Racing Games

Racing games are prime candidates for AA. They follow about as linear a design as you can get, plus the basic design is extremely simple and a lot of bells and whistles can be added on.

Take *SSX* (EA), which remains the most popular snowboarding game out there. (Notice I didn't say sim; it isn't a simulation, but an emulation.)

In *SSX* the soundtrack shifts when someone does a trick. Most notably, the more air you get, the more the volume and low frequencies fade out until you land again, when a transition crash sound plays and everything returns to full volume.

But even before *SSX* was thrashing the slopes, *Need for Speed* and *Road Blasters* were using AA to enhance their races.

Road Blasters (Atari), with a soundtrack by Brad Fuller (http://www.yesterdayland.com/popopedia/shows/arcade/ag1116.php), automatically cues a piece as you approach the finish line and times a finish line piece to play perfectly in time (measurewise) with the approach piece. *Need for Speed 3* (created by long-time IA-SIG member Alistair Hirst) uses a custom sound engine called Pathfinder to fade in and out tracks to a piece as various events take place, such as a chase or as you start to go off the road. This is an example of AA used in very subtle ways, as many reviewers didn't notice how interactive the soundtrack was—and neither did I!

Such techniques raise the question "If a soundtrack is interactive and the player doesn't notice that its interactive, does it make a difference?" I think it does, but what's a shame is that such a soundtrack doesn't win awards, press, or accolades the way a soundtrack based on a symphony orchestra does.

Console Examples: Character Games

The soundtracks to *Soul Reaver 2* and the original, *Legacy of Kain: Soul Reaver*, were written by Kurt Harland, one of the members of Information Society. The genius of *Soul Reaver's* soundtrack lies again in its design. The main character, Raziel, transfers between the spirit world and the real world with a wave of his hands. As he does, the world transforms from a bent and twisted vision in the spirit world to the real world where objects abide by physical laws. The music follows suit: In the spirit world the player is haunted by a warped version of the tracks played in the real world. You can find a demo at http://www.eidosinteractive.com/downloads/search.html?gmid=85.

PC Examples

Deus Ex, and *Unreal* as well, use similar AA models on the PC. During a level an ambient piece plays (anywhere from silence to a grooving techno track to a sweeping symphonic score), and when an enemy approaches, an action music sequence begins. When the enemy is defeated, the music fades back into the ambient piece. In *Deus Ex*, there are different tracks also for when your character dies and when you encounter a person for a conversation. While it is open ended and very much synced with events, the model doesn't always work (an enemy behind you triggers music before you even see it, for example). Still, it was a great place for me to get my feet wet. You can find movies and a *Deus Ex* demo at www.deusex.com.

For another example of this adaptive audio model, check out the *Liberty Island* link (http://www.iasig.org/pubs/features/dxliberty.mp3). The *Liberty Island* main theme is followed by the action track, which is followed by the conversation track, then the death track rounds out the example.

Released two years before *Unreal* and four years before *Deus Ex*, *Fade to Black* followed in the footsteps of *Out Of This World* and *Flashback*, using brilliant techniques in animation to wow audiences and put Delphine Software on the map.

For *Fade to Black*, Delphine uses MIDI to achieve the same model used by so many subsequent titles: Themed tracks—ambient, action, and so on—switch back and forth depending on various triggers in a 3D environment. This, along with music track switching techniques in *System Shock* (http://www.origin.ea.com/ultima/uu/) and *Ultima: Underworld* (http://www.iasig.org/pubs/features/medical_mix1.mp3) helped pioneer mainstream use of AA in the 3D first-person adventure genre. Sure wish I could find some demos of this sucker, but if you want to check it out, you might be able to find it in one or two places under the EA label's "classic" lineup.

Unlike *Unreal* and *Deus Ex*, *System Shock* uses very similar tracks along a single theme per level, and each is cued according to the measure the track is on (switching isn't instantaneous). The example at http://www.iasig.org/pubs/features/medical_mix1.MP3 gives you an idea of how it accomplished this. *System Shock* was one of the best games of its day at using audio to truly envelop the player in a thick and sinister atmosphere.

Taking a different approach to adaptive audio, *The Dig* was one of the most unique game soundtracks LucasArts ever released. The game uses the iMUSE system to achieve stunning interactive results.

In this graphic adventure, characters move around on a static background screen that change when the characters exited. This style of game had been done since the late 1980s, but it still appealed to a large audience because of the ease of play and beautiful graphics. This title is no exception, but Unlike LucasArts's *Monkey Island* titles, which use soundcard-based General MIDI instruments primarily, *The Dig* uses recorded stereo tracks and shifts between them in the same way that the MIDI shifted in previous titles. You can hear two examples of the results at http://www.iasig.org/pubs/features/dig1.mp3 and http://www.iasig.org/pubs/features/dig2.mp3. Even though these are single pieces, trust me, they faded together completely seamlessly.

To finish up, let me say that these few examples aren't necessarily the pinnacle of AA technique. One can hardly claim such a distinction for any title as AA is still a fledgling method, and not a very easy one to pull off. Plenty of composers (who I envy) are very happy to write their music, produce their SFX, and go their merry way. Indeed, most of my favorite titles have no AA at all. However, the titles we have looked at here do set the stage to demonstrate that a great many companies are taking AA seriously enough to schedule it into the already hectic development cycles of top game soundtracks.

Wrapping It Up

So, what conclusions can we draw? Certainly, the public isn't exactly clamoring for adaptive audio, but perhaps that's because there isn't much of it out there to clamor for. If we look at the increase of music-based titles, however, adaptive audio seems to be a good thing to keep your eye on, and if you didn't know all the games discussed above had adaptive audio but enjoyed them anyway, then their creators did a good job.

Techniques and Meditations

Art and
Its Opposite

Techniques
and
Meditations

First Things First, Second, and Third: It's About Repetition

Bits of this chapter, give or take a few changes, first appeared in *Game Developer Magazine*.

The most important thing I can tell you is this:

Repetition is the problem.
Repetition is the problem.
Repetition is the problem.
Repetition is the problem.
Repetition is the problem.

Certainly repeating sound effects are the first thing to clue a gamer in to the fact that he's been ripped off. If you've ever sauntered past a pike with a sound designer's head on it, you can be certain that it was placed there by a gamer who didn't want to hear that one certain sound another time. Regardless of variations in filtering, speed, pitch, reverb, panning, and phase, no matter how huge the game's world is, the third time you hear that bomb blast with the splat at the end, or hear the same guy say "Stand up so I can kill you again," your subconscious is acutely aware that this is not, in fact, Reality. The acceptable film school or design committee way to state that the game's designers deserve to be tortured for all eternity is to say that the repetition of sound effects "compromises the willing suspension of disbelief." In other words, it makes the game an ineffectual joke rather than an immersive alternate environment.

Repetition of music does the same thing as repetition of sound effects, but it sports some special subtleties that are worth emphasizing here.

A normal, intelligent game developer will budget for about an hour of music for his game, more or less. For the sake of this chapter, let's call it an hour. That hour is destined to be stretched over, let's say, a 40-hour entertainment experience. That's the normal, intelligent way to do things, and it's pretty stinking ridiculous.

Think about it. Say there was a law in one of those places outside Texas—like Zanzibar or, say, Canada—that decreed that in order for any citizen to be allowed to hear a piece of music, he would have to commit to listening to it at least 40 times. Tell you what, the population of Canada would consist solely of the beaten, smoking corpses of Canadian composers.

Compare this one-to-forty ratio to your being forced to work a full week as a taxi driver with only one audio cassette in your cab. But remember, it's a cassette that you didn't choose. Perhaps this is the reason that so many game players like to run about shooting and killing things. Sometimes I consider the tragic loss of NPCs and reflect on the possibility that if a few concerned citizens like us could solve the problem of repeated audio in games, perhaps we could save the lives of literally billions of innocent animated characters.

The first step toward solving this problem, saving those virtual lives, keeping our own heads off of pikes, and preventing the eternal torture of our designers is to be aware—and make other members of the development team aware—that the "normal, intelligent" approach to game audio is horribly flawed. Solving the problem might be beyond the scope of this book, but planting the seeds to allow you, dear Reader, to be among those who solve it is certainly not beyond its scope.

To help you on your way to Virtual Saviourhood, here are some of the techniques that have been tried with various degrees of success.

Method 1: Ignore the Problem

Here's what you do: **Nothing**.

Positives: Sadly, this is the best way to keep your job. It's probably closest to the way that any experienced game developers on your team handled audio on the last game. It's easy on the entire development team. It's inexpensive, and it does not challenge anybody's ideas, authority, or sense of confidence. Furthermore, you can rest assured that the game will sound the way a game is expected to sound.

Negatives: The game will sound the way a game is expected to sound.

Method 2: Tiptoe Around the Problem

Here's what you do: Don't use one repeating tune for an entire level of a game. It seems normal and intelligent to have a "first level" tune and a "cave level" tune and an "underwater" tune, but it's just plain old school. There's no excuse, and it will badly injure the ears of anybody playing the game and kill anybody listening who isn't playing the game. So don't do it. Okay? Just don't. If any one tune in your game repeats for more than five minutes, you should do one of the following:

1. Change to another tune after five minutes.

2. Stick a hot fork into your own eye, you evil moron.

Reuse your resources in different circumstances. I know you want special "cinematic" pieces, and "payoffs," and a unique piece for the puzzle with the cute duckies, and such. But the math is simple. If the game's budget is for 20 minutes of music, and the game is constructed so that music plays for an hour in a given session, the music is going to repeat somewhat. And remember that three repetitions of the music would happen only in the best possible circumstances, meaning all music has the same odds of repeating. But suppose you get greedy about special-case music. The more of your music that goes to special one-time cases, the more the other tunes have to repeat to cover for it. Reuse that "Binky meets the cougar" tune as a "tense puzzle-building" or "will we win the pony race?" background piece. The players won't mind; the situation will be different enough that they'll experience it as two different pieces of entertainment. The people listening and not playing will be grateful for one less repetition of that incessant **"riding the pony"** music.

Do not use musical structures that utilize repetition to build familiarity. This is hard to get away from. Sure, conventional musical theory suggests that we play familiarity against variation to achieve tension. That's why conventional music uses forms such as AABA. But in a game, you're going to get 30 repetitions of the tune at least. Think about that. How many times have you listened to the CDs in your house? Even your favorite CD? In a game, you can concentrate on the variation and relax on the repetition. An hour into the game, the familiarity will be there, I guarantee it.

Fade to silence after two minutes of inactivity. Some games don't, and I have one thing to say about that: It's a **strong** indication that everybody on the development team lives **alone**.

Positives: These are brilliant ideas, and I've seen more short-run success come from them than from any other ideas. The costs are low, and the results are good. Do the above, and if your audio content is listenable and your game is playable enough to ship, you will put your game into the top five percent of great-sounding games.

Negatives: You will only be in the top five percent of great sounding games, and with all respect for my chosen profession, that's not yet something that everybody would want to subject his worst enemy to. Because why? Because this: Because even after you've executed all of this earnest cleverness, you're still trying to make an hour of music palatable for 40 hours. Frankly, a miracle is wanted.

Miracle, you say? Surely, Fat Man, that is too strong a word, and you are exaggerating the extent of this problem.

Perhaps you're right. Miracle is a strong word. And all we have to do is make an hour of audio suffice for 40 hours, which isn't that tough. It'd just be like making a loaf of bread suffice for 40. No miracle needed. No need to use such strong, potentially offensive language like "miracle." Let's try another word.

So instead, I'll put it this way. Making one hour of music suffice for forty hours of gameplay is like polishing a turd, and you **can't** polish a turd.

Well, you can, but it's difficult, it gets your rags all dirty and smelly, and in the end, what do wind up with? A shiny turd. And you can't feed the masses with *that*. They prefer bread.

Method 3: Engineer the Problem

Occasionally a producer, designer, programmer, or publisher will look at the one-to-forty problem and recognize it as an issue worthy of his Brilliant Problem-Solving Ability. He will then proceed to decide to solve the problem cleverly. Or, as some might say, "cleverly," in quotes.

I've heard a lot of ideas that qualify as Method 3. From time to time, a producer will insist that the audio for a game be produced using Microsoft Direct Music Composer, a program that will be discussed elsewhere in this book (unless my technical editor forgets to remind me to cover it, which I kind of hope happens because I don't want to get another call from Microsoft like the one I got the *last* time I misinterpreted Direct Music Composer in print). Sometimes a producer has an idea in mind for layering audio, so that more exciting instruments get added as action becomes more interesting. Sometimes there is a more ambitious artist who envisions bringing to fruition his own personal vision of the connection between graphics, gameplay, and audio that will somehow create an ever-varying reactive audio experience. Sometimes these ideas are stinking brilliant, and sometimes they're just plain stinking.

The proposed benefits that tie all the Method 3s together are that somehow the effort and resources that it takes to compose X minutes of music, plus some amount of additional engineering can result in 40X minutes of fresh entertainment. The mood of the developer is always hopeful. The lowest expectation is that a particular chosen Method 3 will affect the results of a composer's efforts the same way that the 39 mysterious "helper" parts of Hamburger Helper affects a single part of hamburger. The highest expectation is that the chosen Method 3 would be like shipping 39 robotic clones of the composer in the game box, each clone brilliantly programmed by the composer to do his precise bidding, responding deftly and with precise real-time artistic insight to every subtle twitch of the gamer's joystick.

Positives: It certainly can look good on paper when a nice, scientific-looking designer struts into the room full of suits and proposes a never-before-heard audio machine that will use science, math, and good old Cutting Edge-ness[1] to allow music to sound different every time it's heard. Money people and marketing people will often sit up and listen, because they respond well to the idea of technological innovation. And well they should. Technological innovation has a history of tending to sell product. Moreover, I like when Method 3 comes up because it's a magnificent change from the ordinary when actual valuable programming resources get moved to the audio realm.

The strongest positive is, however, very, very much more significant than those in the last paragraph. The Big Time Beautiful thing about Method 3 is that *sometimes* the sounds that come from gameplay on these innovative sound engines can actually create audio entertainment experiences that could only have come from a game—experiences that will never be found in movies, television, or CDs. Method 3 thinking is precisely what's needed to break us of our awkward adolescent habit of considering anything "movie-like" to be good.

Hooray for Method 3.

Negatives: Ahem.

Well, my pet theory, which is almost certainly wrong, states that Method 3 is like trying to build a baby-sitting robot instead of being with your kids. My theory states that it is always better to direct all your audio energy toward making lots and lots and lots of warm, exciting, varying, heartfelt audio (see Method 4 below), and that you can do this better with a kazoo and a cassette recorder than with physically modeled 3D interactive vaporware.

[1] My brother Rick was accused of being cutting-edge. He responded negatively. He said he prefers to try to grasp the handle end.

But, theory aside, the problem is that, in practice, it's not music. Wait, that's too strong, of course I don't mean that, I don't even know why I said it. I take it back. I just mean to say, well—it's not *music*. Yet. That I know of.

I am *so* dying to be proven wrong on this point, but so far the *practical fact* is that I have not heard *any* music that has been produced by any "Method 3" engine that I would willingly play on my computer for any reason other than business research. *Please* send me an angry email that proves me wrong!!!

I have great optimism that this is not a permanent situation, nor is it due to a problem inherent in nonconventional, nonlinear composing methods. I merely think that it's a tools problem. The tools are hard to get a hold of, hard to understand, hard to operate, based on a single person's artistic vision of how music should react to games, or all four, and you just can't build a good robot-babysitter from them. The brilliant young composers who would potentially crack this nut are either not exposed to good tools—or any tools—or they're spending so much energy learning the tool they have that by the time they are finished writing a tune, there is no life-force left in them to put the levity and surprise and joy into music that makes it, well, *music*.

Really, I don't mean to make it sound so terrible. I heard one of the great proponents of Direct Music Composer say that the learning curve for that program is more a learning *cliff*. But the view, he said to its credit, is great from up there. Those are strong and wonderful words, and they deserve to be taken seriously. And as I've said earlier, if any game audio guys have jumped from said cliff from sheer frustration, the news hasn't gotten to me. We're all still alive.

Hey, you ever play *Lemmings*?
What a great game.
Oh, sorry. Back to the topic...

Method 4: Throw Resources at It

Here's what you do: In this method, more time, money, attention, and energy go to audio, with all of it going specifically into composition, rather than relying on new technology and the brilliance of our engineers to make things sound better. Instead of composing an hour of music and then doubling the expense by telling the programmer to cleverly make the thing bearable, this method suggests that we just double the amount of careful, intentional, heartfelt composition that happens.

Positives: This method comes with my personal guarantee that the game will be considerably more than twice as good from an audio standpoint. The rationale here is that first you bring twice the amount of entertaining music to the listener, which of course doubles the amount of Beautiful Human Loveliness (BHL) to which he is exposed. Double value, right there. Then, on top of that, you take the worst thing in the game player's life, which is certainly the over familiarity he has with the music he's stuck hearing for the next 40 hours, and you cut that pain in half. Not bad!

Negatives: You've doubled your music costs, and it's far from enough. You've only come a second 40th of the way to your requirements. Even though you've fed twice the music-hungry people that you had before, your crowd is still starving, and you still have to do the work of 40 loaves with two instead of just the one. And there just isn't enough dough to make 38 more loaves. How many more copies of the game will this doubly good music sell, if the music is still, even after doubling, a 20th of what is needed? And now, the budget guy has seen the music department double its expenses. Uh-oh. And then he heard the music guy tell another guy that there is no solving this problem until the budget is multiplied by 40!!! So, you know that Mister Budget Guy is now playing a little game of his own. Like, it's WWII, he's flying over London, heading a squad of German dive-bombers loaded with layoffs, and now he's looking at your music department through a bombsight. "Target spotted, Sir."

NYOOOWWWWWWWWwww Dow Dow Dow Dow Dow...

ka-BOOM!

I can hear the soundtrack even now.

Method 5: Transcend It

Here's what you do: Redefine the industry. Shift the paradigms. Come up with something that hasn't been thought of before.

Positives: You solve the problem completely. You become a saint. Your game is loved by many and makes the world a better place.

Negatives: It's hard, and you will have to pay taxes on a lot of expensive things that you'll suddenly be able to afford. Also, it will be annoying to have to keep telling people who ask you what in the world gave you the courage and the insight to achieve such a thing, "I was inspired by that chapter in The Fat Man's book." What a pain *that* will be.

Repetition is the problem.

Why in the World Would You Want to Write Music for Games?

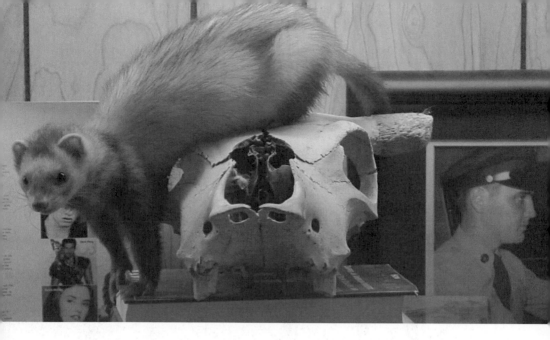

A Fable

Once there was a young raccoon named Sammy. Now Sammy wasn't like all the other little raccoons.... He didn't like to play with all the other little raccoons in the river or steal rotten fish out of peoples' trashcans. Things like that made him nervous. Sammy just wanted one thing, and he wanted it more than anything else. Sammy wanted to write music that would play on a vacuum cleaner.

"I like vacuuming!" said Sammy. "And so do lots of other people. It makes me feel good. If I could write music for a vacuum cleaner, it would be like playing a concert for millions of people!!!"

One day, Sammy decided he would leave Raccoon Town to go make his way in the world of music for vacuum cleaners.

When the other little raccoons heard about this, they laughed. "Why in the world would you want to write music for a vacuum cleaner, Sammy?" they said. "Vacuum cleaners just make that one sound. And they make it all the time, over and over. They're loud and annoying, and nobody likes to listen to them."

In his heart, Sammy knew they were right. But the birds seemed to be singing the Song of the Hoover, and the river was humming a monotonous roar. The call was irresistible, and so he set out on his way!

Wherever he would go, he would try to make friends, and sometimes they would invite him to make music for their vacuum cleaners. He always did the best job he could do, trying with all his might to improve his abilities and hone his craft. He thought hard about the millions of people who might someday listen to his music while they were cleaning their floors. He didn't want to let them down.

In time, he made friends with a Warthog named David, who had great faith in Sammy's talent. Dave Warthog made vacuum cleaners for a living, he wanted them to sound great, and he even paid Sammy a sack of rotten fish every time he finished a tune.

Sammy was in heaven, and he tried even harder to do a good job. He borrowed melodies from the birds. With Dave Warthog's help, he figured out his own special ways to make new sounds and to make the humming sound like all kinds of noises. Together they dropped things into the rotating brushes to make the sound of drums, changed the voltage real fast to change the engine speed and make the sound of an organ, pinched the vacuum tube to make the sound of a didgeridoo, and even flipped the switch off to make the sound of a toaster. That was funny, because everybody knows that toasters don't make much sound.

People who heard the vacuum cleaners loved them. "Hey! That sounds like a toaster!" they would say. It was great!

One day, Sammy met a group of 'possums, all gathered around a piano... and a late '70s Sears Turbo Tornado Wind Winder 1750! "Wow!" said Sammy, "You write music for vacuum cleaners, too?"

"Yup," said one 'possum.

"Can I hear some?" said Sammy.

"I guess," said another 'possum.

What they played him was not really very good at all. It did not sound like birds or drums or anything.

Sammy tried to be polite, but after a while, he said, "I can understand that you don't drop things into the brushes and pinch off the suction tubes and stuff, because those are my special ideas. But why don't you guys borrow melodies from the birds?"

"Oh, we do," said the biggest 'possum of them all. "We do it all the time, and it's really nice music. But when we write something good, well, I mean... why in the world would we ever put it on a *vacuum cleaner*???"

Eventually, it must be said, vacuum cleaner music did catch on. Millions of people did listen to it, and 'possums and raccoons alike learned to do special tricks and borrow music from the birds. Some of them made a *lot* of rotten fish, too.

One day, that biggest 'possum looked at his huge sack of rotten fish, and he remembered Sammy. He wondered where Sammy was. He asked around, but nobody knew. He searched and searched and searched the whole world of vacuum cleaner composers, but none of them had a clue as to where Sammy had gone.

But I bet *you* can guess. Yep, that's right. Sammy had gotten nervous again, and had hit the road, looking for opportunities to write music for...

Toasters.

"And people," said The Fat Man, *wiping a tear from the corner of his eye,* *just read is* **true...** *"the story you have* *that young raccoon* *was* **me**, *and that* vacuum cleaner *was a computer whose* **sound system** **sucked**."

m.

Song idea: ©1998 THE FAT MAN
beep boop poot beep beep boop   boop beep beep boop
beep beep boop beep boot pthththth beep poot beep
boop beep.

Yah!

Sounds like somethin' from a damn VIDEOgame...

Prairie-Granny ©2001

Scrawled by The Fat Man at the meeting with NARAS that led to allowing game music to be eligible for a Grammy. "Yah" was written by Alex Brandon.

Risk and Trivial Pursuit

Lately, our business has generally tended to play it safe in the audio arena.

I expect that phrase, "play it safe," to stab like a sharp wooden stake into the hearts of the "Bad Boy" game developers. Like a long nail. Maybe nine inches. And well it should, too.

We gamers are nasty, rough, and evil. We're about blood, speed, adrenaline, breaking the law, killing the monster, and getting the girl.

But we're scientists at heart, aren't we? And we really, *really* would like to be filmmakers, some of us older guys, wouldn't we, really? C'mon, admit it. At least we long for the legitimacy that filmmakers have. I can tell that we like legitimacy, because when we get little pieces of it, we throw off our bloodied helmets, leap to the top of the mountain, circle our splintered clubs over our heads, and roar victoriously to the sky.

**"Our industry makes more money
than film and television combined!!!"**

"Our ads are on TEE VEEE!"

"We used a *full orchestra* on our game!"

**"I can't believe I used some of the
very same extras *Steven Spielberg* used!!!"**

Guys, these are impressive achievements, but they are not things that seasoned, confident film people, or barbarian warriors for that matter, say. These are things that scared insecure people say when they want their dad to like them.

You want to be compared to Movies? Okay, try this. Once upon a time, the film industry was in that position, too.

Legitimacy was a thing of the future. Working in The Cinema was considered to be not unlike working in The Pornography. "Moving Pictures" were a haven for desperate actors and broke entrepreneurs, and for many of these, it was *precisely* not unlike working in The Pornography. Known stage actors who were reduced to the level of working in film would often deny it, using a different name for the two endeavors. It was common to hear that an actor was working in film "only until something legitimate comes along."

In this way, we *are* like The Cinema. Shout *that* from the mountaintop.

And in our striving to become more and more cinematic, we have taken some of our attention from gameplay and focused it upon some of the outstanding aspects of that noble, flat, tall, and two-hour-long medium. Not "outstanding" as in wonderful. **"Outstanding"** as in like a **sore thumb**.

Black screen with white letters.

A low, throbbing single note builds in intensity.

A deep voice begins speaking, "In a World..."

A scraping, screeching sound effect makes us leap from our seats.

The orchestral score hits really hard!

The car drives really fast.

The Chick is HOT, and man, she says sassy things, and it turns out she can FIGHT, TOO!

The gun points in the guy's face.

The computer-generated alien's jaws open. Look! See how well they can render DROOL now!

Sudden silence...

A drop of blood lands on a white wedding veil.

The screen explodes, and all is quiet. The deep voice is back.

"Kiss-Kiss, Bang-Bang."

"Coming this summer."

"From We Know How to Make Trailers so That Somebody Off-Screen Can Make a Pile of Cash Films."

This is the sum total of what we have picked up from decades of the cinematic art.

There is more to movies than kiss-kiss, bang-bang. There is emotion. There is depth. There is social change and the responsibility that goes with causing that change.

There is the fact that people have given their lives to the medium.

There is innovation—the kind that can only come from risk. And the kind of innovation we see in the great movies is the kind that can come only when many people have given their entire lives over to a medium.

The Cinema can make you cry and change the way you live. Can The Game do that? Not by imitating the worst part of the crappy trailers from the last ten years, it can't.

I guess it would come across well to the scientist in us if I were to say that, particularly when it comes to audio, we game creators can focus fairly well on an object and we can note fairly accurately what it currently is like. In other words, we can notice its position. But we often ignore its velocity, forget about its acceleration, and are surprised to find that there is a formula that governs its motion through space.

Let's imagine that a game's spec calls for "some John Williams, maybe Danny Elfman" (assuming you're not John Willams—John, if you're reading this, this does not apply to you), then you've got a very good starting point. If you treat that as your stopping point, too, you might be able to schedule things pretty well. Poop out a little John, whip up the invoice, connect the dots, bada-bing, bada-boom, done. That's how we do it in The Games Business.

A product made this way could turn out good, and often does, but the odds are very much against its turning out great. Do you have a favorite Elvis impersonator? Is he a truly great musician? Do you have a favorite Beatles cover band? Did they change your life or the course of a generation? John Lennon or maybe George Harrison once said, and I love, ironically, to say this in an accent, "They can't be imitating us, we don't *wear* Beatles wigs."

No, Johnny-or-was-it-George, great performers *don't* wear Beatles wigs. Because people who wear those wigs are only capturing the very sheen of the very surface of the greatness of what's underneath.

On one game to which I had been assigned, I was asked to do "normal game music," (which, for this kind of game, meant Techno) and when I suggested some different approaches, I met with a brick wall. The developer actually *wanted* not to do something that was unlike other games. I was asked, "George, did it ever occur to you that there is a *reason* that all movies use the same kind of sound for certain types of scenes?"

Extreme close up: The Fat Man's face remains polite.

Zoom in, fade to flashback of The Fat Man at USC Film School, sweating his nuts off studying film and music with every bit of devotion he can muster. Split screen. The game developer who asked the question is gargling beer at a frat party, *and* he's still wearing diapers. He shouts out drunkenly that he wishes he could be just *exactly* like John Travolta, then he passes out in the punchbowl. Fade back to The Fat Man's face, and zoom out. Reality begins again. The Fat Man speaks:

"Yes, Friend, but which among those is a great movie soundtrack? They're all imitating *Star Wars*, which was pretty much the first movie to use that sound. *Star Wars* itself, the leader, is a great soundtrack—loved, admired, and imitated. In order to achieve that, wouldn't you think that you would have to innovate?"

He paused for a long time, then said, sincerely, "How does one go about *innovating*?"

It was another *Star Trek* moment. "What *is* this 'Love,' Captain?" "Brain and *Brain*. What is Brain?" "Kiss? Tell me more about this...'Kiss.'" I'm sure I could have explained every bit of it to him quite well, and changed the course of his life, and probably given him religion, too, by simply saying, **"You have to take RISKS,"** but right then I had to use the john.

Anyway, speaking of which, back to Mr. Williams. Yes, John wrote the music for *Star Wars.* Important, substantial music, and *first* of its kind. A person could do worse than imitate him, so go ahead and do it. BUT, to use the "Be Like Johnny" model to be great, you might do well to keep going.

Begin by imitating his compositions, but go on to learn how to create his feelings.

When you imitate his orchestration, continue, and learn how to be evocative of emotions.

When you imitate his greatness, learn how it progresses; learn how it leaves its own roots behind.

A layman might only see the music as an object, frozen in time and space, and he might copy that and think he has done something wonderful. But here, there is no room for the Hand of God.

A more experienced musician would notice that the object has velocity. He would say, "Ah, I see where that came from, and I see where it was going. It represents an improvement on what went before," and he would copy that improvement, too.

But the object also has acceleration, and an overall formula to whose rules it dances across a multidimensional Cartesian plane.

The master learns as much of this formula as he can, admires it, wonders at its unfathomable mysteries. And then he writes his own.

Let's not forget that John Williams is not just credited with *Star Wars.* He also wrote the beautiful solo violin theme of *Schindler's List.* Before all that, he did, without imitating anybody *I* know of, the King of Movie Themes People Like to Imitate: *Jaws*. And you know those hilarious strings in *Gilligan's Island?* Guess what? Look in the credits. Johnny Williams. Same cat.

The guy has history. He changes. He adapts. He makes his own sounds, and they come from his life and the composers he looks up to. Then the sounds come to life, people imitate them, they become a part of who we are. The object has position, velocity, acceleration, and a mysterious formula.

In fact, the story of *Star Wars* is that Lucas had used Holst's *The Planets* as a temp track to the movie, and had liked it so much that he had originally only hired John to reorchestrate that piece. John stood up to him with the suggestion that he be allowed to write some new music.

So I guess that when they ask you for John Williams, don't take it as a request for his melodies and orchestration. The client may not realize it, but he's really asking for a brush with Greatness. The appropriate thing to do is be as great as John, and, like him, do something that moves the player in a way that only *you* would have thought of.

Since I hinted that it is impossible, we know that naturally it *is* possible to be great by wearing the Wig. Once, I asked my friend Michael Land how it was going, and he was sad. For the seemingly endless series of LucasArts *Star Wars* games, Mike had been analyzing and editing John Williams' actual *Star Wars* scores into tiny bits, dissecting them, re-arranging them, composing little bits of filler, and re-creating the most amazing John Williams Hamburger Helper Casserole you'd ever heard. He would have rather been doing what he termed a "creative project," which would call for original music, such as the (great) *Monkey Island* and *The Dig* scores he'd done. But, nonetheless, it was one job for which you would be hard pressed to argue a case *against* John Williams *Star Wars*–style music, and Mike had turned the sights of his Mighty Creative Battering Ram toward that wall. In the end, the music he made was indistinguishable from that created by the Johnmeister.

So I says, "Hey, Mike, you choppin' John?"

And he says, "Yep. I'm choppin' John."

And I says, "I think you're gonna be choppin' John till you're jammin' with Jimi."

A game company was once considering hiring a TV composer whose work they liked. I listened to his work, found it not far out of reach, and offered to imitate his style for half his cost. For a moment, I thought that this might seem like an unkind thing to do to that composer. So I added that they should tell him that if he wanted to imitate *my* style at half my price, that would be fine with me, because, after all, fair is fair.

And how do you do it? How do you **innovate**?

It's easy: You take a risk.

How do you take a risk?

Simple.

YOU DO NOT DO WHAT WORKS.

It's good to *know* what works. It's good to know what people seem to like. But the difference between doing only what works and what *could work* is the difference between following and leading.

Read this sentence:

You cannot
innovate
by only doing what has worked in the past.

This would be a good time for you to consider reading Bruce Sterling's talk in the appendix "Bruce Sterling's Famous GDC Speech," but allow me to sum up its salient points here.

As gamers, we bring to the world some very special gifts. We move forward at lightning speed and embrace technology and invention in a way that surpasses every group of people that has ever come before in all of history. To play it safe in this business is to deny our inner nature. It is to deny our responsibility to the world and to the players. To not take risks is to go against the very principles of fun and risk that define the art of game development.

In short, This Is Gaming. If you're not exposing your players to anything new, then you are just asking them to connect dots. Connect-the-dots is not a game.

God put **you** on this planet along with the other game makers that you might complete your mission, a **crucial** part of which is *scaring the crap* out of your investors.

You are to do this by exposing those investors to your brilliant but untried ideas. And if the thought of that investor walking out the door with his money is too frightening for you, and because of that, you can only bring yourself to propose ideas "that work" and "that people like," then you are not a game maker, you have no idea what makes games fun, and it is morally imperative that you go into another business.

You might try selling soap. People *always* need soap.

And if you don't want to do sell soap, then take risks. Start with the Big Risk, where John and John started: Dedicate your life to your work. And then, you gotta go past them, you gotta innovate, you gotta keep on going. Where? To take the Big Fat Challenge.

The Big Fat Challenge:

Let's make some kind of new sound,
like **John Lennon** did for rock and roll,
like **John Williams**
did for movies, but let's use that
interactive engine,

and that gaming mentality,
and that
unique vision,
and that talent for invention,
and let's by-God make game audio

*do something for peoples' hearts and ears
that movies, that rock-and-roll, that* **EVEN
JOHN WILLIAMS** *could never do.*

I'll even give you the one thing that the True Gamer in you can't resist. I hereby bet you 10 bucks you can't do it.

Art and Judgement

My Prime Directive always has been to figure out what that great thing the Beatles did for me was, and to do it for other people.

If you want to do something great, you have to know what "great" is. To do that, you have to be able to tell when one thing is better or worse than another. Everything hinges on this ability to discriminate and evaluate—to judge.

At the same time, the universe can conspire, sometimes very effectively, to lead a person who is in pursuit of greatness to abandon judgment altogether.

In the very competitive atmosphere of USC film school, we learned the sharpest kind of discrimination in a pretty intense way. Our first filmmaking class demanded that each student write, cast, shoot, and edit five Super-8 films. As sound was to be recorded separately and played back on a reel-to-reel with no sync, dialog was not an option. It was not enough that we merely make the films, either. These films were expected to hold to the high standards of our famous school. The visuals were to tell a story, the main character was to go through a change motivated by forces inherent in the characters, lighting was to be good, camera work was expected to move the story along; it was a laundry list as big and old as film itself, and it went on and on and on. The whole exercise was recognized by class and instructor alike as being pretty much impossible.

At each meeting of the class, we would show maybe four of the films that had been miraculously completed, and we would engage in the Dreaded Critique Process. It went thus: Each student would write five things good about the film (regardless of how bad the film was), then five things that were bad about the film (even if it was *Citizen Kane*). That paper would be graded and given to the film maker. Not so bad, you say? Ah. Maybe you're right. The *first* day.

But here's a funny thing that happens. When your buddy shows his film, and it was, like, really hard to make, it's as though he's handing you his Miracle Baby. And you are required, then, by the Law of the School, to feed it five bottles and stick five knives into it. The more brilliantly you do these things, the better. And the next week, you hand him *your* baby.

As I moved into the world of the recording studio, I repeatedly heard a marvelously helpful phrase from my mentor, Van, that accomplished the goals of the Dreaded Critique in the least painful way. He would step in to the studio, listen to whatever was going on, and pronounce, "That was *won*derful! Now, you know what it needs?"

I tell you what, you can sugar-coat **knives** all day long, but there is just no nice way to stick them in a *baby*. That goes double if you're getting graded.

The suggestions that followed were almost always spot-on—Van has a brilliant ear. But what left a bigger impression on me was that he could use that sentence to introduce improvements with equal effectiveness to the lowest intern and the most sophisticated veteran producer alike.

In later years, I duly brought this concept to Team Fat. For our first few months as a team, we would have "good-but-could-be-better" sessions, in which each of us would play a piece we'd done and the rest would say something good about it and suggest something that could make it better.

In that environment, with the pressures of grades and the pressure to make it in the world's most prestigious film school gone, working with one's own best friends, the critiques became more gentle and encouraging. They often fell away entirely—a piece would be declared perfect, and I found myself helpless to force the team members to stab each others' babies.

And I think we were doing better work and making as much creative progress as the USC students had been.

There arose some interesting thoughts on the subject of evaluation. I began to think that, while indeed one piece of audio might be better than another, all works whose creators were earnest in their pursuit of excellence shared at least one thing in common—they *all* could be seen as good-but-could-be-better. Each artist was at the same point in his process. He was doing his best and pushing forward. And when the listener was a part of that—let's say he was a friend of the artist, or had seen a documentary and understood the where the artist's head was at, or knew how much worse the world's music had been in some area before this artist came along, or when somehow else the listener was able to sense that movement forward from good to better—the listener could be drawn in and have nothing but good feelings about the piece.

Van even hypothesized, on being questioned on this topic, that this was the thing that made the Rolling Stones' music feel so good, even if it wasn't the most sophisticated. One always felt that the band was at the edge of its abilities and moving ahead. I'd even go so far as to say that this kind of at-one's-own-edge art is part of what propels people into an Ed Wood film fest. Ed Wood's film work is loved and famous for its being really terrible, but it always seems like the poor schmuck is doing his best and trying to do more. I wonder if a super intelligent alien with supremely honed aesthetics ("Ah," say the gamers, "Now The Fat Man is talking my language!") upon viewing *Citizen Kane*, or any masterpiece of Earth art, would see it as though it were an Ed Wood film.

"Buzz. Click. Hey, Zeeborg, get over here. We're checking out these paintings by the lame-o Earth painter Rembrandt. They really suck, yet we are strangely compelled to feel the struggle of the artist! Bring cyber-beer. Buzz. Click."

At a time when Brian Moriarty was beginning to drift away from the game business and was in the middle of his self-described "obnoxious Zen" phase, he confessed to me that he no longer had the heart to guide the younger artists under his charge along their paths. It seemed as though they were all good, could be better, and were solemnly engaged in the processes that would inevitably lead them to becoming what they needed to be. To move them along would be like pulling a flower to make it grow or showing them the "whodunit" at the back of the mystery book.

By the time that "Professor" Moriarty and I were having this conversation, my own sense of judgment had become so softened that I had formulated a hypothesis (still unproven) that there has never been a noise made—never a sound, song, or tune—that would not improve some game somewhere, if played at the appropriate moment. This is an important guiding principle of GamePlayMusic, which I will cover later in this book unless it slips my mind.

Team Fat's Joe McDermott figures that art is simply the process of splitting the universe in half over and over again with decisions. You make a decision, it splits the universe in half, and you've made Art. One day it might seem very important to the artist to construct harmonies carefully and leave tone tweaking to the libraries. Another day, the tone might be everything, and it's time to write a one-note piece. When we were working together on a project, some days Joe would come in to the studio as the German ("Ziss mic iss pointink at zee *wronk* part of zee schnare!!!"), and I the Frenchman ("No cables in ze studio today... ze Muzeeque must be free!"). The thing that kept us from ripping each other's skin from the bones was that it was fun and we always moved forward. We each intellectually realized and understood the importance of the other guy's approach, and we realized that it didn't matter which approach became dominant in that project. The important thing was that decisions got made and that earnest efforts were being directed at making wonderful sound.

Sadly, this description of Art stinks. Why? Well, most importantly, because Joe described it best. I mean, even though the whole process of my life seemed to be leading me to that description, my rotten best friend came up with the really good quote. And another nearly as important reason is this: This description of creating Art by splitting the universe in two leaves us completely without the ability to judge our own work. With no sense of what is good, better, or best, how can a poor white boy ever do something Great?

To Be Continued in the Next Exciting Chapter!!!

The Beatles
Solution

Who Buried Paul?

This is where Brian Moriarty and the Beatles come back in to the picture. "Professor" Moriarty is known for giving the best, most mind-expanding lectures in our business. In 2000, the topic of his talk at the Game Developer Conference was the Beatles, specifically, the "Paul is Dead" hoax. The title of the talk was "Who Buried Paul?"

In this lecture, Professor Moriarty outlined what I consider now to be the answer to the Prime Directive. He solved the puzzle. Cut the Gordian Knot. Found the Holy Grail.

He Beat the Game.

No, I can't do it justice here.... Without the benefit of music and copy-rights and clearances, I'll never be able to paint that particular Mona Lisa. But I can draw a cartoon.

The Beatles were big. They were as big as you can imagine anything. They were all we had to look up to. We looked to them for our answers and our questions. They were gods.

One of them—Paul—was missing. We thought he was dead. We discovered remarkable clues all over the Beatle albums—the artwork, the lyrics, the recordings.

There was a hand over Paul's head (reputedly a sign of death) on the cover of *Sgt. Peppers' Lonely Hearts Club Band*. It happens again in several pictures on *Magical Mystery Tour*. No other Beatle had even one such hand over his head. Paul's back was to the camera on the back cover of *Sgt. Pepper*. There's an arrangement of flowers that looks like a left-handed bass (Paul's instrument) at a gravesite, with three strings instead of four, and the flowers appear to spell out the word, "PAUL?" Paul was said to have worn a walrus costume on *Magical Mystery Tour*, and the walrus was said to be a sign of death in certain cultures. Paul's rose was black, the other Beatles' were white. Paul wore no shoes crossing Abbey Road. His shoes are off in a picture in *Magical Mystery Tour*, too.... They are visible in the picture, right over the page number (13) and appear to be bloodstained.

You can hear phrases like "I buried Paul" and "Oh, untimely Death!" in the creepy tune, "I Am the Walrus." And the song "Glass Onion" states, "And here's another clue for you all... the Walrus was Paul."

Backward recording, hitherto unheard-of, became important to us, because if you played certain songs backward, you could clearly hear "Paul is dead. Miss him. Miss him. Miss him," and "Turn me on, dead man."

Moriarty went on to point out some highly original clues—some that he had discovered himself and that were amazing to experience. *But...*

What's the point?

For game developers, the main point might be that "Paul is Dead" was one of the greatest games ever played. It completely occupied us for weeks. We learned the Beatles' music. Our lives were changed.

Yeah, yeah, that's interesting and helpful and all, but how did they do it? That's the question. That's the point. And for game music people, for people on a quest to bring to the world some of the positive influence that the Beatles brought—in other words, for me—the point was encompassed in a single word: *constellation.*

"Professor" Moriarty concerned himself with that word "constellation," not as a noun but as a verb. He pointed out that the process of seeing shapes where they are only implied can be of great value. As one stares into the chaos, one tends to see what he wants to see. What he *needs* to see.

And the Beatles were, more than anybody else before or since, masters of creating just enough order to lure one in, to imply that there is a deep, important, helpful, urgent meaning within the sound, and then to provide enough chaos to allow the listener's ear fall back again on the heavenly voices in his own heart.

And to me,
hearing that lecture was
One Damn Big Fried Duck.

Special Consideration for Children's Games

Son of Repetition:

This chapter, give or take a few changes, first appeared in *Game Developer Magazine*.

Regarding games for kids, there's a lot of money being lost due to poorly constructed audio.

Let's use a military analogy.

There is a great and tragic battle that has raged for decades and has taken a drastic toll on our industry. We have been fighting for dollars, but we have been losing business and alienating customers. And, oddly enough, the key soldiers in this battle are the musicians and the "sound guys." While they themselves may have respect for the unique nature of the terrain upon which they shed their blood, often the commanders of their forces do not.

The most important point that gets missed is this: The person who buys the game (the parent) experiences the game *only* through the audio. This is an important point. History repeats itself, but since I am not yet history, I will paraphrase myself instead: Assuming that the game installs easily, that the kid can play the game mostly by him- or herself, and that the kid pretty much likes the game, all of the customer satisfaction, everything the buyer experiences, all of the motivation to buy the next product comes from the audio. The parents do not see or play the game. They hear it.

Yet due to the inability of the commanders to recognize this fact, never so much as even three percent of the resources has ever been directed to the soldiers at the very important musical front. Historians are still trying to figure that one out.

Atomic Weapon: Use with Discretion

Audio, especially game audio, is a powerful weapon. When used properly, it has the power to involve, immerse, elevate, and reward. It has the power to excite. It can make an artificial world appear to be deeper, older, and much more complex and complete than it actually is. But when misused, audio reveals its most awesome and deadly power—the power to annoy.

The Annoyance Factor for any game is already potentially dangerous. Now add to this dire situation the multipliers that are unique to kids' games, and you have something akin to a combination of friendly fire, toxic waste, and second-hand smoke. For some reason, somebody has decided that any game created for somebody under the age of nine will have the following audio characteristics:

- The compositions will be more repetitive than those in adults' games.
- The tones will be pedestrian.
- The tunes will be shorter and simpler than even normal game music.
- The tunes will all be in the same key, C major.
- Half the tunes will be public domain "favorites," such as "Twinkle, Twinkle, Little Star."
- Characters will yell in high, squeaky voices the following phrases: "Good job!" "Very good!" "Try again!" "Not quite!" "Hey! You're good at this!" "Great job!" "Hey! You're good at this!" "Great job!"

Why? Because it's easy. Because people think kids don't notice these things. **Because people think kids actually like these things.**

But that's insane. None of them is necessary or desirable... ever. Kids like good music, just like you and me. They get bored, just like you and me. And even if they didn't, it doesn't matter because you're never going to drive the kid crazy with good audio. But you're sure to drive the parent crazy with that crap you're giving them, and that's the last sale you'll make in that household.

And again I say, History Repeats.

That is the battle. Repetition is the enemy, so you've got to fight it with everything you've got. Resist the temptation to make audio that sounds like a "kids' game." As with any game:

- Always direct all your audio energy toward making lots and lots and lots of warm, exciting, varying, heartfelt audio.
- Don't use one repeating tune for an entire level of a game.

- Reuse your resources in different circumstances.
- Do not use musical structures that rely on repetition to build familiarity.

Moreover, don't insult kids with poor tones and yelling, squeaky voices. Elmo and Barney are beloved, but so are the softer, lower-voiced characters such as Mr. Rogers, Captain Kangaroo, and Marvin the Martian. Kids' ears are brand new, and they can probably hear better than you. If you want to delight kids, play a pretty little bell for them. Yes, they respond well to high tones. Yes, they even like those little square waves, by God. But even though some little girls might be inclined toward pink, Crayola has not yet rationalized filling an entire box of crayons with that one color.

Somebody Stop Me!

Okay, the knife is in. Now let's get down to the twisting. Picture this typical scenario: Mom works very hard at the office, then barely has the energy to cook. Somehow she manages.

"Dinner! *Now!*" shouts Dad, feeling guilty that it wasn't he who cooked it.

"But I'm right in the middle of my game!" comes the kid's answer. Good. The game is interesting. The makers of the game can be proud. But the parents—the customers—are getting angry.

"*Dinner!* Get in here right now or I'll throw that damn thing through the window."

"Okay! Okay! Okay!" answers the kid, if the parents are lucky.

The kid comes to dinner. What do we hear from the other room all through the meal? Music! It's the ice cream truck, parked in our living room, clanking out "Twinkle, Twinkle, Little Star" over and over and over and over and over again. And what's worse, every 45 seconds, a shrill voice yells out, "Hey! Are you there? Hey! Are you gonna play or what? Snore!!!"

Oh, yeah, the parents are going to love that. Why isn't there a "fade to silence after two minutes of inactivity" feature? Were the designers never in a human family? Are they designing for kids who don't eat, go to school, or play soccer? Is the target kid one who buys his own software and sets his own bedtime?

And do you know why these games sell as well as any other games for kids? It's because even the greatest games in the world have these design problems, and the parent's choice is either to buy no games for their kids or to buy annoying ones. Can you imagine what would happen to sales of kids' games if some of them stopped being deathly annoying?

And Another Thing

I should end the chapter here, but it is my duty as a Texan to go into areas I know nothing about. Here is my non-audio gripe....

Who in the world decided to let this happen: "Mom, I can't come to dinner now! There's no place to save my game until I get out of this battle!" One game even makes you earn a certain object that allows you to save your game more often.

(Long pause, Texas voice, one eyebrow raised.) Now I'm no game designer, but I know financial-suicide-by-greed when I see it. The kid has simply got to be able to save instantly at any time. Whatever the justifications are for having designated places in the game from which the player can save, trash them. If you have to hit your lead designer with a cattle prod until he admits that he screwed up, do it. I'll buy you a new cattle prod. If it's a hardware problem, and you'd have to solder another chip into every last cartridge yourself to rectify the problem, do it. I'll hold the soldering iron. Because that one element of game design has done more damage to our industry than any other.

Parents might say that the problem is the violence, but it's not. It's the fact that games have committed the unthinkable crime: They have made parents' lives even more difficult than they already are. And they have done this by making it impossible to get a kid who is playing a game into a car, into his clothes, to school, to the dinner table, or even out of a burning building if that kid is in the middle of a game with no save screen.

And what are the parents' choices? They can say, "Okay, I'll wait for you," which leads to untold misery and a quick undermining of the family dynamic, because now the sister, who was all ready to get into the car, asks if she can start a game too. The parents can say, "Quit without saving," which even parents know is a mortal sin—besides, it can easily lead to an hour of tears. Or the parents can say, "No more games for you anytime within an hour of when another activity is planned." Which is, when you think about it, exactly what happens, because it's the only option available.

Given the mistakes I've seen and heard, I think it's a damn miracle that games are even allowed in homes with kids. So pay attention to the lessons of your industry's history, and maybe you can make a bundle, and save the world and a family or two.

Money and
Its Opposite

Techniques and Meditations

How Much to Charge

How much should I charge?

The Fat Man

From: Anonymous
Sent: Tuesday, March 18, 2003 11:51 AM
To: The Fat Man
Subject: RE: How Much to Charge

Hi again George,

No problem for the information. I am the president of a new developing company planning its first console game. The name is [withheld] and we are in Montreal, Canada. The pre-prod is completed and we're wondering how to spend wisely the money we mortgaged our very souls with. Our web site is www.[withheld].

We have a full-time composer/musician/sound engineer, but he came up with a budget so outrageous we're wondering if he's not abusing his position just a little.

We would like to know what would be the strict minimum for him to work with in terms of hardware and possibly software. He will do the music and the SX of the entire game (but will benefit from assistants during testing phases).

If you need more details for a better assessment, don't hesitate.

The Fat Man

From: The Fat Man
Sent: Tuesday, March 18, 2003 1:55 PM
To: Anonymous
Subject: RE: How Much to Charge

Ah.

The ballpark budget for game audio is somewhere between zero dollars (U.S.) and infinity dollars (U.S.). I'm not sure how to convert this to Canadian currency.

I think perhaps the breakdown in communication between your audio guy and you would come at the word "minimum." Does your audio guy know that you would go to an expert and ask him for the bare minimum necessary, so that you would be able to come back at him to refute his budget request?

Is he really so untrustworthy to you that you actually suspect he might be abusing his position?

I strongly suggest that unless you work through these difficulties, you not invest a nickel in this relationship; there is no possible way either of you, or your players, will ever be happy with the outcome.

I will attach a chapter from my upcoming book, which will outline a formula for finding a good budget for any project. The formula will work equally well to find ballpark numbers for scoring a game, building a studio, or, indeed, building an actual ballpark.

Sincerely,

The Fat Man

The Chapter I Sent Him

One day in the Deep South not so very long ago, the old white-mustached Colonel was riding his favorite white mare across the fields of his plantation, enjoying the weather, checking in on the workers, and thanking the Lord for a good cotton crop by taking the occasional ceremonial sip from a large flask he carried for such moments.

He paused the mare in the shade near one particularly industrious worker, and upon studying this man's ways, his heart glowed with admiration and pride. Not a movement was wasted. He was a model of efficiency. Surely it was because of the labor of men like this that the Colonel had been able to enjoy such a sweet life. His eyes watered slightly as he was suddenly inspired with the urge to somehow make a gesture of appreciation. He called the man over.

Benevolently sweeping down in a graceful motion halfway between a salute and a bow, he presented the swollen flask to the worker and urged him to take a sip.

The worker, taken aback, cautiously took a sip, eyed the Colonel for no more than a second, and returned straight away to work.

The Colonel was livid. No thanks? No appreciation of the day, the crop, the kingdom they had built together? Hoping to spark a conversation, maybe even a friendship, the Colonel spoke. "Well? How was it?"

"I figger it was just about right," said the worker.

"What in God's name do you mean by *that*, my man?" demanded the flustered Colonel.

"Well, if it was any worse, I couldn't a drank it. And if it was any better, you wouldn't a give it to me."

When establishing a rate structure, game musicians should bear this story in mind. The correct amount to charge is "about right."

How to Get Work

People like to tell you how to get a job. "Do everything I did," they say, "and you can't go wrong."

How nice of them.

I've only become successful in game audio once. I probably can't help you much there. If asked, my advice would be likely to begin something like,

"First, **marry** Linda."

I've gotten a lot of jobs, though. But I only got each one once, so I probably can't help you much there, either. "First, call your brother's roommate and ask him if his boss needs help putting music into an Intellivision game called *Thin Ice*."

On the other hand, I've been in the business since '83, and I'm still in the business. So, advice-wise, I'm probably as good as they get, in theory. Here, for what it's worth, is my advice on getting a job.

I advise you to be weird. There's a good, solid, historical basis for this advice, and it is outlined eloquently in the appendix of this book, in the speech that Bruce Sterling gave to the GDC attendees in March, 1991.

Being weird comes naturally to me, as it does to many of the people in gaming, even the ones in the black clothes and the shades. Black clothes and shades are often an armor coat that we wear to conceal and contain the odd impulses that we were born with. Deep inside, we like to do things that not everybody "gets."

Some things make me laugh harder the more I think about them. It was that way when I was thinking about getting an old beat up Rolls-Royce instead of a normal, good car. I realized that I could take the Cub Scouts to their campouts in a Rolls, and then, when they were old, they'd be able to say, "I remember going to camp in a Rolls-Royce," and their grand-children will be able to say, "You're making that up, Grandpa." I sometimes dressed like Abe Lincoln in high school, and I get confused when people ask me why I did it. Why wouldn't I? I was able to grow a beard, and I had found an old black tux in a paper bag—what's to not do? My brother built a two-story studio recently, and I can't understand why he didn't put in a fire pole. He can't understand why I'd *want* to. So that's just me. Maybe it's you, too.[1]

How I Broke Into the Recording Business

In 1979 I took out an ad in LA's *Music Connection* magazine announcing that I would record anybody on my four-track recorder for $8.50 per hour. I got a lot of jobs in Watts. It was fun.

In 1980 I told audio engineer and futurist Van Webster that I would be happy to intern at his 24-track studio for free if he would allow me to ask questions. He insisted on paying me $5 per hour. It has been a lifelong friendship so far. We won't know for sure 'til one of us croaks.

Van Webster at BBQ 2002.

The "I'll work for free" thing coupled with the "I want to learn" thing is very powerful, and I recommend it. It gives your potential employer clarity about your intentions, expectations, and priorities. It only works when you realize and admit out loud that the person you're wanting to work for is better than you are at the given career.

---

[1] At the first DICE conference in 2002, Joe Kaminkow, VP of Game Design at IGT, described in his lecture some pitfalls that are likely to be encountered if one uses a focus group to make decisions. He cited the story of a focus group commissioned to determine the potential success of the first Dodge RAM trucks, which had a radically different look from any truck before. Reportedly, something like 50% of the people in the test group said they wouldn't be caught dead in something that looked like that, but 15% of the people tested were ready to buy a RAM on the spot. The marketing people were ready to trash the truck based on the embarrassingly high amount of negative reaction. Fortunately, somebody pointed out that the fact that 15% were ready to buy the truck meant that this would likely be the best selling car in history.

Inexperience should bow to

experience.

REEL MOBILE

A Small Recording Studio
Anywhere—Anytime

Dear Customer:

Reel Mobile is a 4-track mobile recording operation serving the
greater Los Angeles area. We offer a musician the luxury of a
complete studio in his home, rehearsal hall, or show at an incredibly low price. As a professional operation, we feature many
services that amateur and semi-professional recordists do not, including a 35-foot, six-channel snake, and a full monitoring system.

Equipment:
    TEAC A-3440 4-channel tape deck
    TEAC Model 2-A 6-in, 4-out mixer
    TEAC A 550 RX Cassette deck w/DBX
    NAKAMICHI and SHURE 57 and 58 mikes
    CROWN monitor preamp and power amp
    ROLAND SRE 555 chorus/echo/reverb
    B & S AUDIO Monitor speakers.

The entire system is mounted in two portable rack-mount Anvil cases
for quick set-up and convenient patching. The system or any part
of it runs for only $8.50 per hour, including engineer: The client
must pay for tape and travel charges (only 30¢ per mile from Eagle
Rock, Los Angeles). Due to the inevitable wear on equipment, it
is necessary to ask that the total charge (excluding tape and travel)
come to no less than $20. Still an unbeatable price.

Please consider the creative possibilities of this offer. Call me at
 [phone number] if you have any questions.

                                    Sincerely,

                                    George A. Sanger
                                    Mgr. Reel Mobile

The First Game Job

I just discovered this document yesterday. It is a draft of a letter sent in 1983 to Sybil at Mattel Electronics. Of course, people didn't have computers in their homes in 1983, so I handwrote this draft in order to not have any mistakes on the typewritten final version.

Evidently, I had not done the ten-second song for $1,200 as I had remembered. It turns out that I did the music as a "free demo" to leverage myself into regular employment.

I did not get the job. Instead, they felt it would be better to pay me off, make the whole thing legal, and forget about me. They asked how much I needed, and I said $1,200. They didn't *want* to pay that much for a ten-second tune, but they did. They went out of business a couple of months later, and I became The Greatest Professional Game Musician of All Time—not counting you, Dear Reader.

Dear Sybil,

Not too long ago, I found out ~~that~~ Dave Warhol, a friend of my family, worked for Mattel Electronics. ~~One when he was writing~~ When I asked how they arrive at music for ~~Intellivision~~ games, he ~~told me that~~ explained the process: the engineers themselves write and program tunes, and if a song doesn't work for, say, a baseball game, they save ~~the song~~ it, until someone comes by and says "I'm working on the Penguin game - do you have a tune that might fit?"

"Penguin game!" I shouted. "I could write you a great penguin song." I wrote ~~the~~ Carnival of the Penguins, and sent it to him, with the understanding that I was not guaranteed to be any payment, recognition, or employment, but, at best, a chance to be played on intellivisions everywhere.

Dave gave the song to the penguin ~~her~~ game designer, who played it for her supervisor, who played it loudly enough for the whole floor to hear. Apparently, the response was good, for Mark Urbaniec, Dave's supervisor, suggested that I write for an interview.

I hereby write for said interview. I have been led to believe that Mark ~~or~~ is involved in a search for a sound effects/music person, capable of learning computer programming and understanding – if not helping to design - Intellivision games. I am immenently qualified for this position. Yea, my entire life has been leading up to it. ~~Plea~~ Scan the enclosed resume (prepared before I spoke with Dave Warhol) and ~~see~~ if you don't agree.

~~To the resume I might only add that my senior~~ ~~thesis was on a Music Synthesis, and that I helped~~ ~~assemble Con Brio Productions, possibly the best-equipped~~ ~~synthesizer-based sound effects and music produ~~

~~Call me at ▊▊▊▊▊▊ to set up an~~

To the resume I might only add that my ~~knowledge of Mathematics include~~ senior thesis was on Music Synthesis, that I helped assemble Con Brio Productions, a synthesizer-based sound effects and music production facility, ~~and that~~ my knowledge of Mathematics includes ~~integral calculus~~, a ~~thorough~~ understanding of integral calculus, ~~and~~ my knowledge of ~~physics~~ extends through thermodynamics, and my high score ~~Call me at~~ on Moon Cresta is enviable.

Call me at: ▊▊▊▊▊▊ for the aforementioned interview, or write me as soon as possible at

▊▊▊▊▊▊▊

▊▊▊▊▊▊▊

Looking forward to meeting you,

Sincerely, etc.,

The First Job I Got In the Computer Business

My brother Rick was making one of the first color paint programs ever. It was to run on the Epson QX-10 as a part of the first-ever integrated software package, Valdocs, by Rising Star. Rick liked my interface ideas and wanted me to get paid by that company as an interface designer. So he took me to meet his boss, Bill Volk.

I had just finished building an off-road radio control car, so I charged it up and brought it over to Bill's house. When the door opened, I handed him the controller, and he said, "What? Oh. This is neat."

Fifteen minutes of laughing and chasing the cat around the room later, the battery gave out and Bill spoke again. "We gotta get you a job at Rising Star."

Other Successful Promotions of The Mighty Fat Man

I had a successful promotion in 1991; let's talk about that. I'm pretty sure that mine was the first promo pack ever sent out for game audio. It had some nice things going for it that might help you if you're thinking about sending out some promo packs.

First of all, it was sent in a fast food container that was about the shape of a french-fries tray. The great thing was that, with its non-parallel edges, it wouldn't fit in a bookshelf or file drawer very well without getting crushed or falling over, so it sat on peoples' desks. In some cases for years, really. I've had people recite bits of the tape back to me.

The top of the fast food box was weirdly cool, too. To help me with the project, I had hired (for far less than he's worth) Bill Narum, a great rock poster artist famous from the era of the Armadillo World Headquarters. Bill had, in fact, designed the Nudie suits that ZZ Top wore, and he'd designed the inside of ZZ's *Fandango* album. (He calls them "ZZ." Isn't that cute?) For my promotion, he stuck a bunch of rubber fishing-lure worms and batteries and circuit boards and things on a color Xerox machine, along with my business card, then glued the results to the top of the fast food box.

Inside was a nice little professionally duplicated cassette, stuck to the bottom with Velcro. One side had samples of my PC work, the other had my Nintendo compositions, and I narrated the whole thing, pointing out my merits and disclosing specific clever things I'd done. So it goes. There were also four little cards listing my work history, awards, bio—that kind of thing—and if the recipient was lucky, there was also a small handful of rubber worms and confetti that didn't get in his coffee.

After we worked together, Bill got into games in a big way. He signed on as an artist at Origin, and got a bunch of the other legendary hippie artists work there, too, which was good for the industry. He started his own multimedia company, Go-Go Studios, which employed a lot of people for a lot of years.

The mailer was a smash hit. It resulted in my getting a lot of jobs. Also because of the mailer, the very first article ever was written about me in a trade paper. The headline was "Fat Man Serves Worms."

Here's another good thing I can tell you about the relentless march to the top of my profession. I got a fabulous reputation at the first Game Developers Conference that I attended (then the Computer Game Developers Conference), and that was the first time I wore cowboy clothes in public. There, at the first GDC awards ever, two of the four nominees for Best Sound Presentation were my projects, *Loom* and *Wing Commander*. That was a great conference. I was the pretty girl at the prom. Everybody wanted to talk to me, and I literally had no competitors. Therefore, I must admit that I really don't know if the cowboy outfit was important or even helpful. I don't know if it would have even been tolerated if my music hadn't been liked.

So, there it is: I sent a bug-covered box to a mailing list, and I wore cowboy clothes to a conference. Genius. Beyond those two things—even including those two things—it's hard to put my finger on anything I've done promotionally that can really be proven successful in the conventional sense.

However, a lot of what I've done has been fun. And somewhat warm. And fearless, I daresay. In the end, I suspect that I have secured much work, and more importantly, a lot of friends, over the years because of the way in which my promotions reflected the values that are important to me.

One such friend, Terry Boyle, from Compton's New Media—the people who had the nerve to patent "Multimedia"—asked me to promote their company in a booth at a trade show. I was asked to compose music while people watched, or something. That sounded boring, embarrassing, and difficult, so I asked if I could do something else:

"Could I just play guitar or something?"

"Sure."

"Could I do something nutty, like Mariachi music?"

"Sure."

"Oh, Man. I just remembered. Kevin plays bass, Joe plays guitar, and Dave used to play drums. If they agree to learn a set of surf music, can you fly Team Fat out and rent them some amps and a drum kit?"

"Sure."

The Fat Man
and TEAM FAT SURF!*
The Biggest Name in Computer Game Music

Team Fat has made musical contributions to over 70 software products, including The Seventh Guest, Wing Commander, Wing Commander II, Loom, Castles, Ultima Underworld, Star Trek: 25th Anniversary, and now, for Compton's New Media...
The Berenstain Bears Learning at Home
*The team has also learned a set of Surf Tunes for this CES show, don't ask why.

Photo by Teresa "Spanki" Avallone

I liked Terry. He was agreeable, a wonderful producer, and a great believer in Team Fat.

We did a lot of trade-show gigs as a cowboy-clad surf instrumental band. Very few people "got" that. They seemed to think of Team Fat as a band, rather than a team of composers. Some got the impression that we only did surf music rather than, say, everything in the world. But we had fun, we sounded cool as hell, and we were bringing something to those trade shows that nobody else had even come close to.

We even crashed a trade show with our band, which was kind of tricky to do. We drove our gear out to the CES show in Vegas, and Kevin drew on his years on the road with bands like The Call and Asleep at the Wheel to convince the guards that we were legitimate. We set up to play at the Papyrus booth (we'd done music for NASCAR racing) and at the Atari booth, where our friend James Grunke let us improvise music to his demo of a skiing game.

In fact, crashing the trade show with the surf band got us a job. Jim Eisenstien, producer of *Twisted* for 3DO, saw the act and hired us to do music for the game's sequel, *Zhadnost: The Peoples' Party*. We were even supposed to show up in the game as a western-style surf-music pit band for a gameshow that had taken over a communist country. 3DO ran out of budget, so video of the band was never shot, and as good as the game was, it was a flop sales-wise. But we kept the rights to the music and made our SURF.COM CD from that soundtrack. So you see how promotion pays off?

Team Fat's Joe McDermott put a lot of effort into creating a coloring book about Team Fat. I don't think that giving out a coloring book to game developers and friends ever directly got us a job, but many people, including ourselves, began to think of Team Fat as having a very special relationship to high-tech entertainment. The Information Superhighway to us was "The Dusty Ol' Info Trail." Our characters were interested in old cars and horses. They wanted to help people. They were idealistic. They found

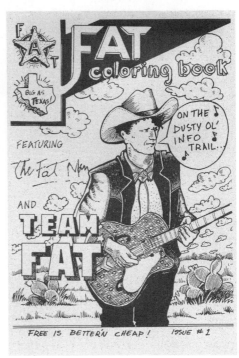

snakes in the computers and put 'em back where they belonged.

Tommy Tallarico was so impressed that at the next trade show he passed out crayons.

Teresa Avallone, a.k.a. Spanki, whose pet snake it turned out to be in the cartoon, was Team Fat's publicist and my very good friend for years. She came up with a lot of fun, good pieces that established a positive vibe around Team Fat.

Teresa did things like make up a limited number of gold "Fat Labs" cards, which went only to very special people who had done something big to help the industry or Team Fat, and made "Fat Ranger" membership cards for fans. She put out several issues of our newsletter, *FATBEAT*, which emphasized the team's friendship and adventures.

Spanki and me, fixing Dr. Cat, creator of Furcadia. *Character designed by Danielle Barry. Which one, you ask?*

She traveled with me to conferences, tirelessly posting banners (back when one was allowed to post banners at conferences) and stocking pressrooms with goodies like key chains and luggage tags that she'd often meticulously handcrafted herself.

Sometimes, life hands you a limo. So you have to make laminate.

As good as she was at all the detailed work over the years, what I think Spanki did best for me and for our team was that, even at trade shows and even in the middle of business dealings, she opened up her heart and was kind to people. She made friends. She danced with our clients. She snuck drinks into stuffy meetings. She brought business enemies together. She giggled.

That's what you need to do to make it in this business;

you need to *giggle*.

Spanki giggles at Project BBQ. Who armed the smartest people in game audio with rubber band guns? Spanki did.

The best promotion we did never brought in a dime, but I wouldn't trade the experience for all the Ferraris in the world. A pretty good friend (that's a good friend of mine who is pretty) told me that she had finally figured out of whom I reminded her; Willy Wonka. That's pretty cool.

I remind Marianna Marino of Willy Wonka. Beat that.

So for the 2000 Game Developer Conference, Linda came up with this idea: Like Willie Wonka, I would pass out chocolate bars, five of which would contain golden tickets. The winners of the golden tickets would receive a ride in the Rolls, a Grand Tour of my studio and zeppelin, they'd be introduced to my friends, and I'd compose a free piece of music for them.

Poster used to promote the Golden Ticket giveaway.
Drawn by game artist 'Manda Dee. The color print of the poster
was confiscated by GDC "flier police," because in 2000,
for the first time ever, distribution of fliers and posters at the
GDC was not allowed except by event sponsors.

That year we weren't financially in a position to pay for flights. Essentially, we were promising magic, and asking the winners of the Golden Tickets to bet the price of a plane ticket that we would actually deliver. Oddly enough, the winners took us up on that bet. Even more oddly, the magic happened.

Golden Ticket day was one of the slowest days in airport history. Everybody who made the trip arrived extremely late—some arrived sleepless that morning—and we had to pack everything into one day.

Everybody was assigned a tent in our yard into which they threw their luggage, and we got going. Noelle was interested in horses—we took all the winners horseback riding.

Patricia and John were very into biking. We rented them some nice bikes and got them down to the Veloway, one of the world's nicest paved bicycle loops. We all took a nice canoe trip on Town Lake. Jay and Brian were happy to talk about illusions of fame and old cars. We drove around in the Rolls. We took everybody to Sheppler's and bought them cowboy hats. We toured the studio. We jammed. We became friends.

Now, just as we were realizing that we'd become friends, and things had just gotten all warm and fuzzy, the Oompa-Loompas arrived. See, my friends The Enigma

and Katzen had agreed to act as Oompa-Loompas. Katzen is the world's only woman with a full-body tattoo: cat stripes. She has plastic whiskers that stick through her upper lip. Her husband, The Enigma, is covered head-to-toe with blue puzzle pieces, and he has surgically implanted horns in his head. They burst in, with the shirtless Enigma blaring polka music on his accordion and grinning like Satan on a rollercoaster, while the lovely Katzen wordlessly handed out Chinese finger traps, kazoos, and little demonic toy figures.

That's what you have to do to get a job. See, Brian and Jay became big fans, and they volunteered to help me with my career. In our discussions of what it is to be famous, we agreed that it doesn't count when you have to chase after reporters yelling that you are famous (see next chapter.) It doesn't count just to have a web page, and then advertise yourself "as seen on the World Wide Web." What counts as true fame is when you are so famous that somebody out there hates you. So Jay and Brian set up "I Hate The Fat Man.COM" (http://www.ihatethefatman.com/) so that I could be truly famous. You can still go there. They posted their pictures of the trip, and a wonderful documentary film of how agonizing their airplane journey to Austin was. You can see the tents.

One no-show was my friend Steve Cooke, who had years before gotten me my first trip to England by securing me a speaking slot at the *Develop!* conference. He chose not to fly in from England, and he's been too polite to ask me for that free piece of music. But someday....

Steve Woodcock, whom I mentioned in an earlier chapter as the guy Dr. Marvin Minsky had quoted to open his GDC lecture, was also a winner but not able to make it. He was hosting a War Game on those dates. Not a war game, but a War Game. For the military. With real tanks. So Steve asked us to find a deserving recipient for the ticket.

Right around then I had heard that Rob Wallace, one of the first game musicians I ever met, was very sick and needed a kidney. I sent out a mass emailing, and game composer David "Tex" Houston, a guy I'd never heard of before, came out of the blue and volunteered his kidney. To a total stranger. Not bad. He had the wrong blood type, it turned out, but risking your health for a stranger is Golden Ticket material, don't you think? He couldn't make it either, so I asked if there was anything I could do for him. He asked me to sign up for the Bay Area Action newsletter, and I did, and I encourage you to do the same. If they ask you why, just say it's because of Rob Wallace's kidney. They won't get it. Rob's okay now, by the way.

The Fat Man

From: Tex
Sent: Sunday, April 25, 2003 1:51 AM
To: Rob
Subject: Potential Kidney Donation

Rob,

Having almost drowned in a surfing incident at Rock Away Beach back in 1992 (had a wave of peacefulness engulf my soul, then saw bright white lights, heard my deceased Grandmother's voice from the other side of life say "Relax, conserve your oxygen and roll with it"). Ever since taking that first breath after surfacing from a 15-foot wave that broke my surf board in two, I have lived every day as if death is only an arm's length away, because it is!

That experience has made me realize that each moment we are alive is more precious than all the diamonds in the world or the fattest FM sounds around!

Look forward to chatting with you today about potential kidney donation.

I will be going out to Arastradero Preserve early this a.m. to monitor cavity nesting boxes as part of the Blue Bird recovery program for the Audubon Society. Then I have a massage from 10:30 am to noon. So just leave a message with phone number and time I can reach you and we'll chat.

Tex

The final Golden Ticket winner was my friend Keith Robinson, who, with my brother's roommate as programmer, had produced *Thin Ice*, the first game I worked on. Keith is the current owner of Intellivision. On Golden Ticket day, Keith waited for hours for his plane to take off. Unfortunately, just when the plane finally got ready to leave, the jetway bumped lightly into the plane, and the flight was cancelled.

In 2002, Keith landed a huge blessing on me. He flew a reunited Team Fat out to the Classic Gaming Expo in Las Vegas to perform our surf music set for the first time in years.

You see, even though Keith couldn't make the trip, he still got a free tune. For that free tune, Keith had asked me to re-work the *Thin Ice* theme in surf instrumental style. He'd put it on *Intellivision's* promotional audio CD, *Intellivision Rocks*, which was the center of their Classic Gaming Expo strategy. And Keith wanted the band to play the song live at the expo. We were so happy to do it, and we had such a great time.... I'm very thankful that we gave out all that chocolate.

So, that's how you get jobs.

Just do everything I did, and

you can't go wrong.

How
Not
to
Get
Work

Tommy T. has very good advice on this topic. He says that you should never say, "I'm new to gaming. I don't really play many games." Gamers will secretly hate you. To that, I would add that you should not say, "I had a great career in [programming, TV, movies, what-have-you], and then fell in love with games, so I thought to myself, 'Why not make money doing what you love?'" Any experienced game producer has heard that story enough times to know that it's code for "I played a game and then it occurred to me, 'how hard could this be? I can get rich the easy way.'"

I get a lot of demo CDs that go on forever. I would advise the reader that his only job is to make life easier and products better for anybody who has the good sense to hire him. His pitches should reflect that. A long CD lets the client know that you have no stinking idea at all how busy and important he thinks he is.

The only thing worse than a long CD is a CD that has nothing to offer. I get a lot of CDs that have nothing to offer. These strike me as pitiful failures. I would advise the reader not to send out any music or any other artistic work that could ever possibly have been done by somebody else.

Doing as I advise will allow you to fail spectacularly instead of pitifully. Let's step into the time machine and go back to around 1991 to take a look at some examples that I have thoughtfully enacted for your benefit.

Having just arranged seven movements of *Swan Lake* for the game *Loom* made me feel as though I was a bit of an expert at the premiere target sound card, the Roland MT-32. Soon thereafter I was told that there was a company in Austin doing a computer game that was to play back on that sound card. So I started writing letters to Richard "Lord British" Garriott, the creative leader of Origin Systems, that read something like this:

"Dear Lord British,

"Call me. I am the composer you need. I am in Austin. I am an expert at the MT-32 sound card.

"The Fat Man"

The game, of course, was *Wingleader*, which was later renamed *Wing Commander*. It was to turn out to be the first game in one of the most successful franchises ever. The first two installments were tremendously significant to audio in games and certainly to my career.

So, when I got the job, I thought that my letter-writing campaign had worked, but I was wrong. Years later I found out that the letters were only frustrating His Lordship. He'd open one, say, "Who *is* this 'Fat Man' guy?" and then pin it on the bulletin board where he displayed his particularly weird and misguided fan mail, which I would reckon to be pretty darned weird and misguided as fan mail goes. It was the Lord British equivalent of being pinned to a dartboard.

No, the reason I got the *Wing Commander* gigs was not my self-assured manner, nor my persistent faith in my abilities, nor my never-say-die show business attitude. No. See, in utter frustration Richard called the best audio guy he knew, and that guy happened to be Dave Warhol, my brother's roommate, the guy in the last chapter who had given me my first job about 10 years earlier. Dave told Richard that he had retired from the music composing business, but now for all his music he used a guy in Austin who goes by the name The Fat Man, and why didn't Richard call The Fat Man? I wish I'd have been there for that.

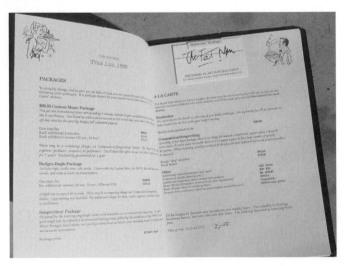

The "Fast Food" mailer was such a success that around *Wing Commander* time I had followed it up with a price list that was made to look like a menu from a fancy restaurant, plastic cover and all. Mailing that out got no results at all. In fact, the price list even caused some confusion in my contract for *Wing Commander* because it mentioned three rates, one rate for non-exclusive use of the music, one for exclusive use for a period of time, and one for a total buy-out, or "work-for-hire." Terms like "rights" and "license" and "exclusive" and such were pretty much unknown in the game business, and Origin gladly hired me at the lowest price. Later, when they figured out what non-exclusive meant, we had a very uncomfortable re-negotiation of the rate. I'm pretty sure that renegotiation damaged the relationship between me and the Origin suits. On the upside, I ended up raising my rate for *Wing Commander* so that I would be getting about 200 glorious dollars per finished minute of music.

For years I mistakenly thought that Team Fat had written enough sound for enough games that people would be aware of what our capabilities were. Not so... that only works when you've written for a mega-hit, and it doesn't work when you've written for lots of small hits. With firmly misplaced confidence, I made *not* sending audio demos the feature of this highly unsuccessful promotion, and shot myself in the other foot by comparing myself to a pretty girl whom the game designer was afraid to ask to dance.

At one GDC, I offered to give my cowboy hat to the first company to hire me for a job that paid $5,000 or over. I think I went about a year without getting such a job, so I decided the offer was void, the promotion was bad, and I'd be better off keeping my hat.

Here's one not to do. I sent this fax to a movie company who was doing the *Texas Chainsaw Massacre III* in Austin. I think the fax speaks for itself. Perhaps it will turn out to be successful in the end. I haven't gotten the call back yet.

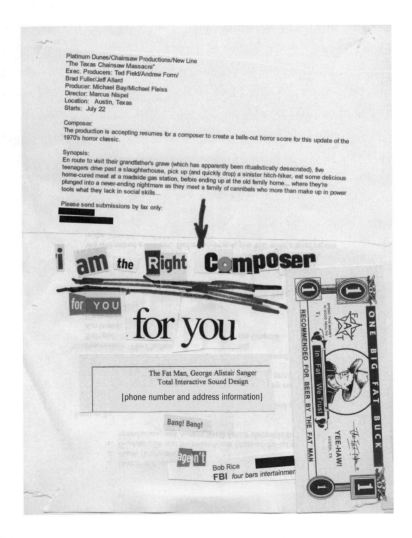

I think the King Daddy of all bad promotional ideas was the Operation Demo. At the depths of my hardest luck, at the time just after I had been forced to let Team Fat go (I promoted them to family, actually), I heard from a company who wanted to make a computer game of the skill game *Operation* for Hasbro. The company hadn't been hired yet, so even if they liked me, the job was uncertain. Their musical plan featured an endless list of stylistic preferences and called for a myriad of styles. Not funky or electronic. There was a jungle scene. Had to play in Iowa. Friendly. Doctor-like. Jetsons feel. There was a haunted house level. And the punch line? I was supposed to audition for the job by submitting custom-composed work.

Now, these guys knew who The Fat Man was, so I talked them into letting me do a special compilation of my previously composed music for them. I even created some voices for characters—The Fat Man and Professor Hochenschtupfer—to introduce the music. But the more I got into it, the more I realized that I was ridiculously qualified for this job. And then I started having a lot of fun. And I guess that I got a little venomous, you might say. So I put more work into that audition than any other and created one of my favorite pieces.

Brother Rick felt that it was a cry for help and advised that I try punching a pillow when I feel that kind of pain, so that it doesn't get on other people too much. Bless his heart. Brother Dave and Sister Wendy thought it was one of the funniest things I'd ever done.

This audio extravaganza begins by suggesting that the huge profits Hasbro makes from games is the "operation" they're talking about. It makes fun of "smart city folks and purty gals such as yourself with cordless phones hangin' off their belts." By the end, regardless of the myriad of demands made by the spec, you've heard enough tunes that are right on the money that it's pretty obvious the only thing to do is hire The Fat Man or be an idiot. Nonetheless, the perfectionist narrator is still not convinced, and he insists that, since we don't have any *one* song that fits *all* of the needs of the spec, well, "we just cain't do it." The demo ends with a suggestion that the client call The Fat Man's competitors, find out how much better they are, then call him back at this number to "laugh in The Fat Man's face."

I sent eight copies to the client, and never heard from them again. So maybe you shouldn't do *that* either.

I was once at the E3 show, and I complimented a guy for the great John Williams-sounding score on his game. Not realizing who I was, he confided in me that it actually *was* John Williams' music. And in answer to my next question, it wasn't expensive at all. In fact, John had let them have it for free.

When he found out who I was, he gasped, apologized, and suggested I send him an email. "Who knows? Maybe I could use you," he said.

The pitch part of my email to him went like this: "...Normally, this is the part of the letter in which I would offer my services. However, given that you're working with John Williams for Free, honesty demands that I put it like this: If you ever want somebody who's a little bit worse and a lot more expensive, give me a call."

The following letter is email from longtime game audio bad-ass LX Rudis to other game audio folks.

The Fat Man

From: LX Rudis
Sent: Tuesday, March 22, 1999 08:34 PM
To: Anonymous
Subject: Re: my most lasting memory…

At 08:34 PM 3/22/99 -0600, [LX Rudis] wrote:
>…my most lasting memory…of this year's CGDC would have to be this:
>two web designers < www.theshaft.net > fleeing in terror as george 'fat man' sanger applied marketing techniques learned from tommy tallarico's keynote address. i've never seen potential clients actually run away from a content provider.

fats, two words: chamomile tea.

:D

"You'll Just **Love** Sticking It In"

GamePlayMusic™

If you can hear your music before you pay for it,
you won't have to trust this man.

The risk we took with GamePlayMusic was to appeal to the brave game developer. We discovered that there aren't that many. I don't think there's a developer in the world who had the nuts to react favorably to the "You won't have to trust this man" slogan, let alone the "You'll just love sticking it in." I have no regrets... it was a great promotion. It just didn't bring any business, because it weeded out the chickens.

With the "big balls" promotion, we went even further towards looking for a developer with courage.

GamePlayMusic™

You'll just love stickin' it in.

Before

After

- **Had to** create a music spec.

- **Had no** time to create a music spec.

- **Had to** manage music creation.

- **Had to** install multiple versions of the music as it evolved.

- **Worried** about the music getting done on time.

- **Couldn't** afford as much music as was wanted.

- **Just** listened to the finished music and picked what sounded the best.

The "Big Balls" Promotion (for a limited time):
⇒ *Up to 30 minutes of GamePlayMusic™*
⇒ *FREE Miles or HAE sound driver license*
⇒ *FREE custom theme up to 2 minutes long.*
Only $9995.

GamePlayMusic™ by all the best game musicians.
Hosted and honed by The Fat Man to perfectly fit the demands of the discerning game developer.
www.GamePlayMusic.com
[phone and fax number]

Even that wasn't enough for Team Fat. We had to go even further. This flier contained...

ONTAINS
NUDITY

This:

GamePlayMusic™

You'll just love stickin' it in.

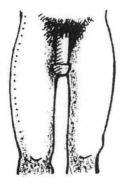 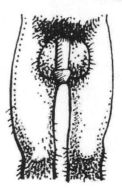

Before

- **Had to** create a music spec.

- **Had no** time to create a music spec.

- **Had to** manage music creation.

- **Had to** install multiple versions of the music as it evolved.

- **Worried** about the music getting done on time.

- **Couldn't** afford as much music as was wanted.

After

- **Just** listened to the finished music and picked what sounded the best.

This won't get you a job, or a phone call, or anything.

Don't even try it.

How to Answer the Phone

When a **developer** finally calls or emails you and says he's ready to put **audio** into his game, what do you do?

1. Say a silent prayer of thanks.

If this is the hundredth such call you've gotten and none has ever panned out, you might be tempted to yell at the guy, telling him how tired you are of the whole abusive business of this supposed "game audio" racket, and extolling gleefully on the fact that there's more security, dignity, and honor in being a serial killer's assistant. Don't. Nothing is forever. You're in a slump, and it will pass. Maybe not in this lifetime, but it *will* pass. Be thankful that the phone rang—maybe this call will be the one that will break your unlucky streak.

On the other hand, if this is the hundredth such call you've gotten this *week*, and *all* the calls have panned out, and you're as busy as a bug tracker at Microsoft, you might be tempted to not even speak to the guy, because the pressure is on. Do talk to him. And be thankful he called, be grateful for his attention, because being busy is a phase as well, and this, too, shall pass. I *promise.*

2. Do not talk about yourself or what you're capable of doing.

This is not resume time. Until he asks, there is no reason to think that this person is interested in your personal specs, what you can do, what you have done, what you're doing right now, or anything. Don't worry what he thinks of you. He's not even thinking about you. Odds are, he's thinking of *him.* He's interested in doing good work on his project, and he's interested in keeping his job. Maybe his dad is sick. Maybe he wants to get off the phone so he can go on the Internet and find a nice chat room full of old guys pretending to be teenage girls. Your job is to find out how you can help him, and it can't be done if you're talking.

3. Ask about the caller, the company, and the project, and *listen to what's being said.*

The developer will likely go on a long tear about something that's important to him. Stay with him. Resist any temptation to just say "uh-huh" while you answer your email. This is where the tone of the project is set. You're learning not just the details of the game, but also the spirit of the company with whom you'll be dealing.

Here are some things you might hear, and ways you might interpret them.

➥ "Um, I was wondering how much **you** usually charge to score a game?"

"Um" means he's young. "I was wondering" means he doesn't make business calls often. "Usually" means he's assuming that he's less experienced than you—he's wondering how this kind of thing is done.

This is almost certainly a first-time developer or a musician thinking about going into the games business, and there's probably little or no money involved. My recommendation, though, would be to remain kind and patient. Find out if he's a musician or a developer.

If he's a musician, he'll think you're amazing for having figured it out, and that's one less person in the business you'll have to impress. Maybe he's a drummer. It never hurts to know drummers... they know where the parties are. Have a chat, find out what he's up to. I think Captain Kirk got lonely sometimes, and especially treasured the rare chats he could have with a fellow starship captain. If he's a first-time developer, that's worth exploring, too. The game might be damned exciting.

New developers are likely to be willing to try new audio ideas. If you're new to the business, you can get experience by working with these people. Your first gigs will almost certainly be with this kind of client. If you're an old hand and you don't think you can learn from him or work with him, you're still in a position to help him out and to be kind, which is a wonderful opportunity for both of you.

This is a new developer or a guy who had a friend score his first game and now is hiring outside help for the first time. He's confident, but uses no jargon.

During negotiation, he'll likely say something like, "We usually pay per minute." "We usually" is a very good indicator of a one- or two-game veteran. Anybody with half a brain realizes after three games that "usually" is not a word that associates well with the business practices of game audio.

➠"How much do you charge to score a game?"

Usually.

Another indicator of the one- or two-game client is that he hasn't lost his love of gaming. Look for conversational elements such as this:

> **"You're the leader of the Quinines, kind of a new-age enlightened species, really sensitive. Your world is destroyed but you excape [sic] in a huge ship, like, the size of most planets. You land on Oxy 10, where you use these Barflys to gather resources. The Barflys are really cool, they have these huge heads and they walk kind of funny. I'll send you the artwork. Anyway, they're kind of your peons, and you use them to build up your strength until you encounter the hostile Babars. Their civilization is almost exactly like 1930's Earth, but dark."**

➠"We've got an MMORPG, looking at six two-minute loopers, menu music, a few victories, and few defeats. What's your per-minute charge? Or do you charge by the hour, or by the project?"

The jargon indicates that you're speaking with an experienced developer—a professional. "We've got" rather than "we're working on" indicates that he's involved in several projects, which means he's part of a bigger company with several games under its belt or maybe even currently in development. At the very least he's not working alone, so he's not *necessarily* a Unabomber-type. (Oh, my God, my spell-checker knows the word "Unabomber.") At best, your doing well on this job could lead to other work. The fact that he's ordering what seems to be "the usual" rather than going into great detail means that he cuts to the chase. Deadlines and cost-effectiveness are going to be high on his list of priorities. He also might be jaded as far as the development process goes. It's likely that the music development process has lost some of its virgin charm as well. This does not by any means indicate that he's uninterested in quality. Often, this kind of pro gets real excited about maximizing the time, quality, and quantity that he can get with his dollar.

Remember "Fast, good, cheap: pick two?" Give him all three and some extras. You *want* this gig.

▶▶ "We've gotten bids from **several** other composers and **sound** designers."

Ah. It's a bidding situation. Super. Cue the next chapter, please.

The Dreaded Bidding Process

Bidding is for the birds. When you go to get a job that requires that you submit a bid, there are some horribly evil things of which you can be instantly certain:

- The client may love your work, but not enough to have come to you first. Any sounds you have made over the course of your career, any friends you have made, any reputation you may have built up over the years, and even those slick Flash movies on your website, have not adequately impressed this company to where they can give you first shot.

- Nobody at the company had the nuts to say "This guy is perfect for this game."

- The company has established a "baseline artistic/technical threshold" and asked for bids from a group of people they consider might possibly meet or exceed that threshold. Now their goal is to find the one who will produce the lowest money-to-ability ratio. This loses them a certain amount of credibility if they say "We're interested in making the best game possible," because they likely aren't. The way to make the best game possible is to pick the best person for the job and negotiate mutually agreeable compensation.

Bidding is the process that allows one to make an **above-a-certain-threshold** game at the lowest price possible. **Better decide** if you want to **participate** in that kind of work.

- There is competition. Somebody is going to lose, probably several people, and you'll either be one of the losers or you'll meet one someday and have to deal with the awkward situation of having taken food from his children's mouths.

- Regardless of how your conversation with the client goes, the person with whom you are speaking is not in a position to make a decision to hire you even if he thinks you're Friggin' Mancini (Hank's brother).

- There's work ahead. Bidding requires that you submit a bio, brochure, and music samples *in addition to* specifying your compensation. Often, the company will request that you do custom bits of audio work on spec. If you have a lot of examples on your website or have had your work appear on 200 games, you still have to create spec work, to keep the bidding process consistent and fair to all the bidding parties. Fair is fair.

I can't help you much with bids. After about 20 years in the business, I just this year won my very first bid. The job was to do sound effects for a PlayStation 2/Gamecube licensed-property game being produced in Austin.

I was warned that the main hitch was that some guys on the committee were dubious as to whether I knew the platforms well enough to perform up to par. I got pretty frustrated about that, because I've learned so many systems, and even helped design them, that I didn't think there could be much doubt as to my ability to keep up.

I think these might be the reasons I won the bid:

- I was local.

- The guy who called me knew my reputation and thought highly of me, and he stood up for me in the decision committee.

- I had a deep knowledge of the licensed property, especially its sound effects.

- I was on the CEO's party invite mailing list.

- I had jammed with the project manager—he's a great guitar player.

- Another exec on the committee had been disappointed in years past that I had lost a bid with his company, and he'd sworn to try to work with me in the future.

- I'm a licensed developer with Sony and Nintendo.

- I called in favors from several friends (including Tommy T., who was really helpful) in order to be certain that I was equipped with all the appropriate tools to properly do audio on the target platforms.

- I did even more spec sound effects than the bid requested.

- I submitted, unrequested, some looping sound effects in the appropriate format for PlayStation 2.

- I did some spec music on top of that for good measure, even though they already had a musician.

- I called every couple of days to see how things were going.

- I charged about $1/3$ of what I need to make to pay my bills.

- I'm The Stinking Fat Man for cripes sakes. I'm good at this stuff. Read the history books!

I have to admit, I was still surprised to have gotten the job. I wasn't so surprised when the company went out of business just after the game was completed. That has nothing to do with bidding, I guess, but let's blame it on the fact that they asked me for a bid. I hate bidding.

The punch line is that after all the fuss the committee had made about my abilities to handle the platform, it turned out that the way their company's sound drivers worked, *no* specific knowledge at all was required to provide sounds for this game. I just FTP'd them .WAV files, and that was it. It was as technically complex as scoring a TV show or film—a piece of cake. In fact, if I had used my newfound skills and provided them with sounds containing embedded normal PlayStation 2 loops, those loops would have crashed their system.

So that's my brain dump on bids and the one that I won. I hope it helps. If you come up with the secret to doing well with the bidding process, *please* let me know, even if it means that you have to write your own book and sell it to me. I'll buy it—swear to God. Fair is fair.

The opposite of asking for bids is "dancing with those that brung you." If you ever, *ever* find a company that is loyal to the workers who started it, that is willing to give a person a little slack now and then in exchange for the difficult crunch times, do whatever you can to get work there. Work for free.

Pay *them.*

There are few things in the industry—or in life in general—that are as rare and precious as the attitude expressed by the phrase "dance with those that brung you." It's kind. It shows respect and compassion. It leads to success for everybody involved. It implies that there are other values present that will make working an enjoyable part of living. It ain't no joke.

The following three slides came from a presentation that my slot machines boss Jeff Lind gave at Multimedia Games here in Austin. In all my years in gaming, I have run into many individuals and several small companies who were smart about things like this, but I've only run into *one* other medium-to-large sized company (Ensemble Studios, also in Texas) that understands as well as Multimedia Games does the importance of treating people with kindness. Take a look at *this* stuff!

Management Beliefs

- Dance with those that brung you.
- Reward people for exceptional effort.
- Let people make mistakes.
- Empower people to make decisions.
- Family first!
- Work must be fun.
- Learning on the job is okay.

GAME DEVELOPMENT · 2003

This is a nice contrast to the usual slide, which reads:

- Management needs new cars.
- If you can find somebody better, hire him.
- There's five artists right outside that door who would take your job in a heartbeat, Deadmeat.

I mean, these beliefs expressed by Jeff would allow somebody with KIDS to work at the company!!! Even *sick* kids!!!

Hey, I don't see "Having five successful games on the market," and "Fluency in C++ and Pro Tools." And where's "Totally knowing what sucks in a game," "Used to work in Hollywood," and "Is a hot babe?"

Jeff says that he hates technical mumbo jumbo because when somebody talks that way, he nods his head as though he knows what they're talking about, but secretly he has no idea, and it makes him uncomfortable.

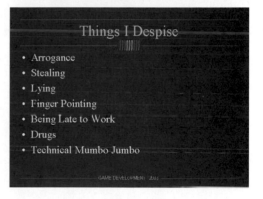

I'm proud to call Jeff my boss. If he ever gives up the gaming business to go into some other industry, say, construction or organized crime,

Planning for Greatness:

Eliminating Schedules and Specifications

Allow me to interrupt the beginning of this chapter by ruining it and giving away the ending. The chapter will build and build until you think, *"Whatever on earth is going to happen in the* second *segment of development?"* The tension will mount and mount until it is unbearable, but I now tell you that the answer is this: In the second segment of development, you will do things normally. You will, by God, stick to schedules, you will stick to the spec, you will stick to the budget, and by so exercising the fundamental disciplines of hard work and mental focus, you will create a great game to which you will be proud to lay your claim in future decades.

I think you can plan for Greatness.

It is sensible to think of game development, including its audio branch, as a process that would respond well to scheduling, specifications, and deadlines. It is reasonable to think that the ideal environment for development would be pervaded by a noble sense of discipline. That the evolving developer who created and held to schedules, met his deadlines, and remained forever under budget and on task would blossom under such conditions into a paragon of productivity, and would proudly walk with his head held high into an illustrious new era of gaming, ever increasing his mastery of dependably and precisely creating environments in which the Unwashed Throngs, the Huddled Masses, and other Wretched Posses would find Brave New Worlds of fun.

Yeah, well, **yes** and **no**.

At the first DICE conference in Las Vegas, Game Developer Mark Cerny quite convincingly threw all such sense out the window. The event gained strength from the fact that in a way, Mark came out of retirement to do the talk. He said that he had looked at the conventional use of schedules and such, and he had felt so strongly that their use had been counterproductive to creativity, that he was compelled to break a years-long oath he had taken to never again speak at a conference. At least, that's what I thought I heard. And what I *thought* I heard was wonderful. So, I think it would serve the community best if, rather than tracking down the troublesome facts of what he actually did say, this chapter incorporated some the ideas I *thought* I heard in Mark's lecture, filtered through my kidneys in such a way as to apply the ideas to audio more than game development in general, thus serving two purposes: First, the ideas will be so loosely reported that Mark will certainly not recognize them and, therefore, not be angry at me for misquoting him. Second, while it was indeed brilliant, I'm not *entirely* sure that Mark's lecture was *quite* as brilliant as my fabulous misinterpretation of it. So, by intentionally misquoting him in this way, You, Dear Reader will get the Great and Useful Advantage of being exposed to my inspiring illusions. Such are the wild leaps of imagination that fool us out of our boundaries.

In creating a game, what are we trying to do? Create brilliance. Capture lightning. Lure the Human Spirit to a deeper world. Show even the most intellectual critics that it's fun to blow people up and run them over— probably even *more* fun than said critics had already fantasized over and over again while staring blankly at the wall during long and tedious breakfasts with their wives. This represents no small contribution to the world. These dark feelings are important; they are a big part of why games work, and bringing them out of the deep, cobwebbed recesses of the intellectual mind is a huge portion of the game community's Gift to Society.

If you want to communicate the game's feelings in an ordinary way, based on a mere imitation of another game with different art, licensed characters, the musique du jour, and the usual kissing of investor butt, that's fine, chuck this book in the trash compactor and stick to normal scheduling procedures. If on the other hand you aspire to Greatness, it's not fine. To be great, a game has to be out of the ordinary. To be out of the ordinary, it has to be different. It has to rise above and leave behind everything that has been done before. It has to be built half by the hand of man, and half by the hand of God. Conventional project management leaves precious little room for the hand of **God.**

These are the "facts":

- **Greatness can't be predicted.** When it comes, it comes with concentration and hard work. And then, just to mess with us, sometimes it comes when we are relaxing or working on something else. Greatness can come when—and because—we're under deadlines, as it did to Douglas Adams[1], but we can't expect that, and we certainly can't demand it.

- **Greatness does not come on our schedule.** Sometimes it doesn't come at all.

I think Greatness is kind of like that girl you dated—the very hot one whom you could never figure out how much, if at all, she actually liked you. I dated her, too. I, too, never knew if she really liked me. But she and I went out a lot, and I think I can give you some tips as to what gets her to show up and put out.

So, if you want to do something great, and you don't want to lose every cent you ever made on fruitless dates with Miss Greatness, this three-pronged approach, this Trident of Brilliance that I somehow feel was suggested by Mr. Cerny might be useful.

Ideally, development is best split into two segments. In Segment the First, the creative team is challenged to create an environment that is ready for Greatness, invites her in, recognizes her, and nurtures her goodwill by offering her the gifts, wine, attention, care, and last on the list as usual music that she likes. In Segment the Second, know what to do with Greatness to turn it into the product you can brag about for the rest of

---

[1] "Don't Panic" was the slogan of the *Hitchhikers' Guide* stories, the first of which originally appeared on the BBC as a radio series. Author Douglas Adams (whom I met at an interactive entertainment installation whose slogan was, ironically, "Panic"), wrote the scripts for the series under great pressure, and this was a source of some of the greatest science-fiction comedy ever created. Remember how one segment ends with Ford Prefect and Arthur Dent floating in space with no possible way to be rescued? As the next episode was to air, Adams had not written the rescue scene, and could think of no way to rescue them that wouldn't violate the laws of physics. He was as adrift as the two heroes. In a moment of, well, panic, he realized that the only way out was to change the laws of physics, so he had a passing ship's "improbability drive" warp the timespace around them and cause highly improbable things to happen... such as rescue from deep space. And from deadlines.

Another thing recommended by the *Hitchhiker's Guide* is that one should always "know where one's towel is." This odd phrase never completely made sense within the context of the book, but today I am quite certain that it represents Mr. Adams' premonition that someday I would write the above chapter.

your life. (Oh, if only I had not typed this chapter's first paragraph, *unbelievable* tension would have begun to build here.) Third, there is the Secret Segment. A tiny, sharp and crucial prong nestled between the first and second segments of the development trident. The G-Prong. It consists of a single sentence, and that sentence goes like this: Be ready to cancel the whole damn party and cut your losses if Snooty Miss Greatness stands you up.

There. We've covered the third segment in its entirety. The second segment was spoiled in our initial paragraph. Now all we have to cover is the first segment, and we're done. See? You *can* schedule for Greatness. QED.

Have I mentioned the importance of scheduling to creativity?

In the first segment, the final one left to discuss in this chapter, *there is no spec, there is no schedule.* What are we trying to do? For Mark Cerny, create a truly great game. For us, create truly great sounds for the game. How can the elements of these things be specified or scheduled? How can you lead a revolution without risking the bullets? How can you be a pioneer without taking a few arrows? How can you make an omelet if you ain't got the stinkin' *EGGS* for it?

More specifically, the question is, what are you going to do in the first segment of development to ensure that God gets His audio riffs in?

Here's the answer: You're going to be brave. That's all. Just brave.

Sounds easy, doesn't it?

Good. Hold that thought. Take the Oath to be a Brave Fat Ranger right now, and stick to it for the rest of your life. Do it and you will almost surely beat even my time in the Greatness department.

Courage is a panacea. Almost anything brave that you, the developer, you, the game designer, and you, the audio guy do in that first segment is likely to help bring Greatness around and brighten the thread that the three Fates are weaving for you in the Eternal Fabric.

Courage breaks the ice and breaks the mold.

Courage paves the way for humor, for a strong team, for friendship, and for admiration. You can't stand up for a person if you haven't got the courage. Dedicating yourself to a project is an empty act if it's not done with bravery.

Courage is the only way to open the door to innovation. There is nothing new that can be done that does not require considerable courage—the safe things have all been done.

I am asking you to be brave, because without courage there is no creative approach to game design. Without it, we are doomed to do all tasks the way they were done in the past.

Is our task to cast aside, at least for a time, old ideas like schedules and milestones, and replace them with a quest for Beauty, Creativity, and Greatness? Without courage, there is no saying "yes" to the Muse. Without courage, there can be no slack, no room for mistakes, no experimentation. No Humanity.

And with an infusion of courage—any courageous act that is sincerely meant to elevate the situation—the project takes on a new life. Bring your dog to the meeting. Wear a turban. Quote Attila the Hun. Challenge the team leader. Turn your parking lot into Disneyland. Make your mansion into a haunted house. Others will catch on, be inspired, help you lead the way, and take over the lead, too, and the pursuit of your great game will feel less like a death march in a cube farm, and will take on the character of the space program, of the arctic expeditions, of the *Scooby Doo* movie, which I haven't seen, but I expect had something to do with courage.

Courage puts, as they say, the "ape" in "apricot."

So why doesn't everybody just be brave? Because the words "brave" and "stupid" are pretty much interchangeable, that's why. Because courage without risk is not really courage, so if your head isn't *really* on the chopping block, you're not *really* being a good, Brave Fat Ranger.

Because, for instance, you and your brand new team are likely being held aloft by the Great Balloon of Venture Capital. In that balloon, safety comes first. The investor's money is the hot air that raises you up, and the delicate mechanism of demos, promises, deadlines, and milestones is feeding a tentative but steady flame to the container above. Passengers on such vehicles who exhibit courage, who suggest tinkering with that mechanism, who begin to climb the ropes and fiddle with the valves are usually looked upon as kindly as though they were, in effect, putting on a burnoose and brandishing a box knife.

In addition to the financial considerations, there's a whole heap of human factors. There's a lot more going on in the first segment of game development than just game planning. Early on, each person on the production team is likely thinking of lots of things that are not related to making a great game. Keeping one's job comes to mind. Showing support, exuding the spirit of teamwork, sniffing out the various personalities involved in the project, and other kinds of kissing up are the order of the day. As ideas are being thrown around, a lot of "Oh, yeah, we can do that" gets said, and in that atmosphere a lot of assumptions get made. And you know what happens when game developers assume? Nothing. Nothing at all. Everybody keeps his job, everybody does things the normal way, and everybody who plays the resultant game is going to have to listen to the usual 40 hours of repetitive, imitative audio hogwash.

That's why you have to leap in there and save that company—every company, in fact, that you ever work for—from themselves. At a time when nobody's sure what level of confidence to have in the project and the team, when they're all cautiously and slowly circling, sniffing each other, and walking on eggshells (See? There's your problem. No eggs. Just eggshells.), you have to bust in there like the SWAT team from Starbucks and shatter their assumptions. "Hold it right there! Creativity Police!" And that's why hardly anybody does it. Because you're going to come across like a kid with a beach towel for a cape who thinks he's Superman. That image isn't for just anybody. People don't like weird kids like that. Intelligent, conservative programmers don't trust 'em. Smart, cautious business people feel uneasy around 'em. Most chicks won't date 'em.

But our business was founded almost exclusively by that kind of freak. And Miss Greatness?

Trust me, Brother, I'm tellin' you; the towel thing drives her wild.

Full-page photo from Das Magazin, the most widely read magazine in Switzerland. Linda says they must have all finished reading Das Buch.

Hitting the Road
with the Rubber

Techniques and Meditations

Methods
(Superstitions)
of
Efficient
Audio
Production

Efficiency is the key. Adopting certain methods will help you make good game audio efficiently. Of course, every one of these methods to which I refer is merely a silly superstition.

Nonetheless, here are some of the key superstitions upon which the Cult of Team Fat was established.

Teams should meet once a week. No more, no less.

Once a week is just the right amount. I can't explain it. Thursdays are best for small teams, Mondays for large teams. Tuesday nights are best for jam bands. Some things are best left a mystery.

If you're not five minutes early, you're late.

Nice, huh? I got it at USC Film School. It goes for film shoots, meetings, recording sessions, lunches. It's what makes showbiz professionals jumpy like poodles.

Miss a deadline, and you break your mother's back.

The Schedule is the Law. If you don't like the pace, change the schedule, but don't miss the deadline. A missed deadline means that the client will lose money because of you. Unacceptable.

Miss a milestone, and you only crack your mother's knuckles.

Be aware of your milestones.

If a milestone is coming up, and you are in danger of making bad noises instead of good noises, call the client and tell them the truth. Perhaps you *can* make the milestone if it is set in stone, but perhaps another week of work will make it sound a lot better. This shows respect for the project and the client, and it shows that you have a good perspective on the importance of the schedule. It can build a sense that you and the client are after the same things. The client will probably tell you that the milestone has slipped anyway. If not, you stay up all night and by-God make the milestone.

Pull your all-nighters at the beginning of the project, not at the end.

The sooner you can fill the spec, the better, regardless of the quality of the first pass. Team Fat calls this "starting the job finished." I have two reasons for liking to do things this way:

- It forces a complete immersion in the whole of the project. Once we've experienced the complete project, at least in a sketched phase, I can then have the team concentrate on making the most significant pieces of audio really wonderful.

- Some sound will just "write itself," and everybody will be happy about that.

- Some sound will be really, really wrong, and that will motivate the artist to re-do it. Since he's already gotten some feedback, he'll be able to proceed with a great clarity of direction.

  This forces a little more re-making, and I've found that at least some members of my team, Joe, sound better and better the more they re-make a tune.

- If the client suddenly needs to ship the product, they can. This makes them feel really, really, really good.

- Linda can bill the client sooner.

You can argue all you want, but I told you at the beginning of the chapter that this was a silly superstition. Okay, five reasons. Jeez, you're so *serious.*

Recording to tape is good. Recording to disk is bad.

I am right on the very, very *edge* of changing my mind about this one. I have been on that same edge for ten years. Probably will be for another five. I like it there on that edge. There's a nice view.

Team Fat tends to record to ADATS, then dump to computers for mixing and MIDI sweetening. I think it's because we can *see* which part of the ADAT tape is chewed up. You can't see that on a disc.

All materials for a job go into a clearly labeled Job Bin.

To keep all of a project's paperwork, floppies, compact discs, action figures, thank-you cards, and tapes in one spot, you need something that can act as a file drawer and a tape filing system. We use Official Team Fat Bins.

The best collection of anything in the bin is marked with a star.

Someday you're going to go back to that bin to pull out that one tune to play for you daughter, and you won't be able to find it. Look for the star.

Remember, when you label something as "best" with a star, you usually have to scribble out the star on some other CD or tape. I'm working on copying all the "star" CDs from each bin, and I'm moving them into a file drawer, which will eventually be a nice "best of" archive.

There may be a nice way to do all this in software, but I don't believe in it. I've seen too many computers turn into doorstops over a short number of years to be able to trust them.

If you use multitrack tape, you must keep two kinds of logging sheets, or you will die a horrible, disorganized death.

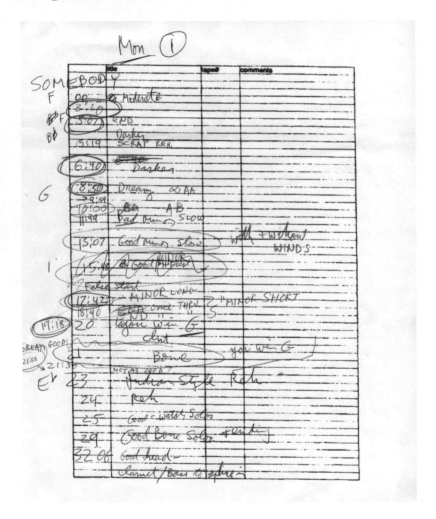

Each tape that you begin to use requires that you start one vertical log to keep track of where each tune is chronologically on the tape. The main use of this log is to help you know exactly which tunes are on it, and where the best, or "circle," takes of each tune are located.

Each tune that gets multitracked needs an appropriate horizontal track sheet to keep track of which instrument is on which track. These sheets save hours of hunt-and-peck mixing, and you should always make them. If several tapes, such as ADATs, are used to record a tune, one track sheet can cover multiple tapes.

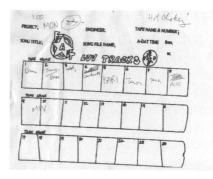

If multiple takes of a tune are made, circling the best take is good luck.

I've saved hours and hours by doing this. It seems that, when you're recording a take, it's easy to tell the difference between a Good take and an Evil one. If for some reason you have to come back to the tape later and find the One True Good one, they will all sound the same.

Never log anything on the track sheet before it's done.

It seems smart to mark on the track sheet the tracks that you're *planning* on doing in that session; resist the urge. The track sheet has to represent what is actually present. If you log a track, then don't record it, or that guy doesn't play any notes, then a label exists where no music exists. Two months from now somebody's going to wonder how high you were when you erased that track, and you're going to have to do some 'splainin'.

Label everything. If you don't label a tape, disk, or other medium, you might as well have not recorded it.

Every time you've found a blank CD on your mixing console, you have re-learned the deep truth in this saying. A properly labeled tape has the job name, a tape number, a description of the nature of the recordings on it (multitrack, master, sketches, that kind of thing) and the date. At the very least, the date and job number, in Sharpie.

Your studio should look like the Bat Cave.

Joe never has gotten the hang of labeling things.

I mean it. Label everything.

All file folders, videotapes, CDs, CD-ROMs, and visible surfaces should be clearly labeled in Sharpie. Your studio should look like the Bat Cave.

Why Sharpie?

Joe's patch bay. Useless.

*Left: Badly labeled DAT tapes. Right: Not as bad.
Joe has a lot of tapes lying around that are marked
"Joe's tape." In an attempt to do better, he changed
one to "Joe's music tape." Then, realizing that it did no
good whatsoever, he advanced to "Joe's music ADAT."
I had one called "Fat Dat." Don't label your tapes with
the few things that you do know about them.
Write the date and the name of the job.*

Sharpies are the only acceptable way to label things.

Buy Sharpies by the dozen. By the gross if you can. You can never have enough Sharpies. Not having a Sharpie is like not having a guitar pick, or a The Thing You Need (see the chapter, "The Culture of Game Audio"), or a friend in the world.

The only bad thing about Sharpies is that they slip so nicely into your pocket that you will accidentally bring one home every day. Another reason to buy more Sharpies.

Sharpies are actually *good* for CDs.

The rumor going around that Sharpies will eventually soak through the surface of a CD and ruin the optical patterns is a cruel lie, spread by evil Infidels.

If you find out otherwise, I don't want to hear it. Sharpies are the only writing implement to use. Ever.

But use pencil for your tape logs.

Using Sharpie on a tape log would be pretty stupid, I think. What if you tape over a track?

File names should be descriptive and different for every iteration of every file.

If a spec outlines that, say, a boomerang sound be named something specific (say, BoomRang1.wav), you should use a different file name, or you will have seven years of bad luck.

Let's say that you come up with a better boomerang sound two days later. How will the programmer know he has the best version? What if you and the developers decide that the first boomerang sound works better as a catapult sound? Now the programmer has the word "BoomRang" in his catapult routine. Even if you had access to the Earth's one remaining programmer who uses comments, commenting the code isn't going to help take the potential for confusion out of that one. What if you come up with 12 variations on the boomerang sound, and they're all good, and you decide that it's best for the player if the game were to randomly pick a sound from the 12 each time a boomerang is thrown?

A spec that assigns specific names to specific sounds is a rookie's spec. It's a noninteractive spec. It's an ignorant spec. It's trouble waiting to happen. And if you get a spec, ten to one it's like that. And if it *is* like that, you should feel lucky that you got a spec at all, you ungrateful sound guy.

Upon receipt of said spec, I would recommend arguing... er... suggesting to the client to get his head out of... er... to consider adding what programmers call a clue... er... a "layer of indirection," to the sorry piece of... er, to the spec.

Perhaps it's better to tell him that when it's time for the program to "call" a sound, it should not call the .WAV file by name. It should go to a lookup table, *which can be a .TXT file that the audio guy can edit*, and in that lookup table, the names of the .WAV files that are associated with the "throw boomerang" sound call are listed. If you can get him to do that, you are actually creating a primitive and fairly effective Audio Integrator. (See the chapters, "Integration for Beginners" and "Everything Comes Together.")

Invoices and audio demos must have contact information written directly on them. Envelopes don't count.

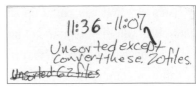

A bad invoice. How am I going to pay it? An invoice like this just sits on your desk making you feel frustrated, until you write a book, and then you put a scan of the invoice in the book, and then you feel a little better.

I also think that an invoice for hourly work should have an end time that comes after the start time, and a little reminder as to what the rate was.

It's Always the Cables

My daughter Sandy gave me a cable for my birthday, along with a handwritten card that bore proof that she'd paid attention to the only truly important lesson her old man had ever bestowed upon her. The cable she gave me is not the one pictured here. It's bright pink.

My brother once tried to stump me as follows: "Let's see if you've still got it, Fat Man. I'm in the studio, the..."

"Cables," I declared.

His jaw dropped.

Any time something goes wrong in the studio, it's the cables. Don't ask why. It's, I don't know, science or something. So if you can't hear the bass, or there's a crackle in the speaker, or the singer is out of tune, the first, fastest, most efficient thing to do is check the cables.

Teach that one to your kids.

Team Fat's File Naming System for Music

Every job has a three-letter abbreviation.

Every file for that job begins with the three letters.

Next comes the composer's digit. I'm 0. Dave is 2. Kevin is 1. Joe is 3. In that order.

Next comes the two-digit tune number.

Next comes the version letter.

Next comes the part letter. Let's say a piece has to fit a three-part drama, so it's split into an intro, a looping middle, and a big ending. These are A, B, and C. Or maybe the spec calls for five "hit the turtle" tunes. We might sketch all five of them on guitar, and then add piano to all five in a session.

If we're limited to eight-character file names, which is often the case because of specific audio drivers, we're done.

If not, next comes the name of the tune, per the spec.

Next comes a name for the tune that, hopefully, acts mnemonically to help one remember how the tune goes when one hears the title.

So, Kevin sits down to write a rough sketch for a game. He looks at the spec. Ah, it's for *Putt Putt Saves the Zoo*. The spec calls for it to be named BoomRang1.wav. Kevin writes a bouncy melody with a heavy drum.

Zoo112aa-BoomRang1-Bouncy Boom Melody.wav

or

Zoo112aa.wav for short.

How to Make Great Sound Effects

That's easy. Get a bunch of the following:

- **Gravel:** For the sound of footsteps.

- **Celery:** For the sound of a monster biting and breaking something.

- **Melons:** For that lovely sound of human heads getting pounded and/ or exploding.

- **Bone-in meat:** For the dulcet tones of breaking bones.

- **Pipes, hammers, and hatchets:** For use on the above.

Then, simply do what comes naturally, and you can't go wrong.

serious. I'm

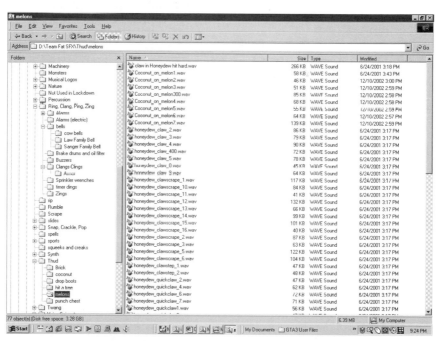

A small segment of the vast Team Fat SFX library.

The essentials of sound effects creation are relatively low-tech. For swords and armor, you're going to need at least one brake drum, a solid old hubcap, and an iron pipe. Use kitty litter containers to store the other necessities out of the way: gravel, coconut halves, horse hooves, animal calls, bells, and broken plaster. You'll break a lot of glass in this business. Keep the broken glass in a safe place. It still sounds like you're breaking it fresh even if you merely drop something into a pile of glass. A tip: Every time you encounter a creaky door, record it right away or make a mental note to yourself as to where that door is. Doors never creak when you need 'em to.

The inside of a clavinet can be played like a slide guitar. Run it through a "golden throat," and you've got some pretty impressive spellcasting sound effects.

I carry a mini-disk recorder with me almost everywhere I go. This Sony mic cost $100 and can capture almost any sound I'm likely to encounter. The fact that it uses the mid-side method of recording makes it especially good for game sound effects. I won't go into the details of mid-side recording and how it works. Suffice it to say that you can record and archive all your sounds in a very natural stereo, and then, when your client requests mono sound effects, which is the norm for game audio, you just merge the left and right signals, and your mono will be perfect, with no possibility of phase shift.

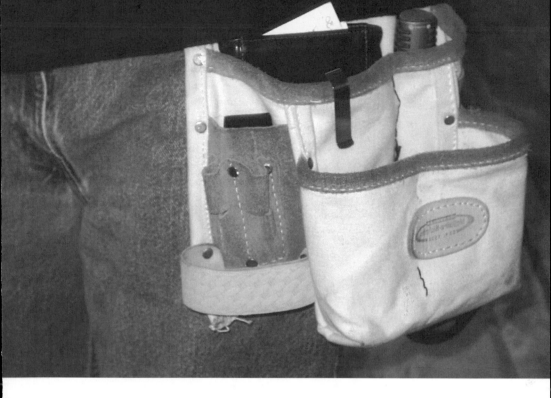

I'm still working out the details of the Utility Belt in which I carry the mini-disk. This latest version allows me to untuck my shirt, but its contents are always getting slammed in my car door.

The concept might work better for you, **assuming** you have a normal, left-hand drive car.

How to Make Great Music

That's easy. While thinking about the game, make music that **nobody** else can make.

Change it somehow, then ask yourself: Is the game **warmer** this way?

If it is, keep doing that. If not, change the music a different way and **ask** yourself the same question **again**.

Repeat until legendary.

Sidebar: Song, Arrangement, Recording—Knowing the Difference

GOOD MORNING SOLDIERS.

STAND UP STRAIGHT.

DID I SAY SOMETHING FUNNY, **PRIVATE?**

WELCOME TO BASIC TRAINING WITH THE FAT MAN.

YOUR SONG

Your song is your best friend. Keep your song clean, and know it inside out. A song is a melody, chords, and lyrics, or some combination of the three, but nothing more. A good song comes across no matter who sings it, and no matter what instruments it's played on. I will now demonstrate a good song by playing Deep Purple's "My Woman from Tokyo" on the autoharp.

Some songs, even though they are hits, are lousy songs. They survive because they have good arrangements or good recordings. You cannot afford to take that chance. All right. Kowalski, you think this is some kind of joke? Here. You take this autoharp, and sing me "Smoke on the Water." *Now,* Kowalski!

Right, that's enough. Now, that's the poorest excuse for a wimpy little song that I ever heard. And every one of you thought that "Smoke on the Water" was a pretty good song, didn't you? But without the riff and the high notes, it stunk like the food in the mess hall, didn't it? Why did I sound so good on "My Woman from Tokyo" while Kowalski here fell right on his butt with a song by the very same group? I'll tell you why, even though any deaf disco dancer could tell you.

My song has something like an ABAC DEDF form. His is more like AAAA BCBC. **THAT'S SISSY STUFF.**

My song has chordal interest and different key centers between the verses and the chorus. This gives motivation and direction. His has a drone on G.

My song has a mysterious bridge section. His has a diddley-waddley guitar solo.

My song has bad-ass lyrics about intriguing human relationships. His reads like a damn school newspaper.

LET THAT BE A LESSON TO YOU.
YOU MAY GET TO THINKING YOU'RE PRETTY TOUGH,
BUT THAT'S WHEN EVEN THE **BEST** SONGWRITERS SCREW UP.

YOUR ARRANGEMENT

An arrangement is the specific manner in which the song is performed.

This includes instrumentation, tempo, rhythm, intro, ending, and seal horn sound effects. What are you laughing at, skinny boy? Someday you may be out strolling in the jungle and find yourself in the middle of an A&R picnic. And what happens? You reach for your song, and find you've got nothing but a jam.

TAKE *THIS!*

I have just demonstrated the value of using the element of surprise in arrangements. Private Jones here was lulled into a false sense of security by my predictable intro, and I won his respect by suddenly dropping a seven-beat bar on him. Get up, Jones.

Surprise. Power. A persistent, relentless groove. These are the elements of arrangement. But they are only good as part of an overall plan. The arrangement *must* support the lyrics, chords, and melody. Otherwise, we find that we are fighting ourselves.

Nobody's going to go out there and win the contract without teamwork. A bold song requires bold arrangement. A quiet song requires quiet arrangement. A cruddy song requires miraculous arrangement, so don't go making things hard on yourselves by writing sloppy drivel, unless you've got a "Smoke on the Water" riff up your sleeve.

So everybody repeat after me:

"THIS IS MY **SONG,** AND THIS IS MY **GROOVE.** ONE TELLS A **STORY,** AND ONE MAKES ME **MOVE.**"

YOUR RECORDING

The recording is a captured performance of a specific song with a specific arrangement, not necessarily accomplished in real time. In other words, it's the real thing—the end result of the song, arrangement, and practice. The final product that will make or break you to the record companies, your fans, your spouses, children, and History.

Oh, yeah, I can see it in your faces... you're all set to jump into combat. You all think you're ready for the big time right now. I can just hear your little voices squeaking, "Lemmie at 'em, Sarge! Put me in that isolation booth. I'll teach them how to record!"

What's that, Van Halen? Well, you drop right now and give me a Top 20.

And while you're at it, you just stop and think for a minute, soldier. You can make it on a grooving arrangement alone, but you'll be damn lucky. You can make it on a song alone, but that's like jumping without a backup 'chute. So you just check and double check and triple check that you have the best song and the best arrangement you know how to write, 'cause once it's on tape there ain't no excuses. And once we get to the studio, well, just leave the recording to me and the engineer.

The music business may be a popularity contest, but producing's not. I didn't come here to be your friend. And I know that by this time, some of you hate my guts. I don't care if you like me or what I have to say. But, by God, if you've learned what I've taught you, you may just survive out there—and that's what's important to me.

YOU'RE AN UGLY BUNCH OF BASTARDS. LET'S GO GIVE 'EM HELL.

An Effective Method of Simulataneous Musical Composing and Recording Using Computer Tools to Full Advantage, or What Be the Workflow du Jour, Fat?

Like the Bible, the Beatles, Shakespeare, and the naked people on the Internet, music is big, and there are a lot of ways to look at it.

Some people are so into The Groove, they forget about melodies. They like to compose on loop-based tools, like Reason.

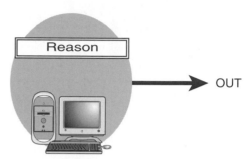

OUT

Some melodic composers can create orchestral melodies and harmonies so strong they'll knock your socks off. But they're often so square they wouldn't know a groove if they were wearing it on their heads like a hat. We used to call these people "classically trained."

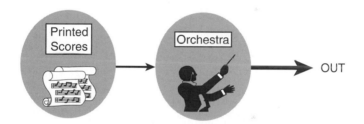

OUT

"Our pianist is classically trained."

"Can't find the beat, eh?"

"Not a clue."

Some people thrive on creating musical "hooks," which happen at a phrase size of about every eight bars or so. Sonic Foundry's Acid is good for that. The program, boys, the program.

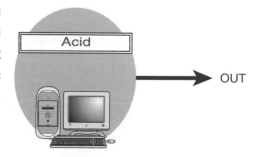

OUT

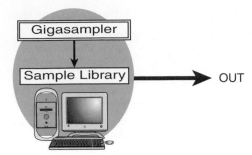

Some people get so hung up on finding perfect sounds and tones, they forget about harmony and composing altogether, and spend their entire lives buying libraries and tweaking knobs. They tend to like the fancy samplers, like Gigasampler, that offer a myriad of sonic choices.

Some compose brilliantly, but when they spend only ten minutes on orchestration the results are

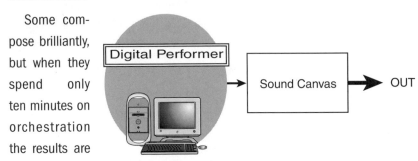

so hokey it's unbearable. They might prefer a MIDI sequencer like Mark of the Unicorn Performer, running to a simple box of sounds like a Sound Canvas.

Some concentrate on composing the large forms, going for the big payoff that comes from the way a piece takes shape over long periods of time. A program like Vegas Video enables such composers to drag and drop their key areas around in relationship to each other, and create orchestral sonorities that sing in huge, magnificent structures. These guys have to watch out for rambling—they might build something that lacks any single moment with the power to speak to the human heart and mind. In interactivity, a genre where any tune can be cut off or changed based on what the user does, this can be a liability.

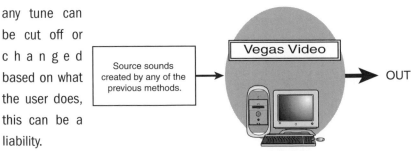

I, The Mighty Fat Man, have developed a workflow that allows me to concentrate my attention in turn on small, medium, and large chunks of time, thus addressing grooves, hooks, and large-form structures, each with appropriate computer tools. It also allows me to integrate simple out-of-the-box tones, carefully tweaked synthesized tones, carefully chosen sampled sounds, and live instruments or ensembles at any of several stages of the composing process. I invite you to examine this workflow and see if you can figure out where it falls apart, 'cause it beats heck out of me.

First, you need to know the basic studio layout, which is this:

- **Fat Mac:** A fairly lame Macintosh computer sporting Digital Performer.

- **Pacemaker Eddie:** A crowded and overworked PC sporting Acid, Vegas Video, Reason, and Sound Forge. Pacemaker Eddie used to be Fast Eddie.

- **Giggles:** Another trailing-edge PC dedicated to running only Gigasampler, never to be upgraded. Giggles hosts the huge library of original sound effects recordings I've made with my mini-disk recorder, as well as a fair batch of orchestral samples.

- **Other stuff:** Some ADATs, a big room, a small handful of really nice mics and preamps, and a whole city full of friends who can play the hell out of their instruments.

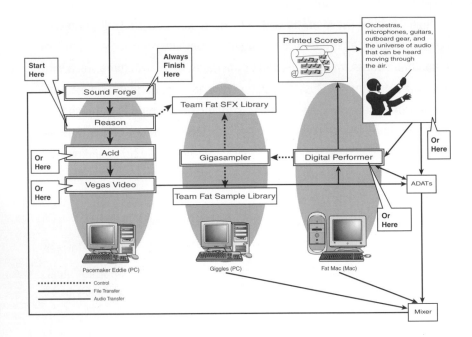

Here's what happens:

Use the drum machine and/or the sequencer/subtractive synth modules in Reason to shape your drum samples and sound effects into little chunks of irresistible groove. Reason's great for that. Basslines and short melodies can be added as desired in a number of Reason-friendly ways. Save these little loops as .WAV files in a directory called loops. Repeat.

Blow the resulting loops into Acid. Acid will be very good for repeating and manipulating those loops, changing tempos and keys, adding effects, and creating nice mid-sized phrases. Save the phrases as .WAV files in a directory called phrases. Repeat. Note where Acid's tempo was set.

Blow those phrases into Vegas Video. Move the phrase-sized chunks around until there's a nice verse-sized or chorus-sized rise-and-fall structure to what you're hearing. You can mix a bit and have fun with layers if you want. This is another good place to add effects if they feel good.

Now you should have a rhythm track that kicks and has a real good structure. Ready for the melody? Play the output of Pacemaker Eddies' Vegas into Fat Mac's Digital Performer. No, silly, don't sync the Mac to the PC—that's too hard, and too much can go wrong. Instead, just set the Performer tempo to the same value as the Acid tempo was, press Play on Eddie, Record on Fat Mac, and patch the analog output of one into the analog input of the other. In Performer, drag the file to where the downbeat sits at the beginning of bar 5 (so you have room for a countoff). Transfer complete.

MOTU Performer syncs nicely to ADATs, and it's a fantastic MIDI sequencer. Kevin once said, "George, you drive that thing like a dune buggy," and that was 10 years ago—I've had practice since then. So from that platform, I can compose the socks off of whatever's left to accomplish on the melody, harmony, and bass using Perfomer's MIDI capabilities. I usually use the Sound Canvas tones, because it's really easy and fast. Once I like the composition, I can reroute the MIDI tracks to Giggles or some other outboard synth and get all particular about the tones. More often, at that point, I move to the Sweet Part.

The Sweet Part happens when music travels through air. Get out the 12-string acoustic guitar, tambourine, and sitar.[1] Print out those melodies, or play them for musicians or yourself, and start adding vocals, fart noises, and any other acoustic sound known to Man. Use the ADATs if you're not in too much of a hurry to wait for rewind times but short of disk space. If you're in a hurry and have loads of disk space, use the digital part of Digital Performer. You can bounce between the two to your hearts content... you'll never hear it. If you claim to be able to hear it, you're either showing off or worrying too much.

---

[1] 12-string, sitar, and tambourine are the three instruments guaranteed to make any song a hit. In a pinch, you can use chimes or a Gang-a-Bong (see next chapter, "Okay, Equipment").

The Sweet Part, as personified by Austin's own famous Marcia Ball Band.
Left to right: Paul Klemperer, master producer Dave Sanger, Dan Torosian,
Marcia, Don Bennett, Keith Robinson, Derek O'Brien, and our own Joe
McDermott. To get a loop-based sequencing tool to sound anywhere near
as good as this group, you'd have to get it the gig as the house band at
Antone's Blues Club for, like, a decade or two at least.

Now, the version I have of Performer is a little bit, er, senseless in the digital realm, and so I've been experimenting with moving the final stage of the process—the linear MIDI/digital part—over to Cakewalk Sonar XL or Nuendo on a PC. Sonar looks promising right now because they're paying close attention to issues of plug-in compatibility, and their target customer remains the "game-audio-level" person.

So, there you have it.

OR

If that doesn't work, two doors down the hall are Team Fat's Dave and Kevin, two of the world's foremost experts on orchestral sampling. Dave was the first person to use a Gigasampler, ever. They have the cutting-edge orchestra sounds months before anybody else, because they're the ones who arrange the tones into the GigaStudio files that other guys buy. I can hum Dave a tune or ship him a Sound Canvas MIDI file and get back the best possible orchestration short of a live recording by the end of the day.

So—do what I do. First, go back in time. Then, when this bartender kid Dave calls you from the bus stop because he had an appointment to see your studio, but didn't have a car, pick him up before I did, and be his friend for about ten years. Then write a bunch of articles on producing hands for a local magazine, but yours have to be better than mine. So, when a student named Kevin asks if he can study under you instead of me, say yes, and again, wait a decade or so.

Long friendships with guys like this can be very gratifying, and small kindnesses pay off big time.

Be **kind**,
      make **friends**,
and you will have *good-sounding* music.

Okay, Equipment

George and his entire "Reel Mobile" studio in 1980 Los Angeles.

Okay, boys and girls, we're going to talk about equipment now. Are you excited? Sure you are! Talking about equipment can be fun—but it can also be very, *very* dangerous, can't it? We can lose track of our... our... anybody?

That's right, Timmy, our Art.

Anything else?

That's right, Omar, schedule.

Anything else?

Oh yeah, our fundamental humanity, that's good, Suzie. But kids, if you know how to do it the Fat Man Way, talking about equipment can be perfectly safe—and really fun!

*Dave Sanger is authentically undaunted by the drums
made available to him during his rehearsal for a TV broadcast
with The Fat Man and the LucasArts Stooges.*

The first and only thing to remember is that equipment is not there to be a stepstool for you to climb on to allow you to go places you wouldn't have gone otherwise. Any equipment that advertises that it allows you to "do things you never dreamed of" is warning you that it's going to take over your life by making you learn the methods and workflows that the creators of that equipment think of as creativity. Ask yourself: Do you *want* to do things you never dreamed of? Have you ever? No, you haven't, because you never dreamed of that.

For my part, and for the sake of my clients, I want to do the things I *have* dreamed of, and I'd really like to do them fairly quickly.

The equipment that I like does not act as a stool of any kind, pun intended. It acts as a doorway or a floodgate. It lets my ideas flow more quickly the more it gets the heck out of the way.

The first place to start in getting the equipment out of the way is by literally getting it out of the way. We can help even poorly designed equipment to get out of our way if we don't buy it.

Another strategy is to use a really nice room.

Rooms, and Racks, Dumb-Asses

Very few game audio houses have a room big enough to comfortably house a mid-sized musical ensemble and the equipment necessary to record them. To play well, people must be happy. A room is big enough for a band and its equipment if, and only if, you can throw a good beer party in it. If you are fortunate enough to be able to use such a room for your audio production, Team Fat recommends constantly monitoring any deviations in the room size by periodically calibrating it with such a party.

To make proper sound effects and music, you'll need enough room to swing a Dobro. Here, "Professor" K. Weston Phelan produces a Joe Richardson blues session for the Cast of 1000's slot machine. It may or may not turn out to be the best blues ever played, but it WILL be the best ever played for a slot machine. Bet on it.

Soundproofing is over-rated. Don't spend a million dollars to block out the sound of the train, just get a place a little farther from the tracks. Book your sessions around the train schedule. Or do a second take for safety; that won't kill you. You only need a small area that's really quiet: Large ensembles usually play loud and nearly always drown out

Hot glue, foam, and Plexiglas make a nice isolation case for loud gear. Remember where your bottom is. It should be clearly labeled.

the occasional loud sounds that happen to leak through normal walls. On the inside walls, certainly only a small area of your room should feel dead and padded.... Dead rooms can be good for voice-over, but they're no fun to play in.

The room should be near eating establishments. Musicians, like human beings, need to be fed. Most studios ignore this fact, choosing instead to host long mic set-ups that plow right through feeding time. I have found that long set-up times for recording sessions are largely an outgrowth of the engineer's desire to prove to somebody, perhaps his father, that he is a good engineer. Given the choice between a long set-up and a relaxed, happy, fed musician, I will take the latter every time. I assure you that all good musicians can make sound that is pleasing when they are fed. All pleasing music can be recorded easily with a stereo pair of microphones placed at the ear-level of the person who is pleased by the music. If one wishes to have both a long set-up time and a well-fed musician, the room must be near eating establishments. QED.

Let's get the gear vertical, too.

To address this problem, Joe pioneered the incredibly efficient Joe Rack, used at one time or another by all of Team Fat. A Joe Rack is a floor-to-ceiling 19-inch-wide rack made entirely of two-by-fours or something close. To keep it from toppling forward, the rear-protruding feet are held down by sandbags or cinder blocks. Other than that, it's pretty much what it appears to be. Joe is an artist, and his medium is two-by-fours. His father taught him that if it's not overbuilt, it's not finished. Somehow Joe took that to mean "never paint furniture."

A vertically mounted amp head takes up little room and serves as a very good amp modeling modeler, emulating the functions of the software that emulates non-virtual amp heads. A couple of tubes placed on top will rattle around, giving you that highly desired "tube sound." You can also use a Pod Pro or similar device to emulate that emulation emulation, or you can emulate all that with the Guitar Port (pictured).

Joe's Joe Racks. Note the speaker and mouse-pad shelves. The equipment is held in place by wood screws. Joe achieves the illusion of black metal rack strips by spray-painting a vertical stripe on the inner quarter-inch of the vertical boards.

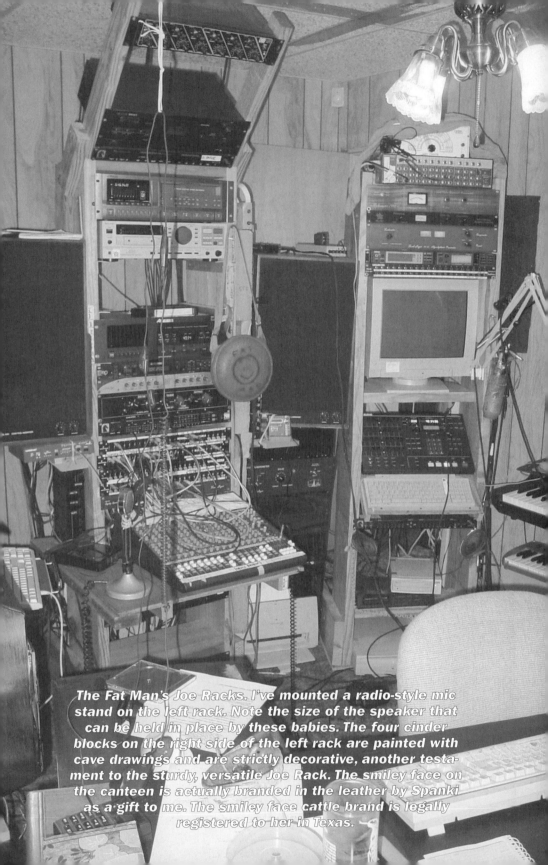

The Fat Man's Joe Racks. I've mounted a radio-style mic stand on the left rack. Note the size of the speaker that can be held in place by these babies. The four cinder blocks on the right side of the left rack are painted with cave drawings and are strictly decorative, another testament to the sturdy, versatile Joe Rack. The smiley face on the canteen is actually branded in the leather by Spanki as a gift to me. The smiley face cattle brand is legally registered to her in Texas.

This Joe Rack is used in our home to hold gaming systems. Note the Intellivision on the top shelf and the Sega Genesis on the bottom shelf. The Atari 800 disk drive is visible in the lower right.

The genius of a Joe Rack reveals itself gradually with use. First, it's dirt cheap and easy to make. Also, floor-to-ceiling rack space is by far the best way we've found to get lots of equipment into a little bit of floor space and into easy reach. Joe Rack users find that they have rack space to spare, and they can be picky about mounting their favorite gear at its optimal height. Furthermore, by running wood screws straight into the rack, your rack spacing is infinitely variable. You aren't limited by the spacing of the holes on those metal rack brackets, and you don't have the problem of having to stock those special rack-sized screws.

Because your Joe Rack is made entirely of raw lumber, you can easily screw more bits onto it, creating shelves for speakers, mixing consoles, keyboards, and mouse pads. I had bull horns on mine before they migrated to the Rolls.

Here's another Joe invention:

the Dumb-Ass.

Joe's Dumb-Ass. That black stick on the left is a mic stand. There's one on the right side, too. Note the plank near the lower left. It features an elevated surface that allows Joe's foot to rest comfortably over his "record" footswitch, making punching in much more quiet.

Joe likes to play quiet acoustic instruments, and he's usually his own engineer. That can present a problem if you're sitting near computers and tape machines with a sensitive mic. The Dumb-Ass is a relatively new creation that holds everything that Joe needs to record his voice and guitar in a quiet corner of his room. The Dumb-Ass Mach I features two fully articulated mic stands for pop

Detail of footswitch holder.

filter, stereo, or guitar/voice micing, a direct box, a tuner, an FMR Really Nice Compressor, an LRC remote for ADATs (not shown), a coffee surface, a power strip (behind the vertical member), six inches of two-by-four that doesn't do anything, and a massive cement block to allow for a minimal footprint. Consider a comparison of the utility per square foot of floor space achieved by the Dumb-Ass to that of the mic stand in the picture.

I can't overemphasize the importance to game audio guys of mounting equipment vertically. Horizontal surfaces are a rare and valuable commodity, and much of what the game musician uses simply *has* to lie flat: music keyboards, computer keyboards, mouse pads, mixing consoles, writing surfaces for track sheets, coffee cups, studio controllers, unlabeled CDs, sleeping bass players, embarrassingly large sacks of cash, and ferret toys. Making all these flat things available at once has been addressed in a number of ingenious ways.

Clint Bajakian of CB Studios cut a notch in his desk to hold the musical keyboard without losing any desk area.

I was lucky enough to be given one of those trays a dentist uses for his instruments. It holds a computer keyboard nicely, and then swivels completely out of the way.

Dentist tray holds keyboard.

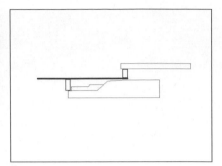

Covert photo and design diagram of the Stooge Mouse Pad,
recovered from the enemy only at great cost.

In my tours of the Bay Area, I noticed a brilliant little invention that all of the LucasArts musicians were using. Each of them had removed the clip from a clipboard, and then had attached right-angles of metal and felt padding all over the board, each in a slightly different way. In each case, they would end up with a mouse pad surface that would sit under the desk surface, but over the music keyboard. The pad covers up about an octave of keys, but here's the trick: The metal and felt pieces slide freely in the slot between the keyboard keys and the front of the keyboard. So when you need those low keys, you just slide the mouse pad up to cover a higher octave.

It's *such* a good idea that it's kind of weird to think that the electronic music industry has come this far with only four of these Stooge Mouse Pads ever having been built. Please make yourself one, and be thankful to the Stooges who paved the way.

*Dave Govett has mounted a mouse pad to the arm of his chair.
The alternatives were to go three levels on the keyboard stand, which
would be wobbly and uncomfortable, or to move his iced tea, which for
this native Texan would have been unacceptable.*

Next, we look at cables. The potential for entanglement is huge in game audio. Like all traditional sound makers, you're likely to be using a lot of things that like to tie themselves in knots: headphones, guitar cables, music stands, guitar straps, pop filters, and microphone cables. In addition, game guys are probably working in a small space, and have got a computer keyboard and mouse, all the wiring to the computer and effects, and most likely a telephone that needs answering in mid-session. Did you ever try to answer the phone when you had your guitar strap on over your headphone cable?

Joe runs **most** of his cables along the ceiling.

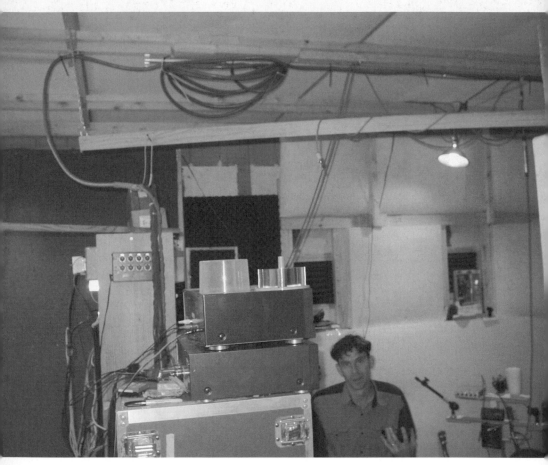

I don't know the function of this particular two-by-four, and I'm afraid to ask.

To get wires out of the way, I hang headphones and my telephone headset from above, using several rubber bands tied together.

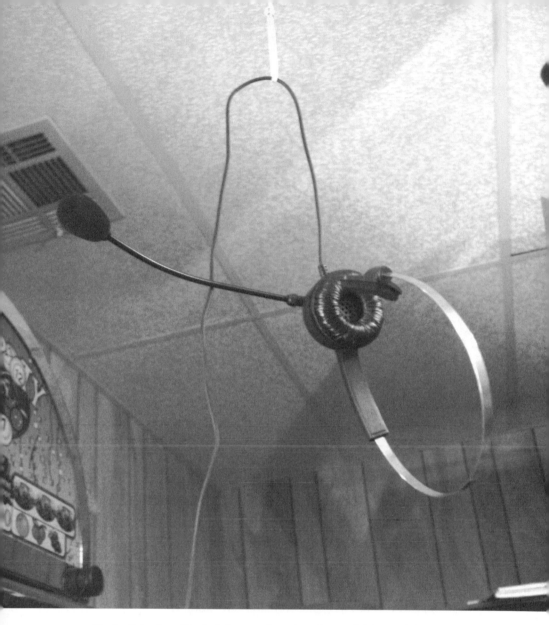

Yeah, it looks silly, but its one less tangle, and I haven't lost my telephone in months. This brings us to an important point. Altogether too much energy is spent in this business on making studios not look silly. Normal, clean, neat, well-equipped wood-paneled studios are like the stiff dress clothes people used to wear to church in decades past. Whom are we impressing? That engineer's dad again?

Team Fat's beloved Booger Buttwell makes a tight punch in Brother Dave's control room. Don't worry, no animals were harmed in the making of this book. A secret passage visible in the back of the oven leads through the wall into a large cage in The Fat Man's office.

The only reason to have your studio look like the cover of *MIX* magazine is if you really, really like that look. For the most part, I believe that people outfit their studios in a manner that is driven by fear of being thought an amateur or being discovered to be a fraud.

Don't beat yourself up if your studio doesn't look like the Record Plant.

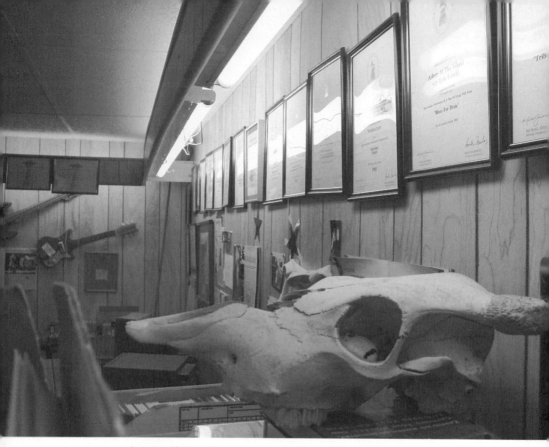

I guess if the clients ever doubt the legitimacy of our work,
they can check out some of Brother Dave's Grammy nominations.
There are more in silhouette on the far wall, and one or two under
the cow skull awaiting hanging, which is too good for 'em.

Team Fat's Abbey Trails studio has been compared many times to a kids' ideal club house. The advantage is that the parents aren't coming home any time soon. I vastly prefer that reputation to the "immaculately professional" thing, which, again, reeks of fear. I like music to sound brave.

Electronic Equipment

Perhaps all this talk of music rooms and cables is making you nervous, because you are operating an entirely computer-based, software-synthesized, direct-to-digital, state-of-the-art, ultra-modern—in other words typical—studio.

"That's a perfectly wonderful, acceptable way of making audio for games" is what you would be reading here if this book had been written by somebody else. You are making sound for games. You will need to record metal banging and rocks scraping and guns going off and all kinds of things that happen in the air. And you know what else happens in the air? Music. That was actually a motto of the Stooges at LucasArts. "Music travels through air. If it's not going through air, there's a problem somewhere."

We have a saying at Team Fat, too. Kevin came up with it when he was running Fat Labs, and he had to deal with all kinds of self-deluded, software-based gimmickry that was being foisted on the public in the early days of General MIDI.

Regardless of the size of your room, use microphones, dammit.

Precious few equipment purchase decisions are easy.

> "When somebody describes an electronic instrument using the words **'as though,'** it's best to run **screaming** from the room."
>
> **—Kevin**

If you're a guitar player, get a Line 6 Pod Pro. The first time I played one in a jam, I threw my old guitar to the ground, raised my arms, and made a declaration. I retracted all the things I'd said over the years about the importance of practice, composition, and playing from the heart. I replaced that wisdom with the statement, "It costs $700, and it's called a Pod."

Here's a purchase decision that has been made easy for you because it was hard for somebody else. Get a Really Nice Compressor by FMR (http://www.fmraudio.com), or three or four. You can read somewhere else what a compressor does, and how to work it, and that kind of stuff. *This* book will tell you the *legend*.

For years, Joe thought that the secret of good recording was good audio compression. He got rid of his DBXs. He bought a pair of Ureis from me. He borrowed other peoples' compressors and listened to them. Compressors became his "thing." He even learned electronics, hoping to someday build his own compressor. He sought out a mentor. Austinite Mark McQuilkin had worked on the Intellicomp digital compressor, back before most people knew what "digital" was. Mark was working on a new compressor, and Joe dug in to study with him. Naturally, I encouraged him to follow his bliss, but I was certain that the fallout of this adventure would be that Joe would learn that equipment is merely a crutch, and there is no substitute for good ears and a warm heart.

Joe's Compressor History. At top, my old pair of Urei 7110 compressors. Center is the Intellicomp, the first compressor McQuilkin worked on. Below it is the pinnacle: three ugly little RNCs.

As a year or two or three passed, I got reports about the progress of the Really Nice Compressor, and the stories were so incredible I couldn't believe it was happening to Joe and not me.

How good is it? Craig Anderton, the world's leading authority on electronics for musicians, took me aside at a party and thanked me for insisting that he listen to the RNC. He wrote to a newsgroup dedicated to arguing the relative merits of various high-end, multi-thousand-dollar compressors, and said, "The debate is over."

How good is it? Many vendors over the years have suggested Mark sell his compressors in the $2,000 to $4,000 dollar range, but they also insisted that he mount the electronics in a big, fancy box, possibly with weights inside. Seriously.

Mark, however, is an idealist. He wanted musicians to have access to good compression and be enabled by it. He wanted musicians to make good music, so that he, Mark, and his wife and children and ferrets could listen to that music. He steadfastly refused to participate in the stupidity of the audio equipment manufacturing community. The RNC, in its ugly little $1/3$ rack box, sells for $200.

I guess I was right. There is no substitute for good ears and a warm heart, and Mark McQuilkin illustrates that fact better than anybody.

So what does Joe do? He decides that the secret to great recordings is not compressors... it's preamps. He built an RCA tube-type preamp himself out of vintage parts, using no labels whatsoever, except the one that is covered up by a dangling piece of blank labeling tape.

*Joe spent about two years building this RCA-style tube preamp.
He overcame his final hurdle—removing the terrible hum—when I leaned over
his shoulder and said, "should those wires be touching?"
He has yet to forgive me for being right on that one.*

Fortunately, Joe's preamp adventure was also headed off when Mark McQuilkin began work on his Really Nice Preamp. Years later, Mark tested the prototypes at Abbey Trails. I think you'll need some of those, too. 'Nuff said.

*A prototype Really Nice Preamp
plugs directly into a Really Nice
Compressor. It heats up slightly, too,
which keeps Joe's coffee warm.*

This Joe Rack sports three modules by Funk Logic.
The upper two units are quite rare. The Holigrailic Interactivator
is in fact a creation of The Fat Man. Musicians who own non-Joe
racks seldom have room for equipment of their own design.

Another man who was disillusioned by the stupid price inflation of the audio equipment marketing world is Derek Van Choice. But whereas Mark responded by making gear that sounds great, looks terrible, and is cheap, Derek responded by creating Funk Logic, a company that makes gear that looks great, is cheap, and does absolutely nothing.

For instance, I am a proud owner of a limited edition (one of 100 made) koa wood Valvecaster 1960 Dual Valve Teleknobic Preampulator with Analogmic Needlator.

Derek was delighted at my idea to hook him up with Mark, and now I'm happy to say, through the combined nonlinear brilliance of these two men, you can buy an RN-Chevy, a cheap rack mount system that turns two cheap RNCs into a unit that looks and sounds like thousands of dollars. Derek let me participate in the design of the RN-Chevy, which sports not only knobs for compression, but brakes, throttle, and the like. It was going to have a working cigarette lighter, but it just didn't look good. So it has a grille.

Team Fat swears by the FMR Really Nice Compressor. Fat put Mark McQuilkin together with the scientists at Funk Logic to create the RN-Chevy. Below that is another Joe masterpiece, the Tube Soul Enhancement Device. Labeled by Fat.

I have great admiration for people who can successfully turn idealism into a business plan. In this regard, Funk Logic and FMR stand alongside Rolls-Royce and Disney. And I hope, Team Fat.

You might notice that I have not mentioned any computer equipment in this chapter. It's a good thing, too, because everything I used when I was writing this book was outdated by the time you read it.

First, let me say that anything made by Sonic Foundry is good.

Here we are with the great programmer Monty Schmidt, who founded Sonic Foundry. He has a tattoo of a sound card on his arm that his mom doesn't know about. His other arm has none. One night in Austin, Team Fat, Monty, and some executives from Miro were celebrating the fact that it appeared that a Miro sound card would be the first sound card ever to get the Fat Seal. The exec was German, and he never cracked a smile until we found a bar with a Jaegermeister dispenser in it. He happened to be from the town in which Jaegermeister was manufactured and had never seen such a thing. He insisted we try it out. We all drank pretty much enough Jaeger to convince us that it was a good idea to get the Fat Seal added to the sound card on Monty's arm. Too bad all the tattoo parlors in Austin are closed at 3:00 a.m., or it would have been a really good story.

Then let me say this:

I can tell you this
about computer gear:

*Kids, computers
are like guns.*

Don't use
them unless
you *absolutely*
have to.

Every computer will crash eventually. I was told by the great audio programmer John Miles: It's not a matter of "if," it's a matter of "when." The hard drive will eventually wear out and lose data. Linda (Mission Control) backs up all her data daily. I make some kind of data or audio CD of every project as it's finished, just to get it the heck off of the computer.

Besides physical wear, there is a thing called "DLL buildup." The more software you put on your computer, the more little bits of software are added to this thing called the Dynamic List Library. The flaw in this system is that each piece of software has a slight chance of not working with some other piece of software. As you add software to your computer, it becomes more and more capable of doing what you want, but it is more and more likely to show you the increasingly inevitable BSD (Blue Screen of Death).

My studio recording mentor, Van Webster, gave a talk at BBQ that inspired a great deal of change in the industry and marked the founding of the School of Appliantology, a philosophical movement that upholds a firm belief in the superiority of appliances, which work, over computers, which don't.

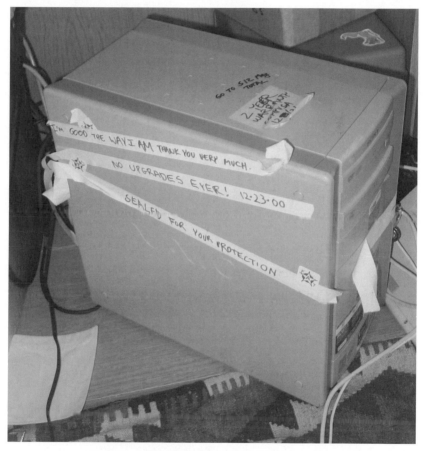

How to combine the advantages of a computer
with the best aspects of an appliance.

You can have your cake and eat it, too, by turning your computer into an appliance. Once your computer is operating well: Wrap three layers of duct tape around it and mark, in Sharpie,

"no upgrades: EVER."

This Fatar Studio 900 was customized to Team Fat's rigid specs using nothing more than black electrical tape and a Fat sticker.

The LitterMaid is still the favorite and most useful piece of electronic equipment in the studio. I got it at a charitable garage sale for five bucks. It sells new for a hundred bucks, so it's gotta be good. Monica Knighton, the woman I bought it from, used me in my red Nudie suit as a model for a card in the western-themed Tarot deck she was creating. Now who's the Fool?

Creating
Your Signature
Sounds

Now that you are equipped with mics and a room, what noises are you going to record? That's easy. Remember, in the chapter about "How to Get Work," we learned that the only acceptable sounds are those that couldn't possibly be made by anybody else.

Let me give you some illustrations of how we at Team Fat have gone about acquiring such sounds, and you can tap into your own inspirations to spin off from there.

Most importantly, we make sure the studio is littered with interesting ways to make noise. If a room is sterile and clean, how can a musical accident happen? And how else, other than through a musical accident, will the Angels be able to speak through you?

It's also nice to have instruments around that other studios don't have—and wouldn't ever if their lives depended on it. Again, it's courage that will allow you to stand when others fall.

Joe got a baritone ukulele for Christmas. Note the other instruments that live within arms' reach.

Detail of Joe's corner. At the bottom is a stocking stretched over a coat hanger, which makes an excellent pop filter. On the right is The Thing That Made That Noise, sort of a lap steel made of two-by-fours and toilet parts. Position markers are the heads of celebrities cut from magazines.

Some very expressive instruments: A Jerry Jones Electric Sitar, a ColorBoy Melodica, and a tenor Bamboo Sax made by Erik the Flutemaker.

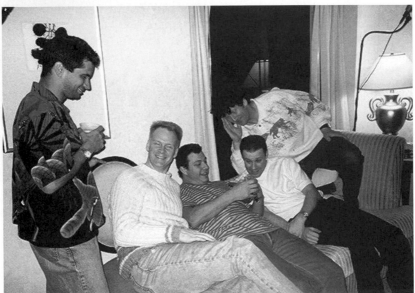

Tommy Tallarico (left) likes to make the BASH sound that goes between the "lie-dee-dies" in "The Boxer" by leaping about wildly with a trash can full of bottles. Most people are not as mentally tough as Tommy, and for them the "trash can method" can cause embarrassment when viewed later, as seen above, on video by game composers Chris Wall, Clint Bajakian, George Sanger, and Alexander Brandon. For those people, the problem is elegantly solved by using the method on the next page.

At Abbey Trails, this long strip of sheet metal hangs by the drum kit for the express purpose of making the crash sound in "The Boxer," without need for a trash can full of beer bottles. We also have plans to hook up a contact mic and a transducer to it, using it as a unique plate reverb. In addition, using the contact mic alone to pick up the drum sound will certainly bear some kind of sonic fruit.

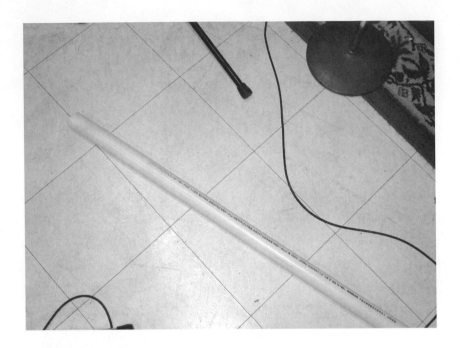

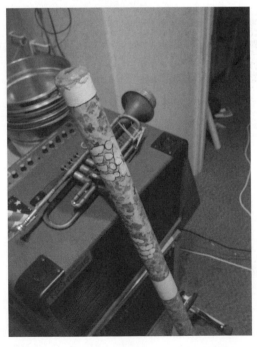

Before and After.
This PVC didgeridoo was
painted by The Fat Man and
game designer/Golden Ticket
winner Patricia Pizer.

You can make a fine didgeridoo out of PVC and beeswax. There are lots of plans for PVC didgeridoos on the web, (for example, http://www.brothermusic.com/didgeridoo.htm), but no plan is needed, really. Just heat up some beeswax and stick it on the end of a pipe. And here's a secret from The Fat Man: If you're only playing for a few minutes at a time, you don't *really* need the beeswax. It's just there for a little fine-tuning and to keep you from wearing out your lip.

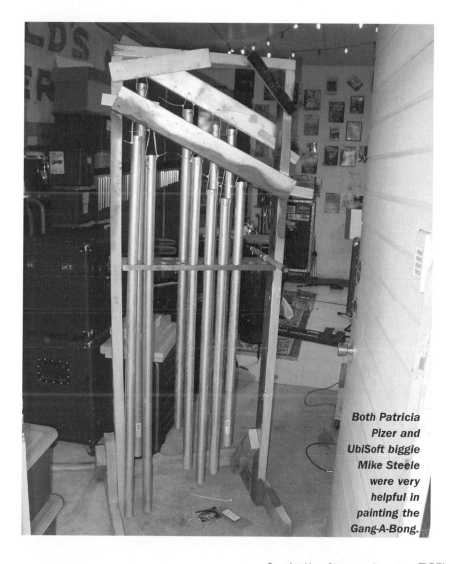

Both Patricia Pizer and UbiSoft biggie Mike Steele were very helpful in painting the Gang-A-Bong.

The Gang-A-Bong was built from conduit pipe obtained from Home Depot, and it sounds as much like proper orchestral chimes as you will ever need.

Not all pipes are there, but note that the ones that *are* there are clearly labeled. In Sharpie.

Linda did the math for the pipes, and every one of them was perfectly in tune when tested. Just in case you want to build your own, the pipe lengths I used are included in the next chapter.

Keep brass instruments handy. Don't worry too much about not knowing how to play them. A little badly played horn can often be much better sounding than no horn at all.

An effective repair of the spit valve
on my favorite trumpet.

A little badly played horn.

   Like fixing Rolls-Royces, fixing old musical instruments isn't as big a deal as some people like to make out. Hot glue, cable ties, and clothespins are every bit as handy in both activities.

   Jam buddy Robert Naishtat sells vacuum cleaner parts for a living. He completely renovated this 1920s C-Melody sax. Where leather is usually called for, he used vinyl from an old chair. Before the World Wide Web, there were modems that you'd drop a phone handset into. Robert tore one apart and used the microphone as a pickup.

This beat 12-string was given to me by Wyte Lyon, (who was overheard telling his friend that I was cooler than God) on the condition that we fix it up to where we could use it. He claimed that it was rare. The action was so bad on this rag that for years it had one string on it, and I used it to make that "plucking out a hair" noise that you hear in cartoons.

The rules changed when I saw a photo of the Beatles playing a Framus 12-string not unlike this one. We got it fixed up, and now it's the best-sounding 12-string I've played. It needed something to hold down the strings, though, between the tuning pegs and the nut. I chose this door hinge, because its screw holes were, like the Beatles themselves, perfectly spaced.

This baritone/six-string double-neck was broken, so I got a great deal. A little Bondo fixed the crack right up, and then I had my daughter Sandy paint it. She was six years old. I show it to six-year-olds and tell them they're old enough to paint their daddys' guitars. The upper neck tunes to a low A, but notes are labeled in Sharpie on the back of the neck so I don't get lost. The very effective trumpet stand in the background is made from a toilet plunger and a mic stand base.

The Hammond is another instrument we already had around, then saw photos of the Beatles using. Joe uses it as a tape shelf and shrine. But, seriously, when the Hammond comes in on any tune, the musicians all give you that highly desirable "Where'd you get that patch?" face.

The nose flute is a highly underrated instrument. It has a huge range, slides better than a slide whistle, and you can hit notes as easily as whistling. Holding up your nose flute is the best MIDI trigger we've come across. Of course, it was invented by "Professor" K.

If you're into using triggers to make percussion sounds, you're reading the right caption. Kevin tested all kinds of woods and found that cedar was the only one resonant enough to allow him to build a trigger that would allow him to tap with his fingers or soft mallets. He added a Radio Shack piezoelectric mic to the back, some rubber padding and Velcro, and voila!

You can stick a bunch of these to anything, like an ironing board or their inventor, and then whack 'em with a stick. Output goes to drum machine. Great for weird performance art.

The desktop Leslie-style rotating speaker, an idea for which the world is not yet ready.

Although this does not involve equipment as such, certain kinds of music can only be made honestly and lovingly if the composer is in a certain headspace. To that end, I recommend that the game composer limber up his attitude by indulging in regular yoga or massages.

Really. Consider these photos. This is me before a massage:

That guy can write certain kinds of music, suitable for certain kinds of games. But here I am writing out the check for a massage I had just gotten:

Pick who you'd like to be most like. If you think you'd like to write the kind of music that would be written by the guy on the left, avoid massages.

Sidebar: Pipe Lengths for Building a Set of Gang-A-Bong Chimes

Note in Scale (beginning at low A)	Ratio of Frequencies (equal temperament)	Frequency (if low A = 60.00")	Length of Pipe (in inches)	Ratio (ideal temperament)
A	1.0000	220.00	60.00	1.0000
A#	1.0595	233.09	58.29	
B	1.1225	246.95	56.63	1.1250
C	1.1892	261.63	55.02	
C#	1.2600	277.18	53.45	1.2500
D	1.3348	293.66	51.93	1.3333
D#	1.4142	311.13	50.45	
E	1.4983	329.63	49.02	1.5000
F	1.5874	349.23	47.62	
F#	1.6818	369.99	46.27	1.6666
G	1.7818	391.99	44.95	
G#	1.8877	415.31	43.67	1.8750
A	2.0000	440.00	42.43	2.0000
A#		466.18	41.22	
B		493.90	40.05	
C		523.25	39.91	
C#		554.40	37.80	
D		587.31	36.73	
D#		622.25	35.68	
E		659.25	34.66	
F		698.46	33.68	
F#		739.99	32.72	
G		783.99	31.79	
G#		830.59	30.88	
A		880.00	30.00	

The numbers in the Length of Pipe column worked perfectly for 1.5" conduit. I'm tellin' ya, ***marry a mechanical engineer!!!***

Hope For The Future

In Which Perspectives, Techniques, and Meditations Collide

Integration
for
Beginners

What the hell is an Integrator?

"Integrator" is a term I coined at the 1998 Austin Road Trip GDC. I was leading a roundtable discussion on "Alternate Business Models for Multimedia Music," and it was indicated by the discussion that there was a missing job description or software tool in our business, somebody or something that would and could *map linear audio into an interactive context.* I suggested that we call it an *integrator*, and I suggested that it would solve much more than the problems it was aimed at.

What problems is an integrator meant to solve?

Primarily, an integrator is meant to solve the somewhat problematic fact that there is no tool to allow music to be composed for an interactive context.

Where can I get one?

You can't. That's the thing. So you can't really do music for games, can you? Man, that's a hell of a thing.

Well, let me correct myself. *I* can't. I'm an independent audio developer, and the only thing available to me that does what we all want to be able to do is Microsoft's DirectMusic Producer. Sure, there are the John Miles drivers and other systems that can actually play music in games, but they can't allow a musician to author or edit any of the interactive/adaptive reactions that the music might have to gameplay.

Microsoft's DirectMusic Producer can act as an integrator; it's capable of doing tons of wonderful things, and it's free. However, it has *so* many features, and it lets you do *so many* things you never dreamed of that it's hard to find the mere integrator functions in there. How hard? Well, the program is free, and yet I can count on the fingers of one hand the people I know who use it. And the sad fact remains that not one piece of music has been created using DirectMusic Producer that is good enough to make people gawk. So, try it, learn it, and be one of the five who do.... Maybe you can break through the Gawk Barrier and make a career of being The DirectMusic Producer Guy.

Another thing you can do to get the fancy tools.... You can go to work in-house at one of several large companies that have created an integrator.

The most famous system is iMUSE, created by the Stooges at LucasArts, at a cost of a million dollars and ten years. It's really good. I think the only three people who ever used it have left the company.

Buzz Burrowes built one for the Sony PlayStation that I reckon is maybe half as good, but it only took Buzz three weeks to create. I asked him once what the one thing is that would make his life easier, and he said if he had more musicians trained on this system he'd be happy. I got a look at the system, and it seemed pretty intuitive to me. But he couldn't give me the system to get good at because I don't work for Sony, and there aren't enough trustworthy smiles and firm handshakes in Texas to convince the Sony lawyers otherwise.

EA has had a couple of reputedly nice interactive engines over the years. One started at Origin Systems as NIMM, or Neno's Interactive Music Machine. Neno showed it to me once around '93 at my house. I haven't seen it or him since, but I know he's in town and if I see him, I'd probably be more inclined to ask him to jam or get a beer or something.

Sandi Geary has one, over at SingleTrac. She mentioned it, cautiously, at BBQ. Nope, can't have it.

There are a couple of nice tools for mapping sound effects to 3D objects. You can have *them*. There's one called Eagle made by BBQ Brother Keith Charley at Creative Labs. There's one built into the Unreal editor (programmed by Carlo Vogelsang). I saw a most promising one this morning—my friends from Sensaura, Mike Clarke and Peter Clare, showed me GameCODA, which does a great job of putting sound effects into a 3D space, and the tool seems like it will hold great potential once it gets all set up to do music, which as of yet it ain't.

Now, I can see that to the beginner, an integrator or the lack thereof may not seem like something that would amount to much more than a hill of beans or the lack *there*of. But from where I'm standing, the game audio guys are a bunch of tall thin Texans holding empty taco shells, and they've been starved for years. A hill of beans might be precisely what's called for.

Why is it so important to game musicians to have special tools? Aren't there enough music creation tools? Isn't music just, you know, music?

Yes, music is just, you know, music. Brian Schmidt gave us a good benchmark for judging if game music is good. He boiled it down to one word: *intentional*. If the music sounds as though it was intended to go with the game's other elements, if it seems to help, and to intensify, and to fool, and tease, and even anticipate what is going to happen, then it's effective. Pretty much the stuff we expect from our movie scores, right? Right.

But just because we expect a certain level of emotional participation from a film's score does not mean that we can expect it—or that it can even be done—in a game's score. To paraphrase a wonderful 2002 GDC talk by interactive storytelling guru Chris Crawford, music is one thing, but music for an interactive game—sometimes called *music for interactivity*, but more recently referred to as *reactive music*—is quite another. A chasm exists between the two "that equals the difference between bits of memory and CPU cycles, particles and waves, nouns and verbs. FACTS and IDEAS. They are as different as a noun is from a verb."

Michael Land suggested once that to compose reactive music at a **serious level of artistry** is impossible.

Now, that's a **remarkable** statement to hear from the guy whose team **created** iMUSE, generally regarded as the **finest tool** ever built for creating reactive music.

It's roughly equivalent to Wilbur Wright saying that powered flight is **impossible**.

A person who knows him might justifiably be inclined to comment that Michael's standards are very high. But there's certainly more than that.

Music is time-based. Events in a game happen at unpredictable times determined by the player's actions. If a composer wishes for his musical brushstrokes to be tied to events in a game, the timing—the very heart of the music—gets scrambled. Imagine spending a month painting a beautiful portrait on the sand on a beach. Then you put all the sand into a jar and send it to a gallery where the viewers are known to be jar shakers.

I've never actually programmed an integrator. Nonetheless, my relationship with game audio and with Michael are such that I was compelled to dispute the idea, however convincing, that my job couldn't be done. I put my ten-gallon thinking cap on and came up with this: Let's imagine that we lived long ago in a special world, where painting was the only art form. Let's say that somebody had the nerve to suggest creating a painting that would be a different piece, constant or changing, depending on what the viewer did. "Impossible," shout the critics.

And then some smartass shows up with the world's first piece of sculpture. It's interactive; it appears differently depending on where the user stands to view it. Yet it is effective, and reflects the artist's intent, regardless of what the viewer does. Amazing! He's solved the puzzle!

Does an integrator solve that puzzle?

Nope! Making an integrator available is like handing a hammer and chisel to the primitive painters in our previous analogy. Are they going to make statues? Maybe yes, maybe no. Just at this moment, all but Michael seem to realize that they're missing the hammer and chisel, but don't realize they're missing the marble. Maybe they're going to chisel a lot of oatmeal and cats and hills of beans before they find how nicely things work with a block of marble. Maybe they'll never find marble. But they're sure not going to carve any marble any time soon until they get out there and start playing with that hammer and chisel.

In other words, the art itself hasn't evolved yet. Nobody can really imagine, yet, what truly successful interactive music sounds like. They don't know how the music would have to act in order to seem as though it was intentional and to feel as helpful to the game as a good film score is to the film.

However, that will only come with time—and the tools.

So, what problems actually get solved by introducing an integrator?

You'd be surprised. But let's start out with the stuff that you wouldn't be surprised at.

First, a tool would exist to allow game musicians to do their job. That's pretty good right there.

For the first time ever, without worrying that the programmer is going to mess it up or be too busy to try it out, the musician would have control over things like which tunes play where in the game. And in what order. And where they stop. And if they fade. And how loud they are. And looping control. And... and just fantasizing about this is giving me seizures of ecstasy. WOO-HOOOO!!!

It's also fairly obvious after some thought that an integrator tool might make things mighty dandy for the programmer, too, since he would no longer have to be constantly changing his program, installing little picky file name and volume changes for that awful musician.

And as we recall that programmer, and we begin to think back on the issues that face him and keep him from being really excited about audio, a thought occurs to us:

We take out the Great List of Insurmountable Problems... and we say

"Hmmmmm...."

Everything Comes **Together,** or

What Are the Remarkable, **Unexpected** Benefits Brought about by an Integrator? **or** There's a Reason They Call It **"Bookending"**

Okay, the first two problems on the Great List of Insurmountable Problems are

- There is no tool for doing what we do.
- Game audio is not on the creative radar.

As we saw in the previous chapter, having an integrator available would certainly seem to go a long way toward solving those two problems. Let's push our luck, and look at the next insurmountable problem on the list:

- Game producers have come to think in terms of a very few styles of music.

All right, this is a bit of a stretch, but as they say, if you run with your old Fat Friend for a while, you'll always come out ahead. I think an integrator could make this "limited styles" liability into an asset, without harming anything along the way.

Look at it like this: How many first-person shooters with nearly identical techno music were made last year? For the sake of illustration and easy math, let's say 100. How many are getting played? Maybe, oh, three. Let's be generous.

Let's say that each of those games budgeted for one hour of music. A kid plays his favorite game for 40 hours, hears that hour over and over, and by the fourth hour, he's sick of the music.

So, I ask you, once the player reaches the point of total saturation with the music in a game, *what is the harm—what is the absolutely worst possible outcome*—if we take little bits of the very best 50 hours of the music not listened to from the other 97 games, and we feed it more or less indiscriminately into his listening mix?

The worst that can happen is that because of variations in musical style, some of the music might not feel intended for to the game. BUT... the "problem" we're dealing with is just that. The music in these games varies little from game to game, and as long as we are not judgmental, as long as we admit the possibility that maybe it's *nice* to have techno music in a first-person shooter, *now* the similarity of styles works *for* us. The more similar music is from game to game, the better this idea will work. The less similar the styles are, the more fun it is to compose for games, so we don't have a problem in that spot on the GLIP.

Now—stay with me—given that we might want to try to do this bizarre, vaguely communistic musical trading, how do we actually implement it?

Well, first you need an integrator. Then you need to add just a one more little thing....

Make sure that your integrator and playback engine can handle this idea: Playfiles that the integrator calls up can not only be .WAV files and .MID files and .MP3 files, they can also be a filter setting for a search engine. Now, instead of calling TECHNO561AB.WAV, your music engine puts a call out to a disk or a central server on the web that has the other 97 hours of music on it, and your engine says "I'll take anything from the best 50 hours, as chosen by me, the game's producer."

DING!!! Now we're cookin'! Insurmountable Problem is solved—even turned into an advantage. Composers are happy—their music is no longer hated as much. Music that would otherwise go unheard is being heard, now, too. Gamers are happy—their music now takes mercy on them, and no longer repeats like a Fat Man talking about how bad it is that game music repeats. Producers are happy, because the game, being tens of times less sonically torturous, gets loved, played, and talked up by players and roommates alike. Parents stop yelling "Turn that damn thing down." Sales skyrocket.

We're on a roll. Do we dare go further down the GLIP?

• Far more audio gets created for games than is ever heard.

Whoops! Looks like we've solved that one, too, at least for techno and first-person shooters. Can we extend it to other, less favored genres?

Yes, let's go and add another bit to our integrator:

Create a big database/library of music that is sorted according to game criteria. Now your game might call for something a little more exotic, and it can be as mainstream or far-fetched as the producer likes. "High-tension Asian battle music, battle going badly, no music by Joe McDermott, look for keyword 'John Williams.'"

Oh, look, I already *have* one. It's called GamePlayMusic. Look it up on the web at GamePlayMusic.com. Subject of another book. 'Nuff said.

Okay, this is getting sweet. What's left on the GLIP?

- Producers are often unfamiliar with the vocabulary and subtle skills necessary to coax a good performance from a composer.

Click-click-click, and the producer has built a temp track to show the composer what he needs and likes.

- There is no business model for game audio.

Okay, okay, we can get that one, too!

Put a little doo-dad into your playback engine such that a central server is notified whenever a player hears any given tune.

Now all you have to do is get one **good-sized** game developer to realize that making games not **horribly boring** for the first time ever will actually **make** the games better, and thereby bring in much **more money**.

The first company to figure this out can put a small percentage of its newfound billions into a little pool. Then, in proportion to how frequently their music is played, musicians might draw out compensation, and thereby benefit fairly for every minute of joy they bring to the hearts of the gamers around the world.

- There is no standard creative "chain of command" for game audio.

Well, well. As you recall, we've seen everybody try to take command of the direction of the music. It's up to the producers, now the distributors, the publishers, the musician, back to the programmers, the girlfriend, and... wait, there's one person who hasn't ever been given the chance to gain control of game audio in a meaningful, interactive way.

Why don't we get over it, and let the player get involved? I don't mean let him stick in his favorite CD, for crying out loud. What I'm talking about is this:

Let's say the integrator turns out to be really easy to use. Let's say that users can get a hold of one for free or at least cheap. Let's say that we add just one more bit to our integrator.

The integrator's authoring tool outputs a *standardized* file type that contains not only information about the playfiles and when and how they're triggered ("downloadable samples"), but it also contains all necessary information about the "rules of interactivity" that govern the audio's playback (The Fat General Solution).

Well, you might raise an eyebrow to find out that an all-star group was formed at BBQ last year to work on this very problem, for this very reason. It's now called the IXMF working group of the IA-SIG.

The A-Team. The BBQ "Neighbors of the Beast" hold the first meeting to explore creating an IXMF Working Group. Left to right: Science Fair Brother Rick Sanger, Mission Control Linda Law, The Fat Man, All Three Stooges (Pete McConnell, Michael Land, and Clint Bajakian), and XMF's creator Chris Grigg, formerly of the band Negativeland, but now of Beatnik.

Now, after this group finishes its work, various integrators can be built on that foundation, the work of any one can be played back on any of the playback engines that read IXMF files, and what do you have? A new art form. A way that any artist can create sounds that flow through time, depending on various interactions that might come from a user, or a thermostat, or a composer, or a ping-pong paddle.

And for games, what do you have? Empowerment of the player. Choices are available: Do I like the way the music is mapped by the jazz.IXMF file that came with the game? Do I like the Native American.IXMF file? Or am I so into it that I want to make my own file?

Now the enthusiast becomes something new: a GamePlay DJ. A player who *really* cares about game audio, he creates an "audio skin," if you will—a custom mapping of "battle in the kitchen is going badly" to his favorite appropriate tunes. He posts it to the web as a standard IXMF file. "Music skin for *Doom 8*," by r337Hvx0r 69. r337 gets some fans, because people like his skins for *Doom 8*, and they go to him for a skin for *Sim Horse Auction.* R337 gets love and attention and power. The player gets good music. The musician gets money. The flow of control becomes totally different from anything it's ever been before. The World is a Better Place.

NEXT PROBLEM? OH, LOOK. WE'VE SOLVED THEM ALL.

People, if I were you, reading this chapter, I'd be thinking just *exactly* what you're thinking. The Fat Man is nuts. Who does this arrogant son of a bitch think he is? He's brought us this huge list of problems that nobody's even recognized yet, let alone done anything about before. He's convinced us of the awful consequences that these problems have had not only for game musicians and producers, but for developers, gamers, and ultimately the health of the game industry. He's shown how difficult these problems are to deal with, and he's even gone so far as to say that they're "insurmountable." Then this Texas butt-head has the *gall* to suggest a solution to them *all* and then he gets all excited and hopeful, and he seems to expect us to take him seriously, get behind him, and implement these ideas.

Yup, I think The Fat Man is nuts. But then I look at the *facts.* I look at the stories, I look at the luck, I look at the predictions that have come true, and the truly unbelievable miracles that have been handed to me over the course of a long career, I look at who my friends are and how they've helped me, and I look at who is on that IXMF team and what they've done, and I just have to say this:

It might be nuts indeed to think that this book has wound its way around to exposing a possible way to approach solving *every single one* of the insurmountable problems that face game audio. But if you've read this book, and if you believe the parts that are true, you'll certainly know that

stranger things have **happened.**

A
Christmas
Wish

From The Fat Man to the viewers of *Electric Playground*, the television show that features Tommy Tallarico:

The Fat Man

From: The Fat Man
Sent: Friday, May 31, 2003 11:59 PM
To: Victor
Subject: A Christmas Wish

Victor,

Thanks for taking this wish list to Santa. Here's what I would like:

- I would like something really nice to happen to somebody somewhere, and I don't even want to hear about its happening.

Oh, wait, I see I already got that one. Okay, okay, okay....

Here we go...

- I would like the ability to tell when somebody could really benefit from my help.
- I would like the courage to act on that knowledge when I see that they really need that help.

In exchange for this, Santa, I will gladly give to anybody you want the Item of Your Choice from my inventory, oh Santa. Ah! I hear your voice! What are you saying now? What is it that you wish, Santa? Give the Gold Key and the Healing Potion to the Mage-Guardian??? But, Santa, the Mage-Guardian is evil... but... but... yes, your Jolliness. I will obey... I have no choice....

Gotta go now!

Holiday cheer,

The Fat Man

Appendixes

Projects

In chronological order:

Project Ranchero

Goal: Get an agent for Team Fat.

Story: I was watching the movie *The Big Picture* at home on TV. There's a scene in which the protagonist, a young filmmaker, finally quits trying so hard to make it in Hollywood and begins to pay attention to his girlfriend. Suddenly everybody in Hollywood wants to work with him. During that scene, I got a call from the agency that handles John Williams. I let the message machine take the call. A few weeks later, we had a pleasant meeting in Hollywood, after which they "re-thought their interactive strategy," and decided not to go there.

A bit later, a good friend of mine from USC film school set me up a meeting with his agent, CAA, the biggest agency in the world. It was a very successful meeting. A week later, the guy with whom I met was no longer working in the business.

I later got a call asking how much we charge for a gig. I recognized the question from my days as a T-shirt salesman, and asked if the caller wasn't a musician, calling to check out our pricing. Indeed, the caller confessed cheerfully that he was Bob the Agent, investigating the possibility of moving in to the area of getting Hollywood musicians work in the field of games.

Bob became our agent. Over several years, we promoted him from "Bob the Agent" to "Bob the Suspected Horribly Evil Enemy" to "Bob the Friend."

Outcome: Success. We gained a friend, learned a great deal about agents, and did very well for 20 years without one. Did you read the chapter "How To Get Work?"

How's an agent going to top *that*?

Project Chaparral

...was Team Fat's original code name for implementing Fat Labs General MIDI sound card certification. See the chapter on Fat Labs, "General MIDI Rides to Texas."

Outcome: Success. We gained no money, made a lot of friends in the hardware business, kept Kevin employed for several years, and made the world a better sounding place.

Project Cuervo

Goal: Get Team Fat's music onto music-only products so that it could be heard in the future, even after the computer on which the game was meant to run would no longer operate.

Story: After many attempts to work out deals with game companies, we finally found a record company with whom we could work. The record company was game designer Brian Moriarty, who had always wanted to be a record company. Respecting Brian's caution that, if word got around that he was involved in a record company, it might appear that he wasn't serious about games, we kept this fact a secret. Now it can be told, because Brian is no longer in the games business, but rather is working for a planetarium, teaching teenaged kids about the heavens. We secured some financial help from good friends at the now defunct *Music and Computers Magazine*, who saw the CDs as a way to promote one of their regular writers—me.

Brian did an excellent job with the art, layout, and the details of financing, logistics, production, and good taste. On his Haight-Masonic label, Team Fat released three CDs of music for which we had kept the rights to do audio-only releases.

Outcome: Success. The CDs sound good and are fun to listen to. There is no significant money coming in, hence no lawyers have intervened to break up Team Fat's friendships. Yet it's nice to know that every month, a few new people out there are buying and listening to a soundtrack from a ten-year-old game.

Project Saddle-Up

Goal: Get decent cars for Team Fat within a year of declaring the project.

Story: I couldn't bear the fact that Team Fat, my best friends and the greatest team of composers for games, were all driving terrible cars. Kevin had no car at all.

Within a couple of months, a big *7th Guest* check came through, and I was able to get my Mid-Life-Crisis car, a Miata named "Sweet Imagination." Three days later Spanki got a nice Jeep. To celebrate, we all rode in the Jeep to the nearest acceptable restaurant, which was seven miles away, since our offices at the time were in Leander, TX. As we finished our meal, we noticed that the sky had gone suddenly black. One of the biggest droughts in Texas history ended just then with a massive rainstorm, and the top was down on the Miata.

When we got back to the ranch, there was Dave Govett, soaked to the skin, and grinning. He had been bailing water out of my three-day-old car, but to little avail. There were still three or four inches of water gathered in the seats and on the floor. "There's only so much you can do without the keys!" Dave beamed.

It was one of the **funniest** things I'd ever seen.

Later, Kevin came into enough money to get a pretty good car. Being a true Texan, though, he opted instead for an ugly $500 pickup truck and part ownership in a horse.

Dave Govett had a terrible car at the time. To close the door, he literally had to roll down the window, reach outside, grab the handle, lift the door three inches, and then close. When enough money came his way to fix the situation, he did what only Dave Govett would do. He just bought the Miroslav Orchestral sample library instead of a car.

The year was almost over, and the only one left was Joe. The car he had his eye on was a Jaguar, and he had found one for sale cheap. The only problem was, Joe has a family, and his money doesn't go as far as the other guys' does.

My grandmother, the wonderful, charismatic sculptress Doris Appel, had died that year, and I had just then received a check for an inheritance... which was exactly the amount Joe needed for the Jag.

I cleared the idea with Linda, signed the check over to Joe, took him to dinner, told him the whole story of my grandma, and gave him the envelope. Actually, it turned out that I had gotten the numbers wrong, and the amount in the envelope was *half* what was needed to get the Jag. So Joe got a Toyota. But at that restaurant that night, a bunch of women whom Joe swears were models came over to sit with us. They were nervous because one of them was going to get married, and they wanted to talk to some men about it. We had one of the best meals ever, and a week later the restaurant disappeared. Joe isn't sure it was ever really there.

Outcome: Success.

Project Bar-BQ

Goal: To solve the Really Big Problems of Game Audio that were too complicated for me to solve alone, by bringing the smartest people in the field together in a very special way.

Story: Mark Miller, then president of the newly-formed IA-SIG, seemed really mad at me. I asked him if he was mad, and he said, "No." Then again. "No." The third time, he said, "Okay, George, come with me."

He took me out into the hallway and read me the riot act about how I had written an article that called the process of doing things through the IA-SIG "slow." After a long, tense discussion, I realized that there were things I would be good at in this community and things I wouldn't be good at. I was not a technical problem-solver. I was not a political player. In that discussion, I re-envisioned my role in the IA-SIG as less a soldier with a gun and more a flag-bearer. "Over here! The smart guys are thinking *this*! Get behind it, everybody! Follow the guy in the funny hat!!!"

The discussion wound down, good tempers returned, and we were approached by Tom White, to whom we told the whole story.

"Well, what article was it that got you mad, Mark? The one where he says the IA-SIG is slow?"

"Yes," said Mark.

"It *is* slow," said Tom.

Anyway, Spanki and I returned to our hotel that evening and over a drink or two envisioned how a flag-waver might best become a good contributor to an industry. We pictured a party in Texas. We pictured making everybody wear cowboy hats, and no company logos, and setting up a place where they could treat each other like people, not business rivals. We imagined the Roland guys actually getting along with their bitter enemies, the Yamaha guys.

We pictured a place where we could really, really attack the problems of game audio, using a giant amalgamation of brain power. It was the only way, I'd figured, because I'd once been asked what was going to come next in the world of sound cards. It made me mad that I couldn't answer. Then I realized that to answer, a person would have to have expertise in marketing, electronics, sound engineering, composition, and games, and be completely up on what was happening at about five cutting edges of technology. I'd met a lot of very smart people through my work in Fat Labs, but not one of them could I recommend as being able to answer the question. Pooling the brilliance of these people into one big Group Brain was the only way.

So we did it.

The first year, IA-SIG showed up mainly to make sure that The Crazy Fat Man didn't ruin the industry by doing anything too out of hand. But it was such a success—so wonderful, so warm, so productive, and so fun—that it's grown to be something that defies description.

Go to ProjectBarBQ.com, or better yet, ask somebody who's been there.

Outcome: Success.

BBQ left.

BBQ center.

BBQ right.

Project Lariat

Goal: To help follow through on BBQ ideas throughout the year, we would launch a program, group, or organization as an annex to BBQ.

Story: Instead of programs, groups, and organizations, after BBQ 2001, Linda, a.k.a. Mission Control, took on the job of setting up list servers for the BBQ groups and personally scheduling and following up on the progress of BBQ-launched projects throughout the year. Nothing more was needed. The woman works miracles, and has run some of the best, most productive discussions and working groups ever to occur in game audio.

Moreover, she has become friends with the BBQ Brothers, and they've given her a community in which she's a welcome and vital part. She has healed the audio world, and in turn, that world has healed her life, blessed our relationship, and made our home a better place every day of the year.

Outcome: Success.

Project Dumbass

Goal: Make the world a better place by doing The Biggest, Nuttiest Thing Yet Done by The Fat Man and Team Fat.

Story: At the 2002 DICE conference in Las Vegas, I heard that some very cool people were forming G4, The Gaming Network. At that time, they were hungry for programming. I thought, if I could tell a story on TV, what would I tell? How could I contribute? How could I spread good lessons without wrecking my career? I had just secured a contract to write a book for New Riders Publishing, too, and at that same time, I was trying to figure out what the book should be about. As I considered it all, many of the elements of my life came together.

1. Tell the tale of The Fat Man and Team Fat as a non-fictional story treatment. It should have a moral that is true to Team Fat:

> Get over **yourself** and your animosities. **Spread the wise words of the sages**, no matter how ancient.

2. Write the book that the character in that story carries under his arm in the final scene, the one that is intended to spread the wisdom of those sages. But what do the sages have to say in the end? Perhaps the bottom line should be that kindness is the secret of music for games. Or maybe that the truth only travels in pairs of opposites. Or maybe that the hero of the story is not the cowboy or the millionaire, but a wonderful tailor.

3. Celebrate the reunion of Team Fat by writing, as a team, a musical CD inspired by the "About the Author" adventure.

4. Shoot a documentary about the creation of that CD.

5. Use material from that documentary to create a trailer intended to pitch to G4 on a TV series about the continuing adventures of the newly reunited Team Fat aboard their alleged radar-cloaked zeppelin, the *Perseverance*, as they spread the ancient words among the New Breed of Game Producers.

Outcome: The story mentioned in #1 is written, and it appears in this book as "About the Author." Indeed, true to the prophecy, the once shattered Team Fat has gradually grown strong again, and the team has come back together in several new and unforeseen ways as a remarkable working unit. The book foreseen in #2 you hold in your hand. The CD mentioned in #3 has been started, but has not seen much progress. The shooting of the documentary, #4, has begun, but our filmmaker has become busy on another project, one that involves exploring the blessings that music has brought to all cultures throughout time. I yield to the importance of that project. Although they'd be fun, #3 and #4 might not be needed anyway, because of Todd Fluhr, a wonderful artist I met when I saved that company in Kentucky. We became close friends very quickly, and he was kind enough to say that if I ever needed anything, he would try to help me. Years later, he moved on to teach an animation class in California, and that class made a project of creating the desired trailer about Team Fat's adventures, which I expect to receive from him within a few hours.

As far as actually getting a TV series based on Team Fat, I'm not even sure I want that to happen. After all... there's already so much stuff. How would we fit *that* into a movie?

Bruce Sterling's Famous GDC Speech

George says: This brilliant talk was the first keynote at the March 1991 Computer Game Developers Conference in San Jose, CA. It captures the best and most outstanding highlights of a weird community and culture that still exists under all that venture capital.

The Wonderful Power of Storytelling

From the Computer Game Developers Conference, March 1991, San Jose CA
Literary Freeware—Not for Commercial Use

Thank you very much for that introduction. I'd like to thank the conference committee for their hospitality and kindness—all the cola you can drink—and mind you those were genuine Twinkies too, none of those newfangled Twinkies Lite we've been seeing too much of lately.

So anyway, my name is Bruce Sterling and I'm a science fiction writer from Austin, Texas, and I'm here to deliver my speech now, which I like to call "The Wonderful Power of Storytelling." I like to call it that, because I plan to make brutal fun of that whole idea.... In fact, I plan to flame on just any moment now, I plan to cut loose, I plan to wound and scald tonight.... Because why not, right? I mean, we're all adults, we're all professionals here.... I mean, professionals in totally different arts, but you know, I can sense a certain simpatico vibe....

Actually, I feel kind of like a mosasaur talking to dolphins here.... We have a lot in common, we both swim, we both have big sharp teeth, we both eat fish... but you look like a broadminded crowd, so I'm sure you won't mind that I'm basically, like, *reptilian*....

So anyway, you're probably wondering why I'm here tonight, some hopeless dipshit literary author... and when am I going to get started on the virtues and merits of the prose medium and its goddamned wonderful storytelling. I mean, what else can I talk about? What the hell do I know about game design? I don't even know that the most lucrative target machine today is an IBM PC clone with a 16-bit 8088 running at 5 MHz. If you start talking about depth of play versus presentation, I'm just gonna stare at you with blank incomprehension....

I'll tell you straight out why I'm here tonight. Why should I even try to hide the sordid truth from a crowd this perspicacious.... You see, six months ago I was in Austria at this Electronic Arts Festival, which was a situation almost as unlikely as this one, and my wife Nancy and I are sitting there with William Gibson and Deb Gibson feeling very cool and rather jetlagged and crispy around the edges, and in walks this *woman*. Out of nowhere. Like J. Random Attractive Redhead, right. And she sits down with her coffee cup right at our table. And we peer at each other's name badges, right, like, "*Who is this person?*" And her name is Brenda Laurel.

So what do I say? I say to this total stranger, I say. "Hey. Are you the Brenda Laurel who did that book on the art of the computer-human interface? You *are*? Wow, I loved that book." And yes—that's why I'm here as your guest speaker tonight, ladies and gentleman. It's because I can think fast on my feet.

It's because I'm the kind of **author** who likes to hang out in **Adolf Hitler's** hometown with the High **Priestess** of **Weird.**

So ladies and gentlemen, unfortunately I can't successfully pretend that I know much about your profession. I mean actually I do know a *few* things about your profession.... For instance, I was on the far side of the Great Crash of 1984. I was one of the civilian crashees, meaning that was about when I gave up twitch games. That was when I gave up my Atari 800. As to why my Atari 800 became a boat-anchor I'm still not sure.... It was quite mysterious when it happened, it was inexplicable, kind of like the passing of a pestilence or the waning of the moon. If I understood this phenomenon I think I would really have my teeth set into something profound and vitally interesting.... Like, my Atari still works today, I still own it. Why don't I get it out of its box and fire up a few cartridges?

Nothing physical preventing me. Just some subtle but intense sense of revulsion. Almost like a Sartrean nausea. Why this should be attached to a piece of computer hardware is difficult to say.

My favorite games nowadays are *SimCity*, *SimEarth* and *Hidden Agenda*.... I had *Balance of the Planet* on my hard disk, but I was so stricken with guilt by the digitized photo of the author and his spouse that I deleted the game, long before I could figure out how to keep everybody on the Earth from starving... including myself and the author....

I'm especially fond of *SimEarth*. *SimEarth* is like a goldfish bowl. I also have the actual goldfish bowl in the *After Dark* Macintosh screen saver, but its charms waned for me, possibly because the fish don't drive one another into extinction. I theorize that this has something to do with a breakdown of the old dichotomy of twitch games versus adventure, you know, arcade zombie versus Mensa pinhead....

I can dimly see a kind of transcendence in electronic entertainment coming with things like *SimEarth*, they seem like a foreshadowing of what Alvin Toffler called the "intelligent environment"...not "games" in a classic sense, but things that are just going on in the background somewhere, in an attractive and elegant fashion, kind of like a pet cat.... I think this kind of digital toy might really go somewhere interesting.

What computer entertainment lacks most I think is a sense of mystery. It's too left-brain.... I think there might be real promise in game designs that offer less of a sense of nitpicking mastery and control, and more of a sense of sleaziness and bluesiness and smokiness. Not neat tinkertoy puzzles to be decoded, not "treasure-hunts for assets," but creations with some deeper sense of genuine artistic mystery.

I don't know if you've seen the work of a guy called William Latham.... I got his work on a demo reel from Media Magic. I never buy movies on video, but I really live for raw computer-graphic demo reels. This William Latham is a heavy dude.... His tech isn't that impressive, he's got some kind of fairly crude IBM mainframe CAD-CAM program in

Winchester England.... The thing that's most immediately striking about Latham's computer artworks—*ghost sculptures* he calls them—is that the guy really possesses a sense of taste. Fractal art tends to be quite garish. Latham's stuff is very fractally and organic, it's utterly weird, but at the same time it's very accomplished and subtle. There's a quality of ecstasy and dread to it... there's a sense of genuine enchantment there. A lot of computer games are stuffed to the gunwales with enchanters and wizards and so-called magic, but that kind of sci-fi cod mysticism seems very dime-store stuff by comparison with Latham.

I like to imagine the future of computer games as being something like the Steve Jackson Games bust by the Secret Service, only in this case what they were busting wouldn't have been a mistake, it would have been something actually quite seriously inexplicable and possibly even a genuine cultural threat... something of the sort may come from virtual reality. I rather imagine something like an LSD backlash occurring there; something along the lines of: "Hey we have something here that can really seriously boost your imagination!" "Well, Mr. Developer, I'm afraid we here in the Food Drug and Software Administration don't really approve of that." That could happen. I think there are some visionary computer police around who are seriously interested in that prospect, they see it as a very promising growing market for law enforcement, it's kind of their version of a golden vaporware.

I now want to talk some about the differences between your art and my art. My art, science fiction writing, is pretty new as literary arts go, but it labors under the curse of three thousand years of literacy. In some weird sense, I'm in direct competition with Homer and Euripides.

I mean, these guys aren't in the SFWA, but their product is still taking up valuable rack-space. You guys on the other hand get to reinvent everything every time a new platform takes over the field. This is your advantage and your glory. This is also your curse. It's a terrible kind of curse really.

This is a lesson about cultural expression nowadays that has applications to everybody. This is part of living in the Information Society. Here we are in the '90s, we have these tremendous information-handling, information-producing technologies. We think it's really great that we can have groovy unleashed access to all these different kinds of data, we can own books, we can own movies on tape, we can access databanks, we can buy computer games, records, music, art.... A lot of our art aspires to the condition of software, our art today wants to be digital... but our riches of information are in some deep and perverse sense a terrible burden to us.

They're like a cognitive load. As a digitized information-rich culture nowadays, we have to artificially invent ways to forget stuff. I think this is the real explanation for the triumph of compact discs.

Compact discs aren't really all that much better than vinyl records. What they make up in fidelity they lose in groovy cover art. What they gain in playability they lose in presentation. The real advantage of CDs is that they allow you to forget all your vinyl records. You think you love this record collection that you've amassed over the years. But really the sheer choice, the volume, the load of memory there is secretly weighing you down.

But if you buy a CD player you can bundle up all those records and put them in attic boxes without so much guilt. You can pretend that you've stepped up a level, that now you're even more intensely into music than you ever were; but on a practical level what you're really doing is weeding this junk out of your life. By dumping the platform you dump everything attached to the platform and, my God, what a blessed secret relief. What a relief not to remember it, not to think about it, not to have it take up disk-space in your head.

You're never going to play those Alice Cooper albums again, but you can't just throw them away, because you're a culture **nut.**

Computer games are especially vulnerable to this because they live and breathe through the platform. But something rather similar is happening today to fiction as well.... What you see in science fiction nowadays is an amazing tonnage of product that is shuffled through the racks faster and faster.... If a science fiction paperback stays available for six weeks, it's a miracle.

Gross sales are up, but individual sales are off.... Science fiction didn't even used to be *published* in book form, when a science fiction *book* came out it would be in an edition of maybe five hundred copies and these weirdo Golden Age SF fans would cling on to every copy as if it were made of platinum... but now they come out and they are made to vanish as soon as possible. In fact, to a great extent they're designed by their lame hack authors to vanish as soon as possible. They're cliches because cliches are less of a cognitive load. You can write a whole trilogy instead, bet you can't eat just one....

Nevertheless they're still objects in the medium of print. They still have the cultural properties of print.

Culturally speaking, they're capable of lasting a long time because they can be replicated faithfully in new editions that have all the same properties as the old ones. Books are independent of the machineries of book production, the platforms of publishing. Books don't lose anything by being reprinted by a new machine, books are stubborn, they remain the same work of art, they carry the same cultural aura. Books are hard to kill. *Moby Dick* for instance bombed when it came out; it wasn't until the 1920s that *Moby Dick* was proclaimed a masterpiece, and then it got printed in millions. Emily Dickinson didn't even publish books, she just wrote these demented little poems with a quill pen and hid them in her desk, but they still fought their way into the world, and lasted on and on and on. It's damned hard to get rid of Emily Dickinson, she hangs on like a tick in a dog's ear. And everybody who writes from then on, in some sense, has to measure up to this woman. In the art of book writing, the classics are still living competition, they tend to elevate the entire art form by their persistent presence.

When you're a game designer and you're waxing very creative and arty, you tend to measure your work by stuff that doesn't exist yet. Like now we only have floppies, but wait till we get CD-ROM. Like now we can't have compelling life-like artificial characters in the game, but wait till we get AI. Like now we waste time porting games between platforms, but wait till there's just one standard. Like now we're just starting with huge multiplayer games, but wait till the modem networks are a happening thing. And I—as a game designer artiste—it's my solemn duty to carry us that much farther forward toward the beckoning grail....

I've noticed, though, that computer game designers don't look much to the past. All their idealized classics tend to be in reverse, they're projected into the **future**.

For a novelist like myself this is a completely alien paradigm. I can see that it's very seductive, but at the same time I can't help but see that the ground is crumbling under your feet. Every time a platform vanishes it's like a little cultural apocalypse. And I can imagine a time when all the current platforms might vanish, and then what the hell becomes of your entire mode of expression? Alan Kay—he's a heavy guy, Alan Kay—he says that computers may tend to shrink and vanish into the environment, into the walls and into clothing....

Sounds pretty good... but this also means that all the joysticks vanish, all the keyboards, all the repetitive strain injuries.

I'm sure you could play some kind of computer game with very intelligent, very small, invisible computers.... You could have some entertaining way to play with them, or more likely they would have some entertaining way to play with you. But then imagine yourself growing up in that world, being born in that world. You could even be a computer game designer in that world, but how would you study the work of your predecessors?

How would you physically *access* and *experience* the work of your predecessors? There's a razor-sharp cutting edge in this art-form, but what happened to all the stuff that got sculpted?

As I was saying, I don't think it's any accident that this is happening.... I don't think that as a culture today we're very interested in tradition or continuity.

No, we're a lot more interested in being a New Age and a revolutionary epoch, we long to reinvent ourselves every morning before breakfast and never grow old. We have to run really fast to stay in the same place. We've become used to running, if we sit still for a while it makes us feel rather stale and panicky. We'd miss those 60-hour work weeks.

And much the same thing is happening to books today too... not just technically, but ideologically. I don't know if you're familiar at all with literary theory nowadays, with terms like deconstructionism, postmodernism.... Don't worry, I won't talk very long about this.... It can make you go nuts, that stuff, and I don't really recommend it, it's one of those fields of study where it's sometimes wise to treasure your ignorance.... But the thing about the new literary theory that's remarkable, is that it makes a really violent break with the past.... These guys don't take the books of the past on their own cultural terms. When you're deconstructing a book it's like you're psychoanalyzing it; you're not studying it for what it says, you're studying it for the assumptions it makes and the cultural reasons for its assemblage.... What this essentially means is that you're not letting it touch you, you're very careful not to let it get its message through or affect you deeply or emotionally in any way. You're in a position of complete psychological and technical superiority to the book and its author.... This is a way for modern literateurs to handle this vast legacy of the past without actually getting any of the sticky stuff on you. It's like it's dead. It's like the next best thing to not having literature at all. For some reason this feels really good to people nowadays.

But even that isn't enough, you know.... There's talk nowadays in publishing circles about a new device for books, called a ReadMan. Like a Walkman only you carry it in your hands like this.... Has a very nice little graphics screen, theoretically, a high-definition thing, very legible.... And you play your books on it.... You buy the book as a floppy and you stick it in... and just think, wow, you can even have graphics with your book... you can have music, you can have a soundtrack... narration... animated illustrations... multimedia... it can even be interactive.... It's the New Hollywood for Publisher's Row, and at last books can aspire to the exalted condition of movies and cartoons and TV and computer games.... And just think when the ReadMan goes obsolete, all the product that was written for it will be blessedly gone *forever*! Erased from the memory of mankind!

Now I'm the farthest thing from a Luddite, ladies and gentlemen, but when I contemplate this particular technical marvel, my author's blood runs cold.... It's really hard for books to compete with other multisensory media, with modern electronic media, and this is supposed to be the panacea for withering literature, but from the marrow of my bones I say get that fucking little sarcophagus away from me. For God's sake, don't put my books into the Thomas Edison kinetoscope. Don't put me into the stereograph, don't write me on the wax cylinder, don't tie my words and my thoughts to the fate of a piece of hardware, because hardware is even more mortal than I am, and I'm a hell of a lot more mortal than I care to be. Mortality is one good reason why I'm writing books in the first place. For God's sake, don't make me keep pace with the hardware, because I'm not really in the business of keeping pace, I'm really in the business of marking place.

Okay... now, I've sometimes heard it asked why computer game designers are deprived of the full artistic respect they deserve. God knows they work hard enough. They're really talented too, and by any objective measure of intelligence they rank in the top percentiles.... I've heard it said that maybe this problem has something to do with the size of the author's name on the front of the game-box. Or it's lone wolves versus teams, and somehow the proper allotment of fame gets lost in the muddle. One factor I don't see mentioned much is the sheer lack of stability in your medium. A modern movie-maker could probably make a pretty good film with D. W. Griffith's equipment, but you folks are dwelling in the very maelstrom of Permanent Technological Revolution. And that's a really cool place, but man, it's just not a good place to build monuments.

Okay. Now I live in the same world you live in, I hope I've demonstrated that I face a lot of the same problems you face.... Believe me there are few things deader or more obsolescent than a science fiction novel that predicts the future when the future has passed it by. Science fiction is a pop medium and a very obsolescent medium. The fact that written science fiction is a prose medium gives us some advantages, but even science fiction has a hard time wrapping itself in the traditional mantle of literary excellence... we try to do this sometimes, but generally we have to be really drunk first. Still, if you want your work to survive (and some science fiction *does* survive, very successfully) then your work has to capture some quality that lasts. You have to capture something that people will search out over time, even though they have to fight their way upstream against the whole rushing current of obsolescence and innovation.

And I've come up with a strategy for attempting this. Maybe it'll work— probably it won't—but I wouldn't be complaining so loudly if I didn't have some kind of strategy, right? And I think that my strategy may have some relevance to game designers so I presume to offer it tonight.

This is the point at which your normal J. Random Author trots out the doctrine of the Wonderful Power of Storytelling. Yes, storytelling, the old myth around the campfire, blind Homer, universal Shakespeare, this is the art, ladies and gentlemen, that strikes to the eternal core of the human condition.... This is high art and if you don't have it you are dust in the wind.... I can't tell you how many times I have heard this bullshit.... This is known in my field as the "Me and My Pal Bill Shakespeare" argument. Since 1982 I have been at open war with people who promulgate this doctrine in science fiction, and this is the primary reason why my colleagues in SF speak of me in fear and trembling as a big bad cyberpunk... this is the classic doctrine of Humanist SF.

This is what it sounds like when it's translated into your jargon. Listen closely:

> "Movies and plays get much of their power from the resonances between the structural layers. The congruence between the theme, plot, setting, and character layouts generates emotional power. Computer games will never have a significant theme level because the outcome is variable. The lack of theme alone will limit the storytelling power of computer games."

Hard to refute. Impossible to refute. Ladies and gentlemen, to hell with the marvelous power of storytelling. If the audience for science fiction wanted *storytelling*, they wouldn't read goddamned *science fiction*, they'd read *Harpers* and *Redbook* and *Argosy*. The pulp magazine (which is our genre's primary example of a dead platform) used to carry all kinds of storytelling. Western stories. Sailor stories. Prizefighting stories. G-8 and his battle aces. Spicy Garage Tales. Aryan Atrocity Adventures. These things are dead. Stories didn't save them. Stories won't save us. Stories won't save *you*.

This is not the route to follow. We're not into science fiction because it's *good literature*, we're into it because it's *weird*. Follow your weird, ladies and gentlemen. Forget trying to pass for normal. Follow your geekdom. Embrace your nerditude. In the immortal words of Lafcadio Hearn, a geek of incredible obscurity whose work is still in print after a hundred years, "Woo the muse of the odd." A good science fiction story is not a "good story" with a polite whiff of rocket fuel in it. A good science fiction story is something that knows it is science fiction and plunges through that and comes roaring out of the other side. Computer entertainment should not be more like movies, it shouldn't be more like books, it should be more like computer entertainment, SO MUCH MORE LIKE COMPUTER ENTERTAINMENT THAT IT RIPS THROUGH THE LIMITS AND IS SIMPLY IMPOSSIBLE TO IGNORE!

I don't think you can last by meeting the contemporary public taste, the taste from the last quarterly report. I don't think you can last by following demographics and carefully meeting expectations. I don't know many works of art that last that are condescending. I don't know many works of art that last that are deliberately stupid. You may be a geek, you may have geek written all over you; you should aim to be one geek they'll never forget. Don't aim to be civilized. Don't hope that straight people will keep you on as some kind of pet. To hell with them; they put you here. You should fully realize what society has made of you and take a terrible revenge. Get weird. Get way weird. Get dangerously weird. Get sophisticatedly, thoroughly weird and don't do it halfway, put every ounce of horsepower you have behind it. Have the artistic *courage* to recognize your own significance in culture!

Okay. Those of you into SF may recognize the classic rhetoric of cyberpunk here. Alienated punks, picking up computers, menacing society... that's the cliched press story, but they miss the best half. Punk into cyber is interesting, but cyber into punk is way dread. I'm into technical people who attack pop culture. I'm into techies gone dingo, techies gone rogue— not street punks picking up any glittery junk that happens to be within their reach—but disciplined people, intelligent people, people with some technical skills and some rational thought, who can break out of the arid prison that this society sets for its engineers. People who are, and I quote,

That still smells like hope to me...

"dismayed by nearly every aspect of the world situation and aware on some nightmare level that the solutions to our problems will not come from the breed of dimwitted ad-men that we know as politicians." Thanks, Brenda!

You don't get there by acculturating. Don't become a well-rounded person. Well-rounded people are smooth and dull. Become a thoroughly spiky person. Grow spikes from every angle. Stick in their throats like a pufferfish. If you want to woo the muse of the odd, don't read Shakespeare. Read Webster's revenge plays. Don't read Homer and Aristotle. Read Herodotus where he's off talking about Egyptian women having public sex with goats. If you want to read about myth, don't read Joseph Campbell, read about convulsive religion, read about voodoo and the Millerites and the Munster Anabaptists. There are hundreds of years of extremities, there are vast legacies of mutants. There have always been geeks. There will always be geeks. Become the apotheosis of geek. Learn who your spiritual ancestors were. You didn't come here from nowhere. There are reasons why you're here. Learn those reasons. Learn about the stuff that was buried because it was too experimental or embarrassing or inexplicable or uncomfortable or dangerous.

And when it comes to studying art, well, study it, but study it to your own purposes. If you're obsessively weird enough to be a good weird artist, you generally face a basic problem. The basic problem with weird art is not the height of the ceiling above it, it's the pitfalls under its feet. The worst problem is the blundering, the solecisms, the naivete of the poorly socialized, the rotten spots that you skid over because you're too freaked out and not paying proper attention. You may not need much characterization in computer entertainment. Delineating character may not be the point of your work. That's no excuse for making lame characters that are actively bad. You may not need a strong, supple, thoroughly worked-out storyline. That doesn't mean that you can get away with a stupid plot made of chickenwire and spit. Get a full repertoire of tools. Just make sure you use those tools to the proper end. Aim for the heights of professionalism. Just make sure you're a professional *game designer*.

You can get a hell of a lot done in a popular medium just by knocking it off with the bullshit. Popular media always reek of bullshit, they reek of carelessness and self-taught clumsiness and charlatanry. To live outside the aesthetic laws you must be honest. Know what you're doing; don't settle for the way it looks just 'cause everybody's used to it. If you've got a palette of two million colors, then don't settle for designs that look like a cheap four-color comic book. If you're gonna do graphic design, then learn what good graphic design looks like; don't screw around in amateur fashion out of sheer blithe ignorance. If you write a manual, don't write a semiliterate manual with bad grammar and misspellings. If you want to be taken seriously by your fellows and by the populace at large, then don't give people any excuse to dismiss you. Don't be your own worst enemy. Don't put yourself down.

I have my own prejudices, and probably more than my share, but I still think these are pretty good principles. There's nothing magic about 'em. They certainly don't guarantee success, but then there's "success" and then there's success. Working seriously, improving your taste and perception and understanding, knowing what you are and where you came from, not only improves your work in the present, but gives you a chance of influencing the future and links you to the best work of the past. It gives you a place to take a solid stand. I try to live up to these principles; I can't say I've mastered them, but they've certainly gotten me into some interesting places, and among some very interesting company. Like the people here tonight.

I'm not really here by any accident. I'm here because I'm *paying attention*. I 'm here because I know you're significant. I'm here because I know you're important. It was a privilege to be here. Thanks very much for having me, and showing me what you do.

That's all I have to say to you tonight. Thanks very much for listening.

—Bruce Sterling
bruces@well.com

Appendix

What Didn't Happen

Here is what didn't happen Sunday afternoon, five miles south of Austin, driving back from the Project BBQ conference. Actually, the only part that isn't absolutely true is the part in italics. The part in bold just hasn't happened yet.

At the side of IH-35, The Fat Man was lying under his Rolls in seven quarts of blood-red transmission fluid—enough to actually make his souvenir BBQ t-shirt so wet with oil that it would later be thrown out rather than washed. *"I will pray, and God will send an angel to help me,"* thought The Fat Man.

Alex Brandon, head of music for Ion Storm, was helping him pass the time by handing him tools, delving deep into philosophy, and reciting from memory long stretches of movies. Dan Bogard of Sigmatel had his truck with him, and he was getting ready to go shopping for more fluid.

Smokey, the Mobile Mechanic, pulled up on his way to the gun show, and asked if he could be of any help. The Fat Man cheerily discussed what could be wrong, and Smokey agreed, adding some advice about adding two teaspoons of brake fluid if it turned out to be that the seal was broken. "You're pretty hardcore to be workin' on a transmission out here," said Smokey.

"Thanks, Smokey! You go on... have fun at the gun show!" said The Fat Man, thinking *"God will send an angel to help me."*

"There's oil drippin' off your ear," he said and drove off.

An hour or so later, a flatbed tow truck pulled up. "Need help?" asked the driver.

"No," said The Fat Man. "I think I've just about got it. The flywheel had come a bit loose from the fluid drive cover, so I tightened them. And the threads of the torus cover plug were a bit stripped, so I put some Teflon tape on 'em. Dan got me some tape, and some transmission fluid to put back in. *And besides, if I screw up, God will send an angel to help me.* So you can take off, it's okay."

After a while, The Fat Man started the motor and drove off, the transmission working beautifully.

Eventually, The Fat Man died, and went to Heaven, and yelled at God, "Where was that damn angel?"

And God said, "Hey, dipshit, I *sent* you Smokey the mobile mechanic and the guy in the flatbed tow truck!!! I gave you a great bunch of attendees at BBQ, and I blessed it with success, so you'd think you could do anything and would try to fix the transmission yourself, which is, by the way, *very* hardcore. Besides, I sent you Alex Brandon to keep your spirits up, and Dan Bogard to let you know you were leaking in the first place, and to go get you your Teflon tape and tranny fluid. And to top it off, I gave you ten extras of that BBQ shirt by making sure attendance was a bit lower this year! Angels? Dude, you're *lousy* with them."

And The Fat Man agreed.

Thanks, Angels!

—FAT

The Nudie Suit Story

Nudie made the greatest suits in the world. He made Elvis' famous gold lame outfit, which was reputed to have cost $10,000. Nudie would add that $9,500 was profit. He made all of Porter Wagoner's rhinestone suits. He is credited with having invented the rhinestone shirt. He made the light-up suit for the movie *The Electric Horseman*. Tammy Wynette found out she was pregnant with George Jones' child when she noticed her Nudie suit didn't fit. Nudie was, not arguably, the greatest cowboy tailor. He had come from the Old Country and made a name for himself. At his peak, he could be seen driving his huge, handcrafted, horse-trophy-bearing limos through Hollywood, passing out dollar bills to kids. His picture was pasted over George Washington's. A special man, and a real artist. He

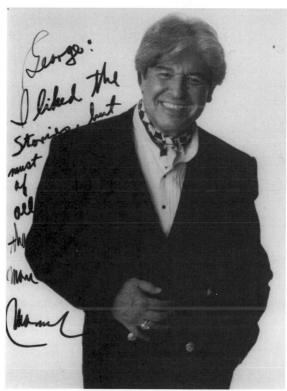

died in 1984 at the age of 81, and his shop closed 10 years after.

In the early '90s, my brother Dave called me from Taos, New Mexico. Dave is the drummer for Asleep at the Wheel, a job which has earned him a small fistful of Grammies. Dave was calling because he had found two Nudie suits in a second-hand clothing store.

Manuel began as Frank Sinatra's tailor.
He was the head tailor under Nudie during
the great age of rhinestone suits, and is
the current king of Nashville fashion.

He whispered into the phone that the owners didn't know what they had. He wanted the "good-looking one," for himself, and I could have the "ugly one" for $250. I told him I didn't care what was on it, what condition it was in, what the pattern was on it, or what size it was, I wanted it. One day, I had a feeling it had arrived. I waited by the mailman's truck until he showed up and handed me the big, brown-wrapped package. When I tried on "The Ugly Suit," which was a perfect fit, I felt wonderful. At last I was where I belonged. I felt, I imagine, the way a transvestite feels when he first tries on a bra.

It was great for my career. All of the pictures of me that are well known were taken in the suit. I wore it to every trade show. After a while, I traded a computer to Dave for "The Good-Looking Suit," but I had to promise that I'd leave it to him in my will. Some folks would say I got pretty famous with the help of those two outfits.

Photo by Teresa "Spanki" Avallone

"The Ugly Suit" is brick red, with about 50 hand-stitched, painted leather silver dollars on it. Each silver dollar is about the size of a pizza or cupcake, and is surrounded with a tightly spaced circle of the finest rhinestones. The dollars on the right side are all stitched tails, and those on the left are heads. It's the best-looking thing I'd ever owned.

"The Good-Looking Suit" is black, with hand-embroidered gold buckets of money dumping out all over it. It's gaudy and elegant. It appears on the cover of Hank Thompson's *Live in Las Vegas* album, which I've heard said was the first live country album. Who knows.

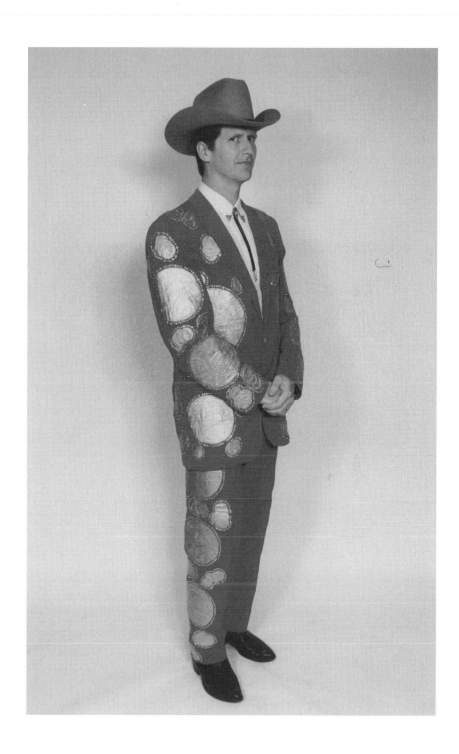

Dave wore the black suit to the Grammies and was the best-dressed guy there. Bonnie Raitt got on the elevator with him and gave him a look. "Heavy suit." "Thanks." At a later Grammy show, Dave ran into Hank Thompson. They talked about the suit as though it were a woman they'd both slept with. "Sure was heavy." "Yup." As Dave was leaving, Hank's wife showed up. Dave thought he heard Hank's wife call after him—something about the suit.

Dominating the fashion scene at the CMA awards with Cledus T. Judd, "the first redneck on the Internet" (cledus.com) and Brother Dave in The Good-Looking Suit.

In *100 Years of Western Wear*, the book about outfits like this, there's a chapter or two about Nudie. A couple of Hank Thompson's suits are shown. Hank is a great Country singer who was one of Nudie's biggest customers (http://www.infocs.com/hank/). Nudies were Hank's trademark. The book says, "If anybody knows the whereabouts of Hank's Gold Nugget Suit, please contact the publisher." I called, got in touch with Hank's manager, and was assured that there was no problem with my owning the suits.

Cousin Ernie

After my first really, really good year in business, I went with my friend Kevin to the Dallas guitar show to buy myself a treat. Maybe a White Falcon guitar. We looked at every guitar in the place, and came back to one very strange one. "Cousin Ernie" (which was its name, for that is what was painted on the pickguard) was a big '58 Gretsch, that much is certain, and as such is worth more than I paid for it. However, there was so much uncertain about it; it was universally known and despised by Gretsch collectors, so I got it for a steal. For one thing, it looks just like a White Falcon,

Cousin Ernie, sitting in with The Propellerheads, the AMD house band, up on the baggage ramp, upon the occasion of closing Austin's Bob Mueller airport.

but its finish was an outrageous gold sparkle. For another thing, there was a little red button next to the other switches. The button did nothing and shouldn't have been there, and the purists didn't like that. What's more, Cousin Ernie is the stage name that Tennessee Ernie Ford used on the *I Love Lucy* show. Nobody has ever shown me pictures of Ford with this guitar, but, in the unofficial opinion of Teisco Del Rey, the great expert on weird guitars, it's too weird not to be real. Who would paint Cousin Ernie on a perfectly good instrument if it weren't for Cousin Ernie? I mean, who would bother to forge something that stupid?

My conversation with the salesman was colorful. I asked him "What's Cousin Ernie's story?" and he told me to sit down. That's a good sign. He said that Mac Yasuda, the famous collector of vintage guitars, had once bought Cousin Ernie for $28,000, but Gretsch wouldn't authenticate that they had made the guitar in-house, so Mac hadn't taken delivery. As for the red button, he swore that it was stock. There was, he said, a picture in some book somewhere of some famous guy with a stock Gretsch Anniversary with that same button.

There is a group of guitar enthusiasts who complain that the Japanese are ruining the world buying up all the "real guitars." It's generally thought that the guitars sit around, collected but unplayed. I have come to believe these enthusiasts are complaining about Mac Yasuda. Mac now also collects Nudie suits. Some folks worry about that.

During what I imagine to be years of disuse, waiting for the collectors to stop arguing, the jack on this poor guitar had fallen into the body, indicating that the thing hadn't been played for a long, long time. I asked the salesman to fish the jack out. I played Cousin Ernie. That was that. I bought Cousin Ernie, for much, much less than the $28K Mac Yasuda had supposedly paid. I pretty much haven't played another guitar since.

One day, a few months later, I decided to explore the vintage guitar store nearest my home. I'd never been in. The owner recognized me. He had a color newspaper picture of me and Cousin Ernie up on the wall. I think I was wearing The Good-Looking Suit in that picture. He was glad I'd come in. He had wanted to get a good look at Cousin Ernie, maybe a photo, and didn't know how to reach me. We talked slowly and appreciatively about guitars for a while. I told him all about Tennessee Ernie Ford and Mac Yasuda. I went home and got the guitar, came back, opened the case—now remember this was, like, a Thursday afternoon—and into the empty store walked a Japanese guy, followed by two guys carrying briefcases.

He pointed at the guitar in the case, and said, very deadpan, "Cousin Ernie. I know this guitar. It's not real."

"You know this guitar?"

"Yes. I once paid $28,000 for this guitar. It's not real. I didn't take delivery." He turned to go.

"Wait! Can I have a card? I might want to get more information on the history of this guitar." He scrawled his name and number on a piece of paper. Mac Yasuda.

"Are you going to the Dallas show this year?"

"No, I've got a guitar I like playing."

"Hmmmm." He left.

"Who was that guy?" asked the store owner. I showed him the piece of paper. "MAC YASUDA?!?!" he screamed, and started wildly flipping off the exit door.

"I wouldn't have **sold** you anything anyway, ya jerk! I don't **NEED** your money!!!"

The Nile Valley

On the way out to the NAMM show in LA in '98, where the rest of this story will take place, I had the good luck to be on a nearly empty plane from Austin to Phoenix. After hauling The Ugly Suit to the airport in a big, heavy Keel case, I was delighted that I might get to sleep, since for the two previous nights I'd been partying hard for business and friendship at the Austin Computer Game Developers' Conference. But the sleeping was not to be, for assigned to the seat across the aisle from me was Awad.

I had seen Awad twice before and each time had a wonderful, though short, conversation with him. He wears white robes, and has three deep scars down each cheek. He sells incense and herbal tea under the brand name Nile Valley (http://nilevalleyherbs.com/). He uses the profits to buy solar power and clean water for the villagers in his homeland on the banks of the Nile. Awad is a Nubian.

My friend Awad Abdelgadir.

We had a wonderful talk, which led to my telling him about a dream I'd had recently. I was in the poor part of town, near some parking lots. There were homeless folks all around. There was money on the ground. I'd pick up a dollar, then a five, then a hundred. It felt pretty good. Then I saw that one guy, one really old guy, was dying. I gave him all my money. It felt *really* good.

Awad said "It's always better to give than to receive." I guess he'd know.

On the next plane, from Phoenix to LA, I was ready to sleep. But I got to talking to the guy next to me, who was into Big Investments and moving money through time and all that cash stuff. He seemed pretty "up." He especially was excited about model trains. When I asked him what motivates him, this is what came out: "I had a rough divorce. My wife set fire to my house, destroying everything I owned. She was convicted of arson, so there was no insurance. She then killed my 14-year-old daughter and herself. That changed my priorities. Now... I have good days and *great* days. That's it."

NAMM. I was There.

I arrived at my hotel room, and found my roommate, Jim Cara, had already arrived. I told him about my having sat next to Awad, thinking he'd love the story. But his airplane story was better—sort of a "Dear Penthouse Forum, I never thought this would happen to me" story. Part of the fun was that Jim, married, acted the perfect gentleman throughout his adventure. So I got really mad at him for beating my story, and that became our running gag. "...and The Forum team is still just a little bit out front—but wait! What's this? Out of nowhere, The Nubians Score!!!"

Every month, the back page of *Music and Computers* magazine (published by Miller-Freeman) features a photo of me in The Ugly Suit, with a few paragraphs of crackpot philosophy, which I narrate in about an hour every month to editor Dave Battino. Dave edits it brilliantly (modest guy, he says he just "takes out the um's"), and the column has gained a bit of a following among computer-oriented musicians. I was at the NAMM show to sign autographs at Miller-Freeman's booth. The slogan for the event was "It ain't over 'til The Fat Man signs." To be recognized, I wore The Ugly Suit. It's interesting to note that the signing event was taking place at the LA Convention Center, the same building in which I had once used the Heimlich maneuver to save the life of a movie producer in front of 300 people, dressed in my "cowboy hero" clothes. (How all those people got in my cowboy hero clothes, I'll never know.)

At the booth, during signing hours, things went slowly. To pass the time, the Miller-Freeman staff and I took to swapping some stories. When my turn came, I opened with the phrase "Amazing things seem to happen to me." I began to tell of opening my guitar case in the little store in Austin. I told how Mac Yasuda had walked up, and how he had said "I once paid $28,000 for that guitar." I was doing my best gruff Japanese accent, which is somewhat thicker than Mac's. At exactly that moment, somebody stopped right in front of me and waved. I looked up. It was Mac Yasuda.

The two or three people who had stayed with me during my story were dumbfounded at this coincidence. I told Mac that I had just been telling a story about him. I even repeated the last line in my awkward "Mac" voice. I don't like to say things about people behind their backs that I wouldn't say to their faces. He touched me on the brick-red, rhinestone-studded sleeve and said only this:

"Hank wants the suits back. I'm seeing him in two weeks."

Horse Trading

I mentioned that I had checked into it, and all I could figure out is that maybe Hank's wife wanted the suits back. For a Hank Museum or something.

Of course, I was a bit stunned. I mean, the suits were my trademark, but they had always been Hank's, too. I'd seen a music video recently of Hank and Junior Brown, which featured a couple of Nudie suits. I told this to Mac. He said "He gave them all away. He doesn't know where they are."

I said maybe we could work something out. A trade. "Mac. You're a famous horse-trader. You could work this out for us."

His reply? "Horses. Yes. White ones. I have five of them. Are you going to the Dallas guitar show this year?"

I went home that evening. I slept, but not a lot. Around four in the morning, I was thinking about Awad and that dream about giving the money to the old man. Suddenly, I felt great. Come to think of it, I've felt great ever since.

The next day, I took the suit to Mac and told him to give it to Hank.

Turns out Mac's a pretty nice guy. He's a country singer, performs at the Grand Ol' Opry, and loves Hank Williams. He wears Nudie suits when he plays out. He gave me a CD of him singing Hank Williams tunes. On the CD, he plays Hank's actual guitars. Sounds good. Looks *really* good.

When I went back to the hotel, I told Jim Cara what I had done. He said I was like Jesus or something. Then he figured maybe that I had an angle and I'd get some kind of reward. Grin. Wink. I told him that the only reason I had done it was to kick the Forum Team's butt.

I had a run of great luck. Our hotel room had been paid for, I guess by Miller-Freeman. I tried to take a cab across town that evening, but the hotel insisted I take a limo. I had a dinner appointment with Dana, whose picture appears in the next chapter. I got to tell her the whole story.

The next day, the hotel's ATM was broken. I checked out, and there was a $9 refund, which they gave me in cash—exactly what I needed to make it to the airport and still have some money left for lunch. I took a cab to the airport. The cab driver, Amat or Ajak—sadly I only remember that he was Armenian and his name was only two letters from "Awad"—asked what I was carrying in the big Keel case. I told my story. He said I was like Elvis.

Amat, the cab driver, had been interested in playing guitar when he was in high school. His dad had said that if he got good grades, he could have a guitar. He couldn't get the grades. My parents and I had made the same deal, and I got my first good guitar that way. I said, "Amat, I'm you. You're me."

Amat and I stopped for lunch at In-n-Out Burgers on the way to the airport, and he paid for my lunch. I told him *he* was like Elvis.

—FAT 2/15/98

As of this writing, my favorite music is Mac Yasuda's

Tribute to Hank Williams.

Sound Man Saves Picture, or What It Takes to Get Work in Show Business

Photo by Teresa "Spanki" Avallone

This happened to me at the E3 Electronic Entertainment Expo Conference in LA, 1996. I don't claim any credit for having been brilliant or heroic. Some generally playful force, like Spirits, Angels, a Higher Power, or what-not, seems to have set me up. Actually, that sort of thing seems to be happening quite a bit lately. The same may be happening to you. Or not. You have to decide for yourself. But this is my story, I'm stickin' to it, and every word is true,

so help me *Texas*.

Because of the E3 show, I had to miss my son Glen's gymnastics show. Glen was five and a half. I called him from the big, well-lit glass-covered cafeteria area of the LA Convention Center. I was wearing a rhinestone cowboy suit covered with gold embroidered buckets of money, made by the great Nudie, Elvis' late and legendary tailor. There were about 200 potential clients who could see me from where I was standing. I told Glen I was sorry I missed his show.

"That's okay, Daddy. Here, I'll do some gymnastics for you right now." He put the phone down for awhile, picked it back up and said "How was that, Daddy?"

"Wow, Glen. That was great!"

"Now you do some," said Glen.

"Okay, Son. I'll fly around the room."

So I put the phone down, yelled real loud, got some looks, of course, from the room full of potential clients, but what the hell. "How was that?"

"Great! You did it! You flew around the room!"

The next morning, I got a call at 8:30 from Bob, my agent. "I got you an interview with the biggest magazine of its kind in Europe. I think what these guys want is a sort of American Hero. They're nuts for that sort of stuff over there."

"Okay, Bob. American Hero. Got it. Thanks."

I climbed out of bed and went over to the show to meet with some chip manufacturers in the Compass Cafe, the same cafeteria area from which I called Glen. I sat in a part of the room that was a little more out in the open, so about 300 potential clients could see me. I was wearing a U.S. Cavalry outfit that had been "Indianized." In other words, it had not only gold buttons and insignia, but intricate beadwork, suede fringe on the shoulders, the works. Had the white cowboy hat too, of course. 10x. Only the best.

Now the chip manufacturers had heard all The Fat Man stories, but they hadn't quite bought into the legend yet. I'll refer to their spokesman as "Chip." Chip had heard that some other chip manufacturers weren't able to sell non-Fat-certified chips in Taiwan to sound card manufacturers. "Don't even think about it" is what the Taiwanese told the salesmen, in one case.

But I think Chip was not fully believing the stories. I think he thought them exaggerated. Maybe I was reading too much into it, but I thought he rolled his eyes a bit when he said, "Oh, yeah, we've heard all about Taiwan and everything."

Other than that, the meeting was going very well, and I thought they had a product that was worth endorsing. I hoped they would understand the value of the Fat Seal as a sign of integrity, and consider associating my name with their product.

It had been hard during the meeting to get down to brass tacks. A lot of folks who knew me were coming by, most of them with some business matters to discuss. I thought this might lend me an air of credibility. Or was it just annoying?

Just then, along came Bob the Agent, wearing Hollywood sunglasses, an FBI hat, and a huge Fat Seal across his shirt. I flagged him down to meet the chip guys. He then launched into an incredible pitch... but maybe not exactly the right one for a skeptical audience. How could he know?

"I've gotta tell ya about this guy. Have you got two minutes, because I'm really gonna embarrass him," he began. "I mean, I work with Alan Sylvestri, James Horner, blah, blah, blah, and all that sort of good stuff, and all those guys."

"And I gotta tell you, you ask the average moviegoer who wrote the music to the movie they just came out of, and maybe one guy knows John Williams, and that's it. But you ask game players about THE FAT MAN, well, that's different. I mean to tell ya, they ALL know about him. I mean, they buy games because of his music. Nobody goes to a movie just for the soundtrack. Not even for John Williams. Have I embarrassed you, George?"

And off he went. I thought it was a swell pitch, but there was that little roll of Chip's eyes again. Damn.

The next thing that happened is that a guy about 12 feet from me threw up a little bit, then stood bolt upright, eyes straight ahead and bugged out, clutching his chest, and began wheezing very loudly. I heard a voice, whose source I have yet to track down, say, "George, do you know Heimlich?" I got up and asked the guy if he was choking, but he didn't seem to notice me. So I got behind him and popped him in the chest. Out flew a piece of chicken the size of a PC mouse. Chip said "You got it, George."

I asked the choking guy if he needed another squeeze, but he signaled weakly that he was okay. I helped him sit down. I stayed with him for a minute, then, when it seemed he was okay, I went back to my table.

There was silence in the room, which is unusual for these trade shows. I tried to be cool and pick up the conversation where we left off. "Now, we were talking about doing something more than the standard endorsement...." But it was hard not to grin.

The chip manufacturers, whose jaws were open to the floor, said "Oh, my God, George. That was incredible! You just saved that guy's life. Do you realize what this means? Now we have to go back to our company and say, 'We gotta work with this guy... bigger than James Horner... can't sell chips in Taiwan without him... and he saves peoples' lives!'"

Some of brother Rick Sanger's medals, including one for saving a guy's life, presented to him by President Clinton. Park Ranger Rick jumped into an icy stream and risked his own life to save a mere doctor. This stands in stark contrast to George's adventure, in which he managed to avoid any inconvenience whatsoever and in the process saved an entire movie producer.

As the sound came back to the room, I tried to get back to business, but people started to come by. "Fat Man! Do you have a card?" (Yes, but I'm out of silver bullets....) "Are you The Fat Man? That was amazing." "I was eating with some Japanese guys, and all I can think of is that they'll be telling their friends, 'I went to America and saw a cowboy save a guy's life!'"[1]

---

[1] Scott Berfield, a.k.a. Info@xbox.com, wrote: "LOL, that version fits pretty much with what I saw. I was at the next table from the choking guy meeting with a Japanese investor. I saw the guy start to choke and started to stand up to do the Heimlich, when in you come and took care of it (faster reflexes I guess). Anyway, all I could think of was this little Japanese businessman going home and telling his kids he saw a cowboy save a guy's life at E3. Still one of my favorite stories."

We actually did get some pretty good business talked about. After about 20 minutes, the floor had been mopped, and the choking guy recovered enough to come over. He said, "I know you're not expecting any kind of repayment, but I'm a movie producer."

He handed me his card. I didn't think anybody would make a card like this one. It said, "Simon Dubinsky: Movie Producer."

He went on, "When you get your script written, send it to me. I'll read it."

I said, "That's great! I don't write, but I do music for those things."

Walking away, he said, "That doesn't matter! You can't have a movie without a script!"

He kept walking, saying "Thanks again."

"Thanks for the opportunity."

At that, the guy behind us piped up. "That's the funniest thing I've ever heard. Do you realize what that says about how hard it is to get your script read in this town? I have a friend who's a reporter. Do you mind if I tell him this story?"

Well why not? That's the kind of day I was having.

Bob came back around to the table. I caught him up on the whole story. I told him that I had been sitting around trying to think of ways to further my career when this annoying guy started making a lot of noise. I told him I had been thinking "Think. Think. Career. What's all that noise? Oh, another damn movie producer choking at E3. Now, what was I thinking?

Oh, yeah. Bob said something... American Hero! That's it! Hey, I know what to do! So I saved his life. I mean, what the hell. There's all these potential clients around. I'm dressed for it. And if it had happened yesterday and I'd been wearing the rhinestone suit—well, who knows? It might have gotten messy."

The first person I got to tell the story to was Dana. Beat that.

Bob looked at me admiringly:

"You know, George. The only thing I expect from you now is for you to *fly* around this room."

PS: At E3 1999, in the same room, I told this story to some friends. I told them that it changed my life. "Things like this happen fairly frequently to me now, and when they do, I'm no longer surprised, just delighted. And I tend to say 'thanks' out loud. Or when a bird flies by in front of me, I wave to it."

At this, Michael Land, who was sitting across the table from me, got an awestruck look. "Uh, excuse me, George, but immediately after you said that, a bird flew by right in front of me."

Indoors.

Curriculum Vitae

"Put that in your pipe and smoke it!"

—Bernard Appel, Professor of Dermatology at Tufts University Medical School and Chief of the Dermatology Department at Boston City Hospital, upon the occasion of handing his Curriculum Vitae to grandson George A. Sanger

Education

Graduated Occidental College with AB in Music, heavy background in Physics.

Did graduate work at the University of Southern California Film School. Studied film writing and production.

Studied Film and TV production at Loyola Marymount.

Took classes in Recording Engineering at UCLA.

Recording

Produced and engineered *Sound Effects of the Future* for Warner Bros. (This was not released. It was meant to be the first sound effects CD ever.)

Engineered first digital aerobics album, *On The Move*.

Engineered projects for Discovery Records, *People Magazine* (on HBO), Cannon Films, Metavision, Mattel, and others.

Staff Engineer at Digital Sound Recording, LA.

Owned and operated Reel Mobile recording studio.

Digital Engineering

Projects for Warner/Elektra/Atlantic (WEA), MCA, and Geffen Records, including albums by Elton John, Peter Gabriel, Michael Franks, Joni Mitchell, and Ray Price.

Producing and Composing

Produced and recorded music for films by World Research, Inc. and Tropus films, award winning films by Hispanic Television Network and Banning Lary, and many others.

Computer Program Design

Designed VALPAINT, a color graphics program, for Rising Star Industries.

Interface design consultant for the Gigasampler, a software sampler created by Nemesys.

Interface design consultant for iMUSE, an audio integrator program by LucasArts.

COMPUTER TOOLS FOR THE MUSICIAN, PART II

RECORDING MUSIC AND SOUND WITH CON BRIO PRODUCTIONS

(Left to right): George Sanger, engineer/producer; Brian Horner, synthesizer programmer/producer; Bob Randles, MuSync creator and operator; Alan Danziger, computer programmer

by Roy Brown

Con Brio Productions is a one-stop music and sound effects production company specializing in Soundtrack accompaniment for video and film. Founders Brian Horner, Adam Holzman and George Sanger have assembled an impressive array of advanced equipment based at Digital Sound, a 24 track Los Angeles recording studio.

The studio houses over a dozen analog and digital synthesizers,

back as a trigger for a Wavemakers synthesizer, which played the unaccented notes. At the same time, the clicks were run through a Kepex, with the oscillator tones at the key, and the output to another synthesizer module, which played the accented notes. The taped pulses played the synthesizer in real time while we recorded. We took the resulting sound and ran it to the live room, and then miked it with a coincident stereo pair of AKG 414's for enhancement.

"The Con Brio ADS 200 digital synthesizer records the actual

compatible with each other and often patched together to produce special, unique effects. Their applications are not always predictable, explains engineer George Sanger. "Once we were required to record a part that was too fast for the performer to play. The part was all rapid sixteenth notes, accented in a non-repeating pattern. It had to be extremely precise, so we set up a sequencer to multiply the click track from quarters to sixteenths. We recorded a tone under the beats we wanted to accent, running at half speed. The clicks were then played

JANUARY 1983   95

Writing and Illustrating

Wrote "Computer Tools for the Musician, Part II—Recording Music and Sound with Con Brio Productions" *The Mix*, January, 1983.

Wrote "Sounds for the Eye: Getting the Most Out of Visuals (and Budget) Through Sound" *Millimeter,* May, 1983.

Wrote and illustrated *Sheep Thrills* cartoon book.

Created cartoons for Fostex Corp. of America, *Follies* magazine, and *The Occidental.*

Wrote "Lunch with The Fat Man" column for *Texas Beat* (formerly *Glitch News*).

Wrote "Ride the Wired Surf" back-page column for *Music and Computers* magazine.

Camera and Video Production

Co-produced *Trashdance* for Tropus Films (shown on HBO). Cameraman for Tropus films and WEA projects. Album cover photos for Bent Records.

Spare Career

Professional guitarist/singer for eight years.

The Fat Man's Game-Related Innovations

First General MIDI score for a game (*The 7ᵗʰ Guest*).

First soundtrack CD that shipped with the game (*The 7ᵗʰ Guest*).

First game music considered a work of art (*Loom*).

First game featuring a live band recorded to MIDI (*Putt Putt Goes to the Moon*).

First game music considered a selling point of the game (*Wing Commander*).

First context-sensitive soundtrack to attract industry attention (*Wing Commander*).

First attract screen audio for a slot machine.

Established Project BBQ, the most prestigious conference for sound on computers.

Established Fat Labs, responsible for helping to make General MIDI a useful standard for audio playback on computers.

Built the Fat Sound System for slot machines.

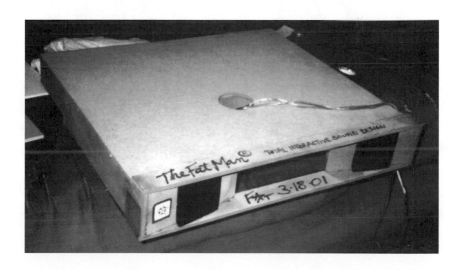

A Partial List of Games to which The Fat Man and Team Fat Contributed

A Partial List of Games to Which The Fat Man and Team Fat Contributed

Release Name	My Role	Other Composers	Software Developer	Publisher	Released?	System
Thin Ice	Composed	Warhol	Mattel Electronics	Mattel Electronics	Yes	Intellivision
Capture the Flag	Composed		Paul Edelstien	Sirius Software	Yes	Atari 800
Dick Tracy	Composed		Realtime	Bandai/ Disney	Yes	NES
Gameboy Dick Tracy	Composed		Realtime	Bandai/ Disney	Yes	Gameboy
Swords and Serpents	Composed		Interplay	Acclaim	Yes	NES
Loom	Arranged MT-32	Tchaikovsky	LucasArts	LucasArts	Yes	IBM
Death Knights of Krynn	Supervised	Govett	SSI	SSI	Yes	IBM
Defenders of Dynatron City	Composed		LucasArts	LucasArts	Yes	NES

Release Name	My Role	Other Composers	Software Developer	Publisher	Released?	System
LHX Attack Chopper	Composed		Electronic Arts	Electronic Arts	Yes	IBM
Maniac Mansion (SNES)	Composed/ supervised	Govett, Hay	Realtime	Jaleco/ LucasArts	Yes	NES
Omar Sharif on Bridge	Arranged adlib	Deenen	Interplay	Interplay	Yes	IBM
Buck Rogers II	Produced	Govett	SSI	SSI	Yes	IBM
Word Hai	Supervised	Bach (Kerkhoff)	Realtime	Meldac	Yes	NES
Cartel	Composed		Access	Access	No	IBM
Battle Chess II	Arranged MT-32	Deenen	Interplay		Yes	IBM
Frogfoot	Composed		Electronic Arts	Electronic Arts	Yes	IBM
Might and Magic III	Produced	Fredrics	New World	New World	Yes	IBM

Release Name	My Role	Other Composers	Software Developer	Publisher	Released?	System
Planet's Edge	Produced	Fredrics	New World	New World	Yes	IBM
Gameboy Double Trouble Ramp	Composed	Hubbard, Govett	Electronic Arts	Electronic Arts	Yes	Gameboy
Total Recall	Composed/ supervised	Govett, Warhol	Interplay	Acclaim	Yes	NES
Track Meet	Composed/ produced	Frantz	Interplay	Interplay	Yes	Gameboy
Heroes of the 357th	Composed		Midnight	Electronic Arts	Yes	IBM
Q Bert (Gameboy)	Composed		Jaleco	Jaleco	Yes	Gameboy
Rocketeer (SNES)	Composed		IGS	Disney	Yes	SNES
Star Trek III	Produced/ arranged/ SFX	Rick Jackson	Interplay	Interplay	Yes	IBM, NES
Lexi-Cross	Composed/ produced	Frantz	Platinumware	Interplay	Yes	IBM
Rules of Engagement	Produced	Govett	Omnitrend	Mindcraft	Yes	IBM
Tony LaRussa Baseball II	Produced	Govett	Beyond Software	Stormfront Studios	Yes	IBM
Chuck Yeager's Air Combat	Supervised	Frantz	Electronic Arts	Electronic Arts	Yes	IBM
Super Pro Pool & Billiards	Produced	Martin	Realtime	INTV	Yes	Intellivision
Monster Truck Rally	Composed		INTV	INTV	Yes	NES
Pools of Darkness	Produced	Govett	SSI	SSI	Yes	IBM
Shadow Sourcerer	Produced	Govett	SSI	SSI	Yes	IBM
The Adventures of Rad Gravity	Composed		Activision	Activision	Yes	NES
Home Alone (NES)	Composed		Bethesda	THQ	Yes	NES

Release Name	My Role	Other Composers	Software Developer	Publisher	Released?	System
RPM	Composed		Interplay	Interplay	Yes	SNES
Marvin the Moose	Produced	McDermott	John Ratcl	Milliken Publishing	Yes	IBM
Spellcraft	Arranged	Beethoven	Tsunami	ASCII	Yes	IBM
Wings 2: Aces High	Produced	Govett, McDermott, Phelan	Acme International	Namco Hometek	Yes	SNES
Magic Candle II	Composed		Mindcraft	Mindcraft	Yes	IBM
NBA Basketball	Produced	McDermott	Sculptured	Tecmo	Yes	SNES, NES
Rocketeer (NES)	Composed	Hayes	Realtime	Bandai/Disney	Yes	NES
The Secret Codes of Cypher: O	Composed		Tanager	Tanager	Yes	IBM
Mario Teaches Typing	Produced arrangements	Govett	Interplay	Interplay	Yes	IBM
Wing Commander	Produced/ composed	Govett	Origin	EA (Origin)	Yes	IBM
Savage Empire	Composed		Origin	EA (Origin)	Yes	IBM
Funhouse	Composed		Realtime	Hi Tech/Wa	Yes	NES
MicroLeague Baseball	Produced some sound effects		MicroLeague Sports Associaion	MicroLeague Sports Associaion	Yes	IBM
Hong Kong Mah Jong	Produced	Govett	9 Dragons	Electronic Arts	Yes	IBM
Martian Dreams	Composed	Hollingshead	Origin	EA (Origin)	Yes	IBM
Castles	Produced	Govett	QuickSilver Software	Interplay	Yes	IBM
Mutanoid Word Challenge	Produced	Govett	Legacy	Legacy	Yes	IBM
Mutanoid Math Challenge	Produced	Govett	Legacy	Legacy	Yes	IBM
Wing Commander II	Composed	Origin Staff	Origin	EA (Origin)	Yes	IBM

Release Name	My Role	Other Composers	Software Developer	Publisher	Released?	System
Castles II	Produced title	Govett	Interplay	Interplay	Yes	IBM
Ultima: Runes of Virtue	Composed	'Manda Dee	Origin	EA (Origin)	Yes	Gameboy
Star Trek: 25th Anniversary	Produced/ arranged/SFX	Govett	Interplay	Interplay	Yes	IBM, NES
Berenstain Bears Learn at Home	Produced	McDermott	Compton's	Compton's	Yes	IBM
Ultima Underworld	Produced/ composed	Govett	Blue Sky	EA (Origin)	Yes	IBM
General MIDI Tones for Yamaha	Produced/ composed	Phelan	Yamaha	Yamaha	Yes	IBM
Faceball 2000 (SNES)	Produced/SFX	McDermott	Xanth	Bullet-Pro	Yes	SNES
The 7th Guest	Composed		Trilobyte	Virgin	Yes	IBM
Q Bert 3 (SNES)	Produced	McDermott	Realtime	NTVIC	Yes	SNES
SEAL Team	Produced/ SFX	Govett	Electronic Arts	Electronic Arts	Yes	IBM
Tony LaRussa's Ultimate Baseball	Composed		Beyond Sofware	SSI	Yes	IBM
Son of M.U.L.E.	Produced	Govett	Danny Bunt	Electronic Arts	No	Sega
SSN-21 Seawolf	Composed/ SFX		John Ratcl	Electronic Arts	Yes	IBM
Zombies Ate My Neighbors	Produced	McDermott	LucasArts	Konami	Yes	SNES
IndyCar Racing	Produced	McDermott	Papyrus	Virgin	Yes	IBM
Putt Putt Goes to the Moon	Composed		Humongous	Electronic Arts	Yes	IBM, Mac
Windows Sound System	Produced/ composed	Govett, Phelan	Microsoft	Microsoft	Yes	IBM
The 7th Guest Part 2: The 11th Hour	Composed		Trilobyte	Virgin	Yes	IBM

Release Name	My Role	Other Composers	Software Developer	Publisher	Released?	System
Battlecruiser 3000 AD	Produced, SFX	Govett, Holzman	3000 AD	Interplay	Yes	IBM
Socks Rocks the House	Produced	Govett	Realtime	Realtime	Yes	SNES
Master of Magic	Produced	Govett	SimTex	MicroProse	Yes	IBM
Master of Orion	Produced	Govett	SimTex	MicroProse	Yes	IBM
Star Trek: Judgement Rites	Produced/ arranged/SFX	Govett	Interplay	Interplay	Yes	IBM, NES
Invaders From Glixer: Rescue	Produced	Phelan	Compton's	Compton's	Yes	IBM
NASCAR Racing	Produced	McDermott	Papyrus	Virgin	Yes	IBM
US Navy Fighters	Produced/ SFX	Govett, Holzman	Electronic Arts	Electronic Arts	Yes	IBM
Freddi Fish	Composed		Humongous	Electronic Arts	Yes	IBM
Mech Wars	Produced	Govett	SimTex		No	IBM
Welcome to Bear Country	Produced		Compton's		No	IBM
1830	Produced	Govett	SimTex	New World	Yes	IBM
Junior's Encyclopedia	Composed		Humongous	Electronic Arts	Yes	IBM
Putt Putt Saves the Zoo	Produced/ composed	Govett, Phelan, McDermott	Humongous	Electronic Arts	Yes	IBM
Zhadnost: The Peoples' Party	Produced/ Composed	Team Fat	3DO	3DO	Yes	3DO
This Means War	Produced/ composed	Govett, Phelan, McDermott	Starjammer	MicroProse	Yes	IBM
Marine Fighters	Produced	Govett	Electronic Arts	Electronic Arts	Yes	IBM
Shannara	Produced/ composed	Govett, Phelan, McDermott	FAR Productions	Legend Entertainment	Yes	IBM

Release Name	My Role	Other Composers	Software Developer	Publisher	Released?	System
ATF	Produced/ composed/ SFX	Govett, Phelan, McDermott	Electronic Arts	Electronic Arts	Yes	IBM
Battle Arena Toshinden (PC)	Arranged GM	Govett, Phelan, McDermott	Digital Dialect	Playmates Interactive Entertainment	Yes	IBM
USNF Platinum	Produced/ composed/ SFX	Govett, Phelan, McDermott	Electronic Arts	Electronic Arts	Yes	IBM
The Incredible Shrinking Character	Composed and Produced title music	McDermott	'Go Go		No	IBM
Azaria	Produced	Govett, Phelan, McDermott	Singularity		No	IBM
No Man's Earth	Produced/ composed		Interworld		No	IBM
Furcadia	Produced music, sound effects	Asikainen	Dragon's Eye Productions	Dragon's Eye Productions	Yes	Network
NATO Fighters	Produced music, sound effects	Govett, Phelan, McDermott, Holzman	Electronic Arts	Electronic Arts	Yes	IBM
Skeletons	USNF tune in it	Unknown			No	Movie
Marry Me or Die	Composed first tune (HockaLoog)		Unknown		No	Movie
Microsoft Network	Produced	Govett, Phelan, McDermott	Microsoft	Microsoft	Unknown	IBM
Dawn of War	Produced	Govett, Phelan, McDermott	Illusion Machines	Virgin	No	IBM, Mac, CDI
WarSport	Produced	Govett, Phelan, McDermott	TimeSink	TimeSink/M	Yes	Network
Qwxyz	Don't remember		Jerry Wong	JW Associates	Yes	IBM

Release Name	My Role	Other Composers	Software Developer	Publisher	Released?	System
Shrewd Move	Produced	Govett, Phelan	The Shrewd Move Games Association	The Shrewd Move Games Association	Yes	IBM
Flabby Rode	Produced, composed, performed	Phelan, McDermott, Govett	Team Fat	Haight Masonic Laboratories	Yes	CD
7/11	Produced, composed, performed	Phelan, McDermott, Govett	Team Fat	Haight Masonic Laboratories	Yes	CD
SURF.COM	Produced, composed, performed	Phelan, McDermott, Govett	Team Fat	Haight Masonic Laboratories	Yes	CD
Unless	Music and Sound effects; voice and camera acting	Phelan, McDermott, Govett	TimeSink		No	IBM, Mac, CDI
Balkan Cauldron	Produced music and sound effects	Govett, McDermott	Confidential	Confidential	Yes	IBM
Tanarus	Arranged	Govett	Sony Online Entertainment	Sony Online Entertainment	Yes	IBM
Hotz Trax II	Composed		Jimmy Hotz	Jimmy Hotz	Yes	IBM
Korean Nightmare	Produced	McDermott	Confidential	Confidential	Yes	IBM
Cyberstrike: The Clan Wars	Composed/ produced	McDermott	Simutronic		No	IBM
Aibo, the Robot Pet	SFX for behavior program	Joe	Sony	Sony	Yes	Aibo
Intellivision Lives	Composed	Others	Intellivision	Intellivision	Yes	IBM
Jungle Legend	SFX	Carl Leon	Valu-Soft		No	IBM
Clue Chronicles: Fatal Illusion	Composed		Hasbro	Hasbro	Yes	IBM
Pajama Sam IV: You Are What You Eat	Composed	McDermott	Humongous	Infogrames	Yes	IBM
Castle Wolfenstein	Sound engine consulting		ID	Muse Software	Yes	IBM

Release Name	My Role	Other Composers	Software Developer	Publisher	Released?	System
Sports Squad.com	Composed		Ron Gilbert/ Hulabee	Hulabee	Unknown	Internet
Shadowbane	SFX	Others	Wolfpack		No	IBM
Dmania	SFX		Zform		No	IBM
Tux Racer	SFX		Sunspire Studios	Sunspire Studios	Yes	IBM
Zform Poker	SFX		Zform	Zform	Yes	IBM
Josh's World	Composed	Others	MRI	MRI	Yes	IBM
Worth the Wait: Teen Sex and the Law	Voice talent		Ellen Guon Beeman	Scott & White Sex Education Program	Yes	IBM
Monsters, Inc.: Mike's Big Adventure	Composed		Hulabee	Disney	Yes	IBM
SpongeBob SquarePants: Revenge of the Flying Dutchman	SFX/ voice talent	Oldziey	BigSky	THQ/ Nickelodeon	Yes	PSII/ Gamecube
Dransik	SFX	Phelan	Asylumsoft	Asylumsoft	Yes	IBM
Crown Jewels	Sound design and music composition		Multimedia Games	Multimedia Games	Yes	Casino console game
Diamond Crown Jewels	Sound design and music composition		Multimedia Games	Multimedia Games	Yes	Casino console game
Dirt Track	Sound design and music composition		Multimedia Games	Multimedia Games	Yes	Casino console game
Dragons Luck	Sound design and music composition		Multimedia Games	Multimedia Games	Yes	Casino console game
Goin' Ape	Sound design and music composition		Multimedia Games	Multimedia Games	Yes	Casino console game
High Noon Stud Poker	Sound design and music composition		Multimedia Games	Multimedia Games	Yes	Casino console game

Release Name	My Role	Other Composers	Software Developer	Publisher	Released?	System
Kona Keno	Sound design and music composition		Multimedia Games	Multimedia Games	Yes	Casino console game
Megabingo	Sound design and music composition		Multimedia Games	Multimedia Games	Yes	Casino console game
Mixed Fruit Magic	Sound design and music composition		Multimedia Games	Multimedia Games	Yes	Casino console game
Red Hot Diamonds	Sound design and music composition		Multimedia Games	Multimedia Games	Yes	Casino console game
Star Struck	Sound design and music composition		Multimedia Games	Multimedia Games	Yes	Casino console game
Thunder Reel	Sound design and music composition		Multimedia Games	Multimedia Games	Yes	Casino console game
Tiger 7's	Sound design and music composition		Multimedia Games	Multimedia Games	Yes	Casino console game
Wacko Gekko	Sound design and music composition		Multimedia Games	Multimedia Games	Yes	Casino console game
Who's Your Froggy	Sound design and music composition		Multimedia Games	Multimedia Games	Yes	Casino console game
Meltdown	Sound design and music composition		Multimedia Games	Multimedia Games	Yes	Casino console game
High Noon Poker	Sound design and music composition		Multimedia Games	Multimedia Games	Yes	Casino console game
Zippity	Composed, produced sound effects	Phelan, McDDermott, Govett	Zippity.com		No	PC and Mac
Diamond Cherry Bell Magic	Sound design and music composition		Multimedia Games	Multimedia Games	Yes	Casino console game

Release Name	My Role	Other Composers	Software Developer	Publisher	Released?	System
Fruit Cocktail Deluxe	Sound design and music composition		Multimedia Games	Multimedia Games	Yes	Casino console game
Spinning Cherries Royale	Sound design and music composition		Multimedia Games	Multimedia Games	Yes	Casino console game
Reel 'Em In	Convert files		Multimedia Games	Multimedia Games	Yes	Casino console game
Filthy Rich	Convert files		Multimedia Games	Multimedia Games	Yes	Casino console game
Keno Magic	Sound design and music composition		Multimedia Games	Multimedia Games	Yes	Casino console game
Dragons Wild	Sound design and music composition		Multimedia Games	Multimedia Games	Yes	Casino console game
High Noon Poker (5-coin)	Sound design and music composition		Multimedia Games	Multimedia Games	Yes	Casino console game
Vortex	Sound design and music composition		Multimedia Games	Multimedia Games	Yes	Casino console game
Wild Spinner	Sound design and music composition		Multimedia Games	Multimedia Games	Yes	Casino console game
Jackpot Party	Convert files		Multimedia Games	Multimedia Games	Yes	Casino console game
Boom!	Convert files		Multimedia Games	Multimedia Games	Yes	Casino console game
Lockdown	Sound design and music composition		Multimedia Games	Multimedia Games	Yes	Casino console game
Winning Bid	Convert files		Multimedia Games	Multimedia Games	Yes	Casino console game

Release Name	My Role	Other Composers	Software Developer	Publisher	Released?	System
Freedom 7's	Sound design and music composition		Multimedia Games	Multimedia Games	Yes	Casino console game
Top Banana	Sound design and music composition		Multimedia Games	Multimedia Games	Yes	Casino console game
Double Jackpot Black and White	Sound design and music composition		Multimedia Games	Multimedia Games	Yes	Casino console game
99 Bottles of Beer	Attract screen		Multimedia Games	Multimedia Games	Yes	Casino console game
Bunch O' Luck	Sound design and music composition		Multimedia Games	Multimedia Games	Yes	Casino console game
Cherry Pop	Sound design and music composition		Multimedia Games	Multimedia Games	Yes	Casino console game
Jungle Juice	Sound design and music composition		Multimedia Games	Multimedia Games	Yes	Casino console game
Paddy's Luck	Sound design and music composition		Multimedia Games	Multimedia Games	Yes	Casino console game
Fruitstand	Sound design and music composition		Multimedia Games	Multimedia Games	Yes	Casino console game
Starstruck	Sound design and music composition		Multimedia Games	Multimedia Games	Yes	Casino console game
Moonstruck	Sound design and music composition		Multimedia Games	Multimedia Games	Yes	Casino console game
Rainbow 7's	Sound design and music composition		Multimedia Games	Multimedia Games	Yes	Casino console game
Bad Monkey	Sound design and music composition		Multimedia Games	Multimedia Games	Yes	Casino console game

Release Name	My Role	Other Composers	Software Developer	Publisher	Released?	System
Gold Coast Keno	Sound design and music composition		Multimedia Games	Multimedia Games	Yes	Casino console game
Five Card Frenzy	Sound design and music composition		Multimedia Games	Multimedia Games	Yes	Casino console game
Sun Dogs	Sound design and music composition		Multimedia Games	Multimedia Games	Yes	Casino console game
White Hot Keno	Sound design and music composition	Phelan	Multimedia Games	Multimedia Games	Yes	Casino console game
Cast of 1000s	Sound design and music composition	Richardson, Phelan	Multimedia Games	Multimedia Games	Yes	Casino console game

Great Fat Moments in History: An Illustrated List of Cameo Appearances by The Fat Man

In *Zombies Ate My Neighbors*, for Super Nintendo, the last level takes you to the offices of LucasArts. I don't have a shot of the game, but look for the two guys in cowboy hats. When you bump into them, it'll tell you that you've just met Joe McDermott and The Fat Man.

(The cheat code to get to that level is **XWJR**.)

In *Putt Putt Saves the Zoo*, by Humongous Entertainment, there is a billboard near the road. Click on it until you see the ad for The Fat Man and Team Fat!

Stay tuned. We hear that the producers might take Fat's son Glen's advice. An upcoming Putt-Putt game is going to have the billboard again, but this time the star of the billboard will be a familiar Rolls-Royce with cattle horns on its grille. Team Fat might be the band at the party in the final scene, too.

The hilarious Rhymin' Monkeys in *Putt Putt Saves the Zoo* are actually the voices of The Fat Man, "Professor" K. Weston Phelan, and two-time world free-style Frisbee champion "Rappin'" John Houck.

Just about nobody knows this one: "Professor" K. Weston Phelan wrote lyrics for the theme for Compton's *Invaders from Glixer: Rescue the Scientists*. Team Fat recorded it in Gino's Bar and Grille in front of a live audience, and it kicks butt! You have to put the CD into your audio CD player and advance past the first track. There's no indication in the game's documentation that this tune exists.

Of course, everybody knows that The Fat Man's portrait is hanging in the portrait gallery in Trilobyte's *The 7th Guest*. That was his first cowboy suit, which he took back to the store the next day because he decided he couldn't afford it. The cigar is a Davidoff.

Fat's portrait is there again in *The 11th Hour*, covered with mold and mildew. He's also in the doll house, we hear. The rule at Trilobyte during production and testing was that you had to say "Fat Man" every time you saw the portrait.

The Fat Man himself is the main pilot voice in EA's *U.S. Navy Fighters*. He's the one saying all that "Pilot S--" that kids aren't supposed to hear. Dave Govett's in there, too, as the ground control voice.

Well, I guess that goes for *Marine Fighters*, too!

Hey! There it is again in *Advanced Tactical Fighters*. Is this a trend?

Here's some modern news: The Fat Man is the voice of the "Clown" and the "Eel Thug" in Blue Sky Productions' *Spongebob Squarepants: Revenge of the Flying Dutchman*. He was also "Male Fish A"—that part was cut. The game won a Nick Kids' Choice award for best game, but the company had already disbanded by then. It's hard to know what to cut; fish or bait.

In some early versions of EA's *SSN-21 Seawolf*, there's a secret key that plays a movie of The Fat Man singing the lyrics "Blow them out of the water" to the theme tune. He's dressed in a Navy uniform, sunglasses and all. As the camera zooms out, he falls backward into a hot tub. It's truly one of the industry's great moments.

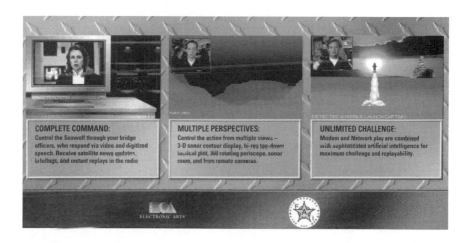

COMPLETE COMMAND:
Control the Seawolf through your bridge officers, who respond via video and digitized speech. Receive satellite news updates, briefings, and instant replays in the radio

MULTIPLE PERSPECTIVES:
Control the action from multiple views – 3-D sonar contour display, hi-res top-down tactical plot, 360 rotating periscope, sonar room, and from remote cameras.

UNLIMITED CHALLENGE:
Modem and Network play are combined with sophisticated artificial intelligence for maximum challenge and replayability.

Linda Law, Team Fat's beloved Mission Control, plays the newscaster in *SSN-21 Seawolf*. Her picture is on the back of the game box.

Don't miss the team's car in Papyrus' *Nascar Racing*. It's got the Fat Seal on it, and Joe McDermott's listed as the driver!

In Spring of '96, newspapers across the nation ran the cartoon strip *Making It*, which showed the Sprites of Spring romping through the strip. Their tune, shown in musical notation trailing behind them, may look familiar. It's Fat's first game tune ever, *Thin Ice* for Intellivision! Seems the producer of the game, Keith Robinson, has gone on to be one of America's favorite cartoonists... and owner and caretaker of the Intellivision name and games!

The little winged angel in the last frame of the *Making It* strip above has the face of Dave Warhol, programmer for *Thin Ice*. Dave, now CEO of Realtime, "discovered" The Fat Man and got him his first game gig, rediscovered him for his first Nintendo gigs, got him *Loom*, and even, we recently found out, helped get Fat the *Wing Commander*  gig. Hats off to you, Dave! Need a career? Team Fat owes you a few.

Web and Print Resources

For more crackpot wisdom from The Fat Man, you might try these:

1. Skreed.com

This website is an art/literature project of 7th Guest co-creator Rob Landeros. Moreover, it features reprints of the 1980's series *Lunch with The Fat Man,* in which a younger but no less insane George Sanger explains all the mysteries of audio production to the aspiring bands of Austin, Texas.

2. Brian Moriarty's Homepage
http://www.ludix.com/moriarty/

Contains the text versions of some of the most powerful talks ever given at Game Developer Conferences. It might eventually contain a video posting of the "Who Buried Paul?" lecture that answered the Prime Directive for The Fat Man.

Take special note of "The Point Is..." in which the Professor explains clearly the relationship between games, the Internet, and humanity's return to a collective consciousness.

3. *The Power of Myth*
by Joseph Campbell, Bill Moyers (Contributor),
Betty Sue Flowers (Editor)
Anchor, 1991

This book contains enough information to show an amazing similarity between all cultures and all religions. This is an excellent first step for the aspiring Game Audio Guy, because it even allows him to glimpse a tiny, remote thread of similarity between game audio and game programming.

4. *The Game of God: Recovering Your True Identity*
by Arthur B. Hancock and Kathleen J. Brugger
Humans Anonymous Press, 1992

This book uses poorly drawn cartoons to illustrate a wonderful philosophy based on the similarity between a game and life. If, like The Fat Man, you've been playing games in hopes of getting some insight into Real Life, this book will sew it all up for you.

5. ***Understanding Comics***
   by Scott McCloud
   Kitchen Sink Press, 1994

   A must for cross-disciplinary crackpot pop philosophers.

   Among other things, this book helped justify The Fat Man's not connecting the chapters of his book to each other, because of its theories of the wonderful things that happen in between the panels of a comic.

   It will also allow you to understand why the "bad" drawings in *The Game of God* work so much better than "good" drawings would have.

6. ***The Complete Guide to Game Audio: For Composers, Musicians, Sound Designers, and Game Developers***
   by Aaron Marks
   CMP Books, 2001

   Aaron actually answers questions in *his* book.

7. **www.dadgum.com**

   Here the reader will find James Hague's giant list of the Gaming Sages, including many wonderful interviews. Perhaps it is our equivalent of the Dead Sea Scrolls. Perhaps it won't be there by the time you look for it. The Dead Link Scrolls.

8. ***Who Dies?: An Investigation of Conscious Living and Conscious Dying***
   by Stephen Levine and Ondrea Levine
   Anchor, 1989

   This book explains how patience and accepting everything exactly how it is everywhere is the same as God and Love and what-not. Very practical. I give it my highest rating: one thumb up and one thumb down.

Index

www.informit.com

YOUR GUIDE TO IT REFERENCE

New Riders has partnered with **InformIT.com** to bring technical information to your desktop. Drawing from New Riders authors and reviewers to provide additional information on topics of interest to you, **InformIT.com** provides free, in-depth information you won't find anywhere else.

Articles

Keep your edge with thousands of free articles, in-depth features, interviews, and IT reference recommendations—all written by experts you know and trust.

Online Books

Answers in an instant from **InformIT Online Books'** 600+ fully searchable online books.

POWERED BY

Safari

Catalog

Review online sample chapters, author biographies, and customer rankings and choose exactly the right book from a selection of over 5,000 titles.

HOW TO CONTACT US

VISIT OUR WEB SITE

WWW.NEWRIDERS.COM

On our web site, you'll find information about our other books, authors, tables of contents, and book errata. You will also find information about book registration and how to purchase our books, both domestically and internationally.

EMAIL US

Contact us at: **nrfeedback@newriders.com**

- If you have comments or questions about this book
- To report errors that you have found in this book
- If you have a book proposal to submit or are interested in writing for New Riders
- If you are an expert in a computer topic or technology and are interested in being a technical editor who reviews manuscripts for technical accuracy

Contact us at: **nreducation@newriders.com**

- If you are an instructor from an educational institution who wants to preview New Riders books for classroom use. Email should include your name, title, school, department, address, phone number, office days/hours, text in use, and enrollment, along with your request for desk/examination copies and/or additional information.

Contact us at: **nrmedia@newriders.com**

- If you are a member of the media who is interested in reviewing copies of New Riders books. Send your name, mailing address, and email address, along with the name of the publication or web site you work for.

BULK PURCHASES/CORPORATE SALES

The publisher offers discounts on this book when ordered in quantity for bulk purchases and special sales. For sales within the U.S., please contact: Corporate and Government Sales (800) 382-3419 or **corpsales@pearsontechgroup.com**.
Outside of the U.S., please contact: International Sales (317) 581-3793 or **international@pearsontechgroup.com**.

WRITE TO US

New Riders Publishing
201 W. 103rd St.
Indianapolis, IN 46290-1097

CALL/FAX US

Toll-free (800) 571-5840
If outside U.S. (317) 581-3500
Ask for New Riders
FAX: (317) 581-4663

VOICES THAT MATTER

New Riders

WWW.NEWRIDERS.COM

Maximize Your Impact

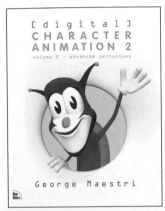
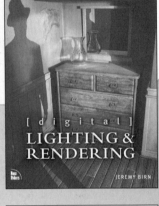
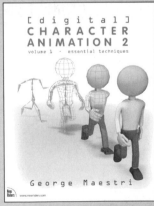
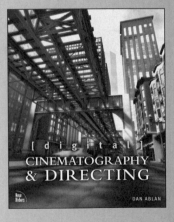